LEN HARVEY
Prince of Boxers

LEN HARVEY
Prince of Boxers

Gilbert Odd

FOREWORD BY
MRS FLORENCE HARVEY

*'It is a far greater blessing
to give than to receive.'*
LEN HARVEY'S TEXT

PELHAM BOOKS

First published in Great Britain by
PELHAM BOOKS LTD
52 Bedford Square
London WC1B 3EF
1978

Copyright © by Gilbert Odd 1978

ISBN 0 7207 1026 x

*Filmset by Northumberland Press Ltd,
Gateshead, Tyne and Wear and
Printed in Great Britain by
Billings and Sons Limited
Guildford, Worcester and London*

CONTENTS

ILLUSTRATIONS

Between pages 144 and 145

Polhilsa Farm Cottage
School at Stoke Climsland
School at South Hill
Ted and Ada Harvey
Devonport and Devonia Boxing Club Mascots
Father and son
Nipper Harvey
The Straight Left
Members of the DDBC, 1921
The Blackfriars 'Ring'
Mrs Bella Burge
Harvey's arrival in London
Harvey *v.* Joe Rolfe
Harvey *v.* Jack Hood
Harvey *v.* Leo Frick
Fathers and sons
Prince of Boxers at his prime
Harvey and his ukelele
Wedding day
Thirtieth anniversary
Len, Terry and Florence
The growing-up Harvey
Weighing-in for Moody
Winning the British middleweight title

FOREWORD

It is not usual for a wife to write the Foreword to a biography of her husband, but Gilbert Odd has pressed me to do this because the most important twelve years of Len's boxing career we shared in marriage. I was therefore closer to the boxer and the man than anyone else, had his whole interests at heart, and made him the focal point of my existence. I was steeped in the sport from girlhood and, perhaps more than any other boxer's wife, could understand and appreciate the working of a fighting man's mind and the way he responded to the colourful atmosphere of his arduous profession. Len never had to explain anything to me: I knew his decision was always right.

Not that Len Harvey was like the average boxer of his day. In my view he was unique, both in and out of the ring. He was a true professional, subjugating everything else to his vocation, yet at the same time being able to forget it completely once he was away from it all and conducting the life of an ordinary citizen; quietly, modestly, pleased at the public esteem that was showered on him, yet often finding it embarrassing. Much as he enjoyed being a professional boxer and all that it entailed, he was just as happy and contented with the simple things of life, and could become another personality entirely.

I always thought Len was very much like his father in character. Both disliked an argument, preferring to let things go by that were of no great importance. Quiet, unassertive, reserved in their judgment, they accepted life as it came and never wasted time thinking about the past or regretting what might have been. Even when it came to business, the fixing of terms for a contest, Len would not indulge in long-drawn-out arguments. He knew his worth and the value of each bout as it was proposed, would state his terms and stick to them, never demanding more than he thought the promoter could afford.

He always maintained that if a man gave of his best, no more could be expected of him. Immediately after a fight he wanted to dismiss it from his mind and look ahead to the next one. If his friends wanted to hold an inquest after one of his contests, he would put a time limit on it. After that he did not want to hear any more about it. It was over and done with. He showed no wild exultation over victory, no bitterness about defeat; asked for no favours, expecting only honesty and justice in return.

There are many things about Len's boxing life that stand out in my memory. After the first contest with Jack Hood, someone suggested that he should bring me with him the next day so that I could see him paid in actual cash. The sight of all that money on the table was a tremendous thrill for a twenty-two-year-old wife and I had the impression that it was done so that I would realise the earning capacity of my equally young husband.

When we were at East Sheen, after his retirement from the ring, Len would go to the Barnes Boys' Boxing Club and help train them. One day, after looking hard at a very small boy, he asked his name and was told it was Humphries. 'I knew it. You are the very image of your father, whom I twice fought at Kensington,' Len exclaimed. 'That was my grand-dad,' replied the lad, whereupon Len, then forty-five, burst out laughing. 'Of course, it must have been, because it was nearly thirty years ago. But you are just like "Pop"; the resemblance is remarkable.'

At the time when Len was looking after his own affairs, Harry Levene suggested that he should become his manager. 'It's a nice idea, Harry,' replied Len, 'but we could not possibly get on together. You talk too much and I don't talk enough. It just wouldn't work.'

After the John Henry Lewis contest, some of Harvey's most ardent admirers booed the American when the decision was rendered in his favour. It was most unfair and Len came from his corner into the middle of the ring and waved his hands to indicate that they should stop and that he was satisfied with the verdict. When we got home I told him that a lot of people thought he had won and he replied that he thought he had just done it. But the matter was never mentioned again.

Len never liked to hear a manager refer to himself and his boxer as 'we'. It jarred on him whenever he heard it, as he felt that each had his individual job to do: one to arrange the matches, the other to fight them. He recognised that great partnerships can exist between manager and boxer, but liked to feel that the fighter's personality should not be lost by being welded into that of a man who, after all, was his employee.

After a contest Len made a practice of going to see his opponent, mainly to find out if he was all right, but also to make him a present of the set of gloves they had used, which in those days were the prerogative of the winner. He was always greeted well; in fact his opponent sometimes gave the impression that it was a pleasure to have been beaten by him. He was always so kind to men he had defeated, saying the right thing, telling them how well they had done and that they should not be discouraged, because they might turn the tables next time.

On the night he beat Steve McCall, he visited the Scottish boxer, and as we were leaving Olympia – by the back door because of crowds in the street outside – two elderly ladies approached us and one asked if Steve was all right. 'I am his aunt,' she told Len. 'They tell me he's been knocked out.' 'He'll be with you in a minute or two,' answered Len. 'He's perfectly all right and did very well indeed.' That cheered them up and we walked on. Neither of the women knew it was Len himself they had spoken to.

I often observed during a contest that if Len's opponent got in a good punch or made a clever move, Len would smile his approbation and lightly touch the other man's arm in acknowledgment of his skill. I saw this happen many times and thought it a most sporting gesture.

His training camps were always the happiest of places, his sparring-partners regarding it as a privilege to be there. He never took liberties with them and was always concerned for their welfare. No work was done on Sundays, everyone being free to do as they pleased, and parents, girl-friends, wives and children were allowed to come if they wished to enjoy a communal tea. Everything was very informal and the atmosphere wonderfully cordial. It was all so casual and carefree, yet the training sessions could not have been conducted in a more serious vein.

When they relaxed they played cards or listened to the gramophone, sometimes having a sing-song with someone at the piano and Len playing his ukelele, at which he was quite expert. Nothing was more enjoyed than the swapping of stories and the relating of comic incidents connected with their individual careers, boxers having their own special brand of humour. As Len always had lengthy training spells – six to eight weeks, according to time of lay-off – they all got to know one another; in fact, it was such a happy family they were reluctant to have to break it up.

I remember Eddie Phillips, an exceedingly nice person, coming to help Len, who treated him like an equal, as he did all his sparring-partners, never letting them feel that they were in any way inferior to himself. Aware of this thoughtfulness, Eddie left Len a 'thank you' note on leaving, whereas it was he who had done Len a great favour by offering his services, he being a top-line boxer himself, but, like Len, eager to render assistance to anyone when having no contest himself on hand.

Champion boxers of Len's generation trained in a much more relaxed atmosphere, going to old inns out in the country when preparing for an important contest. Such places were geared to Len's way of life and revolved round him while he was there. They were comfortable without being luxurious and were ideal for roadwork which he carried out with his customary conscientiousness and zeal. Usually, if one was available, he would take the hotel dog with him and thoroughly enjoyed its company as he trotted round the lanes of Totteridge (while staying at the *Black Bull* at Whetstone); the Heath at Hampstead (*Jack Straw's Castle*), or Windsor Great Park (the *Star and Garter*).

Looking back, I recall the free and easy way Len dealt with the selling of tickets for his fights. He would take whole blocks of these at all prices so that his supporters were sure of getting those they could afford. These could be bought from him at the training camp, the money being tossed into a drawer in his bedroom, not even locked, until someone from the promotion would call to take it away. Hundreds of pounds would be involved, but not a penny ever went astray. How simple it all was – or perhaps it was Len's way of doing things that made it seem so uncomplicated.

Len was immensely proud of his profession. He hated to see it brought into disrepute in the newspapers by the actions outside the ring of anyone connected with it. He always dressed moderately and neatly, changing into a lounge suit immediately after finishing his day's training to become an ordinary citizen, and not wanting to talk or think about boxing. In the ring his appearance was neat and trim, carrying the dignity of a proficient and leading example of his trade.

It was he who introduced the wide-sleeved dressing-gown, which enables a boxer to remain covered and warm while the gloves are being fitted. He was also the first to wear insignia on his shorts. He kept his fighting kit in immaculate condition because he disliked parting with it. It seems strange that a man of his calm disposition should be in any way superstitious, but he wore his famous crimson dressing-gown for twelve years and would never change it for a new one, nor put on a pair of new boots until the others were not fit to wear any more. He even avoided putting in new laces if he could.

After his retirement from boxing, Len refused several offers from commercial firms to join them as a representative on the sales side, but he preferred to be his own master, no matter in how small a capacity. He turned down an offer to coach the Oxford University team and could have gone to Russia as an instructor had he so wished. After the war the German authorities invited him to stay for an unlimited period to see how sport was conducted in their country and to gain his approval, but he had no desire to get involved. He was quite non-political and could never be influenced into lending his name to any party or cause.

Once, when the famous Folies Bergères from Paris were performing in London, Len declined to be photographed among the chorus girls, feeling that boxing should not be cheapened by the wrong sort of publicity. He was well aware of the value of publicity, but preferred it to be of a nature that would not give a newspaper reader the wrong idea.

Excuse My Glove was a full-length movie in which Len played a leading role. It was made in 1934 and achieved some success, but he did not take to the life of a film star and during the eight weeks it took to make he lost ten pounds in weight. The peculiar atmosphere, with no set meal-times and the haphazard way of getting things done, did not suit his orderly way of living, and he wanted no more of it. He also appeared in *On With The Show*, a revue at the Prince's Theatre in London, but again he was out of his element, only being happy with anything connected with sport, like the contest for the World's Grip Record, which he won with a pressure equivalent to a quarter of a ton which remains unbeaten. In recognition of this, Thomas Inch, the famous strong-man, presented him with a magnificent silver cup.

A very good horseman, he also played tennis well and was a fine golfer, once holing out in 'one'. He was a wonderful snooker player, in fact excelled at all sports with the exception of swimming, the arm action for which he did not think was beneficial for boxers. He loved shooting and was always invited to Scotland every year for the 'Twelfth'. Nothing pleased him more, however, than a day at the races when he could pick his fancy and indulge in a mild flutter. He was also an excellent dancer, being extremely light on his feet, which was understandable in view of his remarkable speed and footwork in the ring. He enjoyed social parties, but did not drink during his boxing years. Yet he was equally at ease over a cup of tea in a cafe as he was in a fashionable restaurant or night-club.

He enjoyed the theatre, a good play or musical, and despite his natural reserve, had a polished, gentlemanly manner that made him liked and at home in any company. Perhaps best of all, he loved reading, one of his favourite authors being Edgar Wallace, whose *Sanders of the River* stories gave him great pleasure. He was also a magazine addict in the days when these were so well produced and filled with good reading matter. After a weigh-in he would return home for a meal, then relax with the *Strand* or the *Argosy* until he dropped off to sleep, calm in mind and utterly relaxed. No one seeing him in such circumstances could believe that in a few hours he would be involved in an important and exacting fight. And what confidence he had in his defensive abilities, for throughout that long and strenuous career and all those tremendous fights, he never once wore a gum-shield.

On his way to the arena, usually in an open car, he sang quietly, usually 'Oh Boy, I'm Lucky', one of Harry Richman's songs. But as soon as we got into the stream of fight traffic, he would stop and enjoy a quiet ride with no one recognising him. Then he would slip in unobserved and go straight to the dressing-rooms.

One night I shall never forget was when he fought Jock McAvoy at the White City for the vacant light-heavyweight championship of the world. The next day being Len's birthday, I had bought a silver Victorian beer tankard, which I gave to a friend of mine to have suitably engraved. Just before the last round started, he suddenly appeared at the ringside and thrust it into my hands. Taking a look at it I was horrified to see he had added, without mentioning it to me, the words: 'Light-heavyweight Champion of the World' under Len's name. 'That has finished it,' I thought, 'what a thing to have done before the fight, and here am I sitting with it and still another round to go.' Only bad luck could result.

Fortunately Len got the verdict and when I presented him with the tankard in the dressing-room, he looked at me in amazement, wondering how I had managed to get it inscribed in such a short time after the contest. When I told him how it had happened, he took a deep breath, and said: 'Some people are lucky.'

Reading through this story is like reliving my life with Len and no one is better fitted to be his biographer than Gilbert, who has an unequalled knowledge of the technique of boxing and being of Len's day and age, is a contemporary. It has been a pleasure to furnish the little connecting links and to read what is a truly accurate life story of a one-hundred-per-cent professional fighter, with nothing added for frills or effect. Just the true facts – the way it all was. Len would have endorsed this very realistic account of his career and, I feel sure, considered it superb boxing reporting, something totally different from pure journalism.

Len had been asked many times over the years to write his life story, but could never face the work involved. Gilbert, however, has undertaken the colossal research and writing and I am grateful to him for placing it on record. I am sure all lovers of boxing, past and present, will read it with pleasure, reminding so many as it must of their own youth, when boxing was of such a very high standard, and had so many great boxers on its stage. As an onlooker during those years, I pay homage to all the boxers of that era. They were magnificent. My privilege was to share with dear Len his terrific campaigning years, often under the most difficult and frustrating circumstances. He was noble in character, of great humility and courage, a credit for ever to the Noble Art, of which he was so proud to be an exponent.

FLORENCE HARVEY

ACKNOWLEDGMENTS

My grateful thanks are due to the following kind people who came to my assistance during the researching for this book: Vera Habart, Len's second sister, of Willesden, London NW6; Ted Harvey, Len's eldest brother, of Basingstoke, Hants; Ruth Pascoe, Len's cousin, of Golberdon, Cornwall, for valuable information and early photographs. Clive Mumford of Yelverton, Devon, for permission to abstract information from his book *Fighters of the Old Cosmo*; Graham Houston, Editor of *Boxing News*, for publishing a request letter in his columns; John Rapson of Liskeard, Cornwall, for supplying photos of Len's birthplace; Jack Hall of West Croydon for supplying fight poster of 'The Ring' at Blackfriars, London. Also, George Holder of Cricklewood, C. Taylor of London, N1, John Burt of Holloway, London N7, Lilian Mitchelmore of Plymouth, P. J. Dingle of King's Lynn, Norfolk, Muriel Searle of Plymouth, Eric Webb of Barrow-in-Furness, the Revd A. G. Robins of Plymouth, Harold Beckett of Haworth, Yorks, Alec Williams of Romiley, Cheshire, John Muggeridge of Forest Hill, Young Phil Brooks of Millwall, Ruth and Tommy McArdle of Liverpool, S. W. Barrett of Plymouth, John Bettie of London EC1, Daniel F. Wood of Cheltenham, Glos, Jack Fox of Ilford, Essex, one-time sparring partner to Len Harvey; Tom Jewell of Plymouth; Charlie Crook of London W2 for the loan of photographs to help illustrate this book.

INTRODUCTION

I first *saw* Len Harvey in April 1924 when he had his initial contest at the Blackfriars 'Ring', the place where I spent my apprenticeship as a boxing reporter, being then in my third year. The first time I *spoke* to him, other than in a dressing-room, was in the King's Bench Division of the London Law Courts when his manager, Dan Sullivan, was sueing the weekly paper *Boxing* for libel.

As the defendants were my employers, I was subpoena'd as a witness and in due course presented myself in the appropriate court. Being somewhat apprehensive and disliking my task intensely, I arrived much earlier than demanded and was surprised, delighted and nervous in turn, to find the only other occupant was the young Cornishman, much more a man of the world than myself, he being married while I was not, as no girl was interested in someone who spent every night of the week and Sunday afternoons watching and reporting on the Fight Game.

Naturally we got talking, not – I hasten to say – about the impending action nor, for that matter, about the sport in which we were both deeply involved, if from entirely different angles. Instead, we chatted about our pastimes, hobbies and reading matter, finding that we had much in common. As he liked to say on many occasions afterwards, he interviewed me for a change.

When the court began to fill and we had been separated by our respective and highly indignant parties, Harvey, just twenty-two and as ignorant of legal procedure as myself, proceeded to win the case for his side, which saved me the embarrassment of testifying against him, for which I was grateful; and we remained firm friends for ever after. I spent many delightful hours in his pleasant company, both during and after his brilliant ring career, and we played thousands of games of darts as partners, rarely losing because of his amazing skill and my ability to get finishing 'doubles' from sheer terror.

Only about one boxer did Harvey break his golden rule not to talk 'shop' when I was in his company on these occasions. The exception was Bob Fitzsimmons, who had been his father's hero and the man on whom Len measured his ambitions. Fitz won world titles at middle, light-heavy and heavyweight and Harvey set out to emulate this astonishing record. That he fought for the middle and light-heavyweight world crowns, albeit unsuccessfully, was an indication of his firm and avowed intention, while the fact that he won British championships at these precise weights was a praiseworthy compromise.

' "Old Bob" never got the full credit that was due to him,' Len always maintained. 'Plenty of books have been written about the other heavyweight champions of the world, but no one has written a biography of this amazing character. As a fellow Cornishman I resent this. You can do it, what's more you ought to do it, if only because he was the only Englishman ever to win the big title.' After this unusually lengthy speech, I promised I would, but only if he would contribute a Foreword. This he did and *The Fighting Blacksmith*, published a year ago, was the last boxing book he was to read before his tragic and untimely death. I treasure his approval of it.

As my position on *Boxing* increased in importance and I rose to Assistant Editor,* so my association with Harvey became closer, especially when he was managing his own fistic affairs. Then it was essential that we discuss boxing matters and I was able to supply him with information that came more readily into my hands than his. Over the years it resolved into a profitable partnership for us both.

In the following chapters I have emphasised the greatness of Len Harvey as a superlative boxer, one who epitomised the real conception of the Noble Art of Self-Defence, while at the same time proving himself a destructive fighting machine when the right moment presented itself. Considering the innumerable contests and the many years they covered, it is a tribute to his remarkable boxing skill that he emerged from them all without a mark to show the arduous nature of his profession.

What is even more amazing is the fact that he never wore a gumshield during a contest, a protection no modern boxer would dream of being without, neither did he wear any form of head-guard when training, maintaining that to do so made boxers careless. His sparring-partners, however, always used head-gear for protection, and it says much for Harvey's immaculate defensive skill that he never suffered cuts or facial damage of any sort during the hundreds of rounds he boxed in the gymnasium.

How fortunate he was to marry Florence when he did. It was at the point in his career when he most needed a courageous supporter and confidante; a time when he was facing the world in a hard, exacting pro-

* After the war I became Editor when the paper was known, as it is today, as *Boxing News*.

fession, beset with every conceivable hazard. She proved an intelligent and forthright companion, who put his interests before everything else and did her full share in all that he achieved in his illustrious ring career.

Everyone knew her as 'Blossom', a most applicable name bestowed on her by Sir Charles Higham (by whom she was employed as a sixteen-year-old junior secretary), because of her honey-blonde hair, rosy cheeks and real country colouring. 'That girl looks just like a blossom,' he said, and the name stuck. She stood up to all those whose ideas she considered detrimental to her husband's interests and was a boon to a man of his reserved disposition. Len disliked talking about himself, but she was full of information for those who came searching for stories about his past history.

Her help has been invaluable in filling out the data at my disposal and it is for her, as much as for that vast army of admirers that he enlisted during his momentous life, that this book has been written with such pleasure.

GILBERT ODD
Northiam, 1977

CHAPTER 1

The 'Old Cosmo'

On 2nd January in the year 1920, the Cosmopolitan Gymnasium in Mill Street, Plymouth, was pretty well crammed, as was usually the case on a Friday night. Ever since its opening as a place of sporting entertainment thirteen years earlier, Boxing had been a regular attraction and on this particular occasion the chief item of interest was a contest between the local lightweight hero, Ben Callicott, who was to be tested over fifteen rounds by Sammy Lane from Pontypridd.

Perched on a small rostrum on top of the tiny dressing-rooms was a three-piece brass band, led by Charlie Penny, a one-armed cornet player. They had marched the spectators into their places, either occupying the chairs arranged in rows around the 16-ft. ring, or the standing places behind them, including the raised portion on one side known by the habitués as 'Spion Kop.'* The coke braziers used for heating the barn-like arena were glowing abortively, trying to keep out the many draughts; the referee was sitting on his high-chair outside the ropes, the usual position for such an official in those days. Harry Jenkins, proprietor as well as promoter of the 'Old Cosmo', as the place was known to the local fight fans, had just given a nod to the chief whip to get the first pair into the ring and start the night's performance.

They emerged from the screened-off alcove used by the preliminary boxers as a dressing-room: two small boys, gloved-up, wearing shorts, socks and plimsolls, each followed by a second with a towel over his shoulder. They walked importantly to the ring and ducked through the ropes, but no one took the slightest notice, nor did the babble of conversation decrease. Most of those in the audience were summing up the probable outcome of the main event and it was not until the two youngsters were seated in the opposing corners, and the Master of

* The name of a hill in South Africa where a famous battle was fought during the Boer War, 24th January 1900.

Ceremonies had instructed the timekeeper to clang loudly on his bell, that there was sufficient quiet for the announcement of the first item of the evening's programme to be heard.

'A six-rounds paperweight contest between, 'pon my right, Nipper Harvey,* of the Devonport and Devonia Boxing Club, and on my left, Young King, from the Caprera Boxing Club. The referee for this evening's contests is Mr Frank Marshall.' There may have been a few among the spectators who knew something about these two schoolboy boxers, but to the majority they were just another pair of kids from the two foremost clubs in the city that formed the nurseries from which the able Mr Jenkins recruited the participants for his preliminary bouts each week.

'Let him come to you, Len,' said his father as the order came for 'Seconds Out' and the bell sounded to start them off – and this his dutiful twelve-and-a-half-year-old son did. His opponent was eager for battle and the two put up what one ringside reporter described as 'a smart contest, well worth watching'. At the finish Young Harvey was declared a points winner; they received well-deserved applause, plus a shower of coppers, then left the ring to return to the primitive dressing-room. The promoter came to see Len and his dad while the boy was getting into his clothes; told him he had done very well in his professional début and promised him another contest in a fortnight's time. Mr Jenkins then handed Harvey Senior the agreed five shillings for his son's efforts, it being understood that this amount would be raised as progress was achieved.

How much of that princely sum the 'Nipper' received is unknown, but as working-class children of that era usually received only a few pence a week as pocket money, it must be assumed that the residue went into his money-box, or to the assistance of the family budget, if same was necessary. More than likely Young Len had to be content with his half share of the 'nobbings'.

William Henry Edward Harvey, known throughout his life as Ted, was of Cornish stock, his father being a tin miner at Redmoor who lost his life in a pit accident when still a young man. The son, born in the nearby Parish of South Hill in October 1882, was employed as a farm labourer in the district. At the age of nineteen he married Ada Jane Penny, a native of the neighbouring village of Stoke Climsland, she being older than her husband by five months. They set up home at Trewood-low and children came at regular intervals.

*His weight was 4 st. 12 lbs.

First Edward (also Ted) in May 1902, then Wilfred in January 1903 and Winnifred in June 1905. Later the Harvey family moved to Polhilsa Farm, on a small estate owned by Squire Rattenbury, where they occupied a tiny tenant's cottage, and here, on 11th July 1907, a third son, Leonard Austin, was born. The father continued to work as a farm hand and later drove a traction engine in the course of his employment. Life was very simple, as can be imagined, in the cramped accommodation, but food, if of the plainest, was plentiful, and with other large families in the near locality, there was never a shortage of playmates for the children. As each reached the required age they attended the council school at South Hill.

In 1911, when there were rumours – and these spread quickly in rural areas – that the Polhilsa farmland was to be bought up by the Duchy of Cornwall Estate, which owned most of the surrounding countryside, there was a sudden upheaval in the Harvey home. Fearful of being unemployed, a catastrophe to be avoided at all costs in the early part of the twentieth century, the father decided to emigrate to Canada, to find work there and save sufficient money to bring over his wife and children in due course.

Financial aid for this project was obtained from Squire Rattenbury in the form of a loan,* which not only helped towards Ted's passage to Canada, but left enough to sustain Mrs Harvey and the children until her husband could contribute towards their keep. This he did with regularity, sending monthly money orders which were cashed at the Post Office in Callington, a market town three miles away from Stoke Climsland, where he had secured a cottage for the family at a place called Bowling Green. Only a few steps away was the local council school to which the children transferred. By now their mother was twenty-nine, Young Ted was nine, Wilfred eight, Winnifred six and Leonard four. Also, by that time, there was a one-year-old, Vera.

By 1914 the father had established himself in Edmonton, Alberta, and wrote to his wife, instructing her to sell up their home and join him. She did this and with the passages booked, was all packed up and ready to leave England, being due to sail on 14th August. Ten days before their departure was due, however, war broke out and, as the result of a cablegram from her husband, she cancelled the planned voyage. It is interesting to ponder on whether the boxing world would ever have heard of Len Harvey had this trip to Canada been scheduled for a fortnight earlier, or if the First World War had begun two weeks later than it did.

* This money was paid back in full in due course.

Harvey Senior returned to England by October, travelling with the first contingent of Canadian troops. But, having no wish to revert to the land when the war had come to an end, he moved his entire family to Devonport, about a mile from Plymouth. Here he found a home and war service work for himself as a blacksmith in the Naval Dockyard. By this time his two eldest sons, Ted and Wilfred, were old enough to earn money in after-school occupations and so augment the family income.

From his youth the father had been interested in Boxing, being fifteen when Bob Fitzsimmons defeated James J. Corbett for the Heavyweight Championship of the World at Carson City in 1897. The news had excited all sporting England, especially in Cornwall, for the Fighting Blacksmith had been born at Helston, some sixty miles to the west of Callington. Whilst in Canada, Harvey had been attracted in 1913 to the town of Calgary, about two hundred miles south of Edmonton, where a big fight was being staged between Luther McCarty and Arthur Pelkey. It was widely advertised as being a contest for the 'White' Heavyweight Championship of the World.* Harvey made the long trip to see this highly publicised event, but did not get much for his time and money as the contest ended fatally for McCarty in the very first round. But the atmosphere of the professional ring created a big impression on the Cornishman and his enthusiasm was further increased in Devonport, where he formed a friendship with a certain Kit Carson, who had spent many years as a boxer in South Africa. They began to attend the weekly shows at the Cosmopolitan Gymnasium, and Carson, who was already a member of the Devonport and Devonia Boxing Club, one of the best in Plymouth, soon persuaded Harvey Senior to join.

In due course the latter became a trainer of repute at the club and among those he looked after were such local boxers as Bugler Harry Lake and his brother Percy, Petty Officer Jim Cartlidge, and a host of other popular boys who were to make their mark in British boxing. Young Ted joined the club at the age of fourteen and boxed at the 'Old Cosmo', first as Young Lark's Nipper,† and later under his real name. In 1918 Wilfred became a member, as did the very youthful Leonard, then being

---

*The legitimate Heavyweight Champion of the World was coloured Jack Johnson and every effort was being made to discover a 'White Hope' capable of beating him.

†His tutor was Young Lark, a local preliminary boxer, it being the custom in those times for a novice to adopt the name of his mentor when having his first few pro fights, as it was considered to have prestige value.

only eleven, but showing such a keen interest in physical exercise and the use of boxing equipment that, because of his somewhat frail appearance, it was considered that such training could be only of benefit to him.

Of course, the father was delighted at having three sons so interested in Boxing, hoping perhaps that one of them might become a champion some day. He may have had doubts about his youngest, however, for the first time he took him along to watch the fighting at the 'Old Cosmo', Len was not impressed by a pair of slugging middleweights, who stood toe-to-toe exchanging savage punches with no pretence at defence. He felt that Boxing was much more of an art than this crude exhibition of brute fighting and the sight of their faces and chests covered with blood, which apparently delighted the onlookers, only made him feel thoroughly sick and he was glad when the time came to go home.

This obnoxious experience did not deter Len from his delight in physical culture and in sparring with other boys of his age. He possessed such a calm disposition, and was so thorough in everything he attempted, that it soon became apparent to his father that, young as he was, the boy had all the requirements that go to the making of a class boxer, one who could be moulded on the lines of famous 'Gentleman Jim' Corbett, who had been one of the first to prove that science would always prevail over brute force when he won the world title by knocking out the redoubtable John L. Sullivan.

Len was taught the correct fundamentals of the Noble Art, understood them, practised them and perfected them. His cool disposition enabled him to suppress the natural youthful urge to go in and have a fight, to swing punches and attempt to subdue an opponent by sheer aggression. He knew that the shortest distance between two points was the straightest; that controlled hitting with the knuckles part of the glove was far more effective than the wild, haphazard flinging of punches.

He learnt footwork, how to outbox an aggressive rival whilst on the retreat; the use of every square inch of a ring; the blocking of blows with the gloves, forearms and shoulders; the way to avoid being hit by adroit movements of the head, and the way to handle a forceful opponent at close quarters.

It did not take him long to realise that the more he improved in his boxing ability, the severer would become the opposition; that progress meant the extra tightening of defence, as well as widening the range of his repertoire of punches. Above all, he extended his knowledge of ring-craft by watching others, closely observing their faults as much as their virtues, studying the methods they used to attain success, taking heed of the errors that brought defeat. He got to know that self-control was of paramount importance; that the boxer who lost his head, either when victory or defeat seemed imminent, was an almost certain loser.

Perhaps Young Len's greatest asset was the early realisation that only with a healthy, disciplined and unimpaired body could a boxer hope to achieve the maximum of success. That, just as important as preserving the tools of his trade — his hands — it was essential to maintain a clean body and mind, and to develop himself both mentally and physically to the utmost of his power; to bring to fulfilment the basic desire to grow strong and to use to full effect the bone and muscular framework with which he had been endowed from birth. Although at the tender age in which he commenced Boxing he was far from robust in appearance, there were all the indications that he would grow to perfect manhood. Johnny Williams,* who managed the Devonport and Devonia BC at that time, thought very highly of Nipper Harvey and predicted a great future for him. 'He could grow into a heavyweight,' he prophesied.

Knowing him so intimately throughout his long boxing life, it is safe for me to say that the promise of a second bout at the Cosmopolitan Gymnasium did not excite Len in the slightest. What the other boys at the County Council School in York Street, Devonport, thought of having an embryo boxer in their midst can only be guessed. Those who were keen on the sport were no doubt impressed as he made progress; the remainder thought no more of him than they did of others who shone at football, cricket or similar pastimes.†

Undoubtedly, he was too reserved to talk about his out-of-school activities, for it was no rarity for boys of his standing to have a wage-earning occupation, both before and after their classroom studies. Perhaps his quiet disposition prevented him from being a 'bright' pupil, but he had the desire and the ability to learn and once won a prize for painting, which showed an artistic sense.

In a city such as Plymouth, a colourful and unpredictable sport like Boxing was bound to flourish, and there had been numerous venues for it as a spectacle for entertainment before the Cosmopolitan Gymnasium came into being. Originally the Gymnasium had been a place of amusement known as Hancock's Winter Garden, presided over by a one-legged man, affectionately known as 'Peggy', and his wife Sophie. When they

* Williams took up farming and closed down the DDBC in 1923, but returned to re-open it and promote at Plymouth Drill Hall two years later.
† When he boxed on a Friday evening he did not go to school that afternoon.

departed a certain Silas Alger and his partner, Billy Bennett, took over, and when it was decided to hold boxing shows there, they appointed an American named Bert Dorman as manager. He renamed the building 'The Cosmopolitan' Gymnasium, after a club he had run in London, and just as public house names become corrupted by their regulars, so this palace of punch was soon known by all as the 'Old Cosmo'. As a fight arena it was an assured success from the start as, apart from the nearby dockyard workers, there were the naval and military barracks from which performers and spectators could be drawn in abundance.

As already intimated, it was a rough edifice that let in the elements at various points. The ring was postless and was held in position by being lashed to the many stanchions that kept the dilapidated roofing in place. It was opened as a boxing hall in 1907, but two years later Harry Jenkins, a former butcher from Saltash who now kept the Talbot Hotel in Union Street, joined the promoting syndicate, together with his friend Frank Marshall, and with their influence the place was altered to accommodate five thousand spectators.

Jenkins, an enterprising individual, became a member of the National Sporting Club in London and also served as a steward on the British Boxing Board of Control, which in those days was merely a committee of the National Sporting Club (NSC) members formed to govern the sport in an autocratic fashion. Being thus associated gained Jenkins considerable power and influence, and eventually he took over the proprietorship of the 'Old Cosmo' and did his own matchmaking.

Marshall acted as referee at the start and on ordinary evenings, but for special contests the services of London referees were engaged, in particular John T. Hulls, who was on the staff of the *Sporting Life* and was also a prominent member of the NSC. His presence was of great value to the local boxing fraternity, who thus enjoyed a ready-made introduction to London rings. In fact, Plymouth boys received as many opportunities to make good in the metropolis as did those from any other part of the country.

Soon after Len's début at the 'Old Cosmo', his older brothers joined the army, Ted going into the Royal Engineers and Wilfred into the Duke of Cornwall's Light Infantry. Both served a good deal overseas, but by the time they returned to civilian life, they had given up their boxing careers. They could, however, follow the fortunes of Young Leonard, who by now was an established boxer in London.

Len lost his second bout at the Cosmopolitan Gymnasium, being outpointed by Young Fern, from the rival Caprera BC, but he was becom-

ing increasingly popular because of his upstanding boxing and undoubted skill, and the frequency with which he appeared. He also had
engagements in various other West Country towns during these early
days and although there are no details available of these contests, they
undoubtedly took place. When in later years Len claimed to have been
engaged in between three hundred and four hundred contests, it was
no idle boast.

In those times many small boxing shows, especially those in remote
parts of the country, were never reported outside their local newspapers,
and not even then, if the sports editor had no special liking for Boxing.
Len once told me of being taken by cart to fight at Barnstaple, the
jolting vehicle causing him to be sick on the way. It is also known
that he fought at such places at Bridgwater, Truro, Taunton, Wellington,
Torrington, Stroud, etc., using various forms of transport; buses, trains,
borrowed cars – in fact, any conveyance that could be secured, travelling
costs having to be kept down because purses were so low, especially for
a youngster.

Len's early contests at the 'Old Cosmo' did not receive more than
the barest mention of their results in *Boxing*, the so-called trade paper
of the sport. One report described him as being auburn-haired; another
made mention of the fact that he had a long reach. Against Kid Roberts
he was 'a clever little one, who had to do battle against a hefty opponent',
but when opposed to Young Mac, he scored his first knockout win –
how we are left to guess. Perhaps the boy's interest in Boxing was increased by watching a series of silent films entitled *The Leather Pushers*
at the local cinema. The manager, who liked Len and admired his boxing
ability, gave him a free pass which was used until it dropped to pieces.
Being too shy to ask for another, he paid for admission thereafter.

Young Paul held him to a draw, and to start off 1921, he had four
successive bouts with Young (Harry) Jinks of the Caprera BC, all of
which Harvey won on points. Their third meeting was over eight rounds,
the first at this distance in Len's record. Apparently those behind Jinks
thought he would do better with two extra rounds against the not yet
fourteen-year-old Harvey as they fought for a side-stake. The Caprera
boy was very aggressive, especially in the concluding rounds, but he was
brilliantly outboxed and lost on points.

No doubt by now Len's wages had risen above those initial five shillings and his father was becoming even more immersed in making a livelihood from the Fight Game: an advertisement in *Boxing* invited young
boxers to contact Ted Harvey for training and tuition. The address given

was No. 46, Union Street, Stonehouse, but this is not taken to mean that the Harvey family had moved from Devonport into Plymouth. Another one round victory was scored when Len knocked out Young Richards of the Richmond Boxing Club, after cleverly demonstrating his superiority, and the following week, in the same ring, the youthful Harvey scored yet another victory over Young Jinks.

As soon as he was fourteen, Len left school to work at a garage which might or might not have been selected as a place of employment because it happened to be situated right opposite the Devonport and Devonia BC premises. But the proprietor, Bert Barker, was a great boxing enthusiast and encouraged his youthful employee as much as he could, letting him off to cross the road and go into the gymnasium whenever Len was training for a contest. He remained a firm friend of Harvey's for the rest of his life.

At that time Plymouth simply oozed with boxing talent, which was very encouraging to aspiring youngsters. Harvey's particular hero was twenty-year-old Ted Moore, who came from a district known as Prince Rock, and, to quote a local reporter was, 'a clever boxer possessed of remarkable strength, whose adventures with both bare knuckles and the gloves would read like a Jack London* story.' Moore did go the full distance with Harry Greb for the world's middleweight title in America and when Harvey was knocking on the British middleweight championship door in 1928, there was a lot of talk about a match between him and Moore, but nothing came of it. The brass band at the 'Old Cosmo', to which reference has been made, usually played the participants in the chief contest into the ring with appropriate tunes, much to the delight of the fans. In the case of Arthur Taylor, an agricultural worker, they rendered 'To be a Farmer's Boy' and for Ted Moore they blared out 'Samoa – Samoa'.

Young Callicott, of the Caprera Boxing Club, gave Harvey his second and only other recorded defeat at the 'Old Cosmo', just before Len's fifteenth birthday, gaining a points victory over eight rounds. But, in a return contest over the same distance three months later, Harvey scored revenge for his club with a well-deserved points verdict.

Ever since its formation in 1891, the National Sporting Club, with its headquarters in Covent Garden, has been regarded as the controlling body of British Boxing. It had risen from the ashes of the one-time notorious Pelican Club and under the strict supervision of its founders,

---

*American author of tough adventure stories of the Klondike gold-rush days, many autobiographical.

John Fleming and Arthur 'Peggy' Bettinson, a former ABA lightweight champion, had acquired a membership of successful London citizens, including also some of the landed gentry who patronised the sport, with the Earl of Lonsdale as its President.

The Club ruled its members with a rod of iron. Silence had to be preserved during the actual boxing; the referee, who was god-like in his interpretation of the rules, sat outside the ring, and the boxers were regarded in the light of performing animals, never daring to protest against the feudal treatment they received, and knowing full well that if they failed to please they could be ordered out of the ring for 'not trying', even in the twentieth and final round, and find themselves docked of all pay and blacklisted so far as any future engagements were concerned. The same dire fate awaited them in the event of disqualification.

The Club controlled the championships by the power of the Lonsdale Belts, trophies highly valued and regarded as the final word in the claiming of a British title. To be invited to box at Covent Garden was considered the highest honour a fighter could receive, even though the financial rewards were low because the theatre that held the ring could accommodate only eleven hundred people. But most boxers would willingly fight for nothing for the sheer privilege of appearing there, and would forgo other and perhaps more lucrative engagements, rather than miss the chance of displaying their wares before the dignified, dress-suited and affluent NSC members.

Ted Harvey Senior, who had taken a number of Plymouth boys to the famous Club over the years, was no doubt delighted when he was offered a ten-rounds engagement for Young Len to box at a special show there in aid of Johnny Summers, a former light and welterweight champion, who was in need of financial help. Harvey's opponent was Young Bill Lewis, of a famous Bethnal Green family. It was two years to the day since Len had made his pro start and probably his first ever visit to London. Well, he came, saw and conquered, being awarded a points verdict after what was described as 'a good set-to, fairly evenly fought, but the decision going to the Plymouth boy because of his better style'.

Back at the 'Old Cosmo', Harvey was described as a flyweight when boxing an eight rounds 'draw' with Young Callicott, although this did not mean that either or both of them had reached 8 st. in weight. At a Saturday afternoon show held at Home Park, Plymouth, promoted by a Mr Chiswell of Devonport, Len met his old rival, Harry Jinks, and at the end of a fast six-rounder received the award from referee Joe

Palmer of London, who comes into this story far more prominently at a later stage.

When Len reached the age of sixteen, it appears that his dad considered he had finished his novitiate and was ready to be regarded as a top-line boxer and command the money that such eminence deserved, probably £1 a round to begin with. In his next bout Len was elevated into 'second billing' at the Cosmopolitan Gymnasium, being paired with Kid Socks (real name George Stockings) who hailed from Bethnal Green and had all the promise of a champion of the future.

The distance was fifteen two-minute rounds, and it seemed to be asking a lot of a lad who had only once before travelled ten rounds. But Len's father must have known what he was doing, although the *Boxing* reporter had no hesitation in saying that he thought it was a strain on the Plymouth lad's stamina and was a severe test for him. Thanks to his longer reach and his undeniable cleverness Harvey gained a points win, but he was hard pressed to keep ahead after the tenth round.

Having proved that his talented son was capable of staying fifteen rounds, Harvey Senior next accepted an offer for him to box at the Baths Hall in Lancaster Road, Kensington, on the opening night by a new promoter who, to add to the attractiveness of the programme, had engaged the services of former middleweight champion Roland Todd to act as referee. Len's bout topped the bill, his opponent being 'Pop' Humphries, from Barnes, a worrying little warrior, who battled away with both hands from start to finish, but was forever running into a straight left that was plied so efficiently that at the finish the youngster from Plymouth had won a well-deserved victory.

A month later he outpointed Bill Riley, a smart lad from St Pancras, over the fifteen-rounds route at the 'Old Cosmo', but the reporter remarked that Len 'was not so fresh as I have seen him'. As he also emphasised that the London flyweight was a hard hitter, it says much for Harvey's defensive abilities that he was able to escape trouble and also pile up sufficient points to earn the decision.

Understandably, Len was given a rest of ten weeks before making a return to Kensington. It seems that Humphries had not been satisfied that Harvey was his superior and asked for a second chance, this time over twenty rounds of two-minute duration. Again 'Pop' tried his hardest to batter down the lanky Leonard, but his short stature proved too much of a disadvantage and Harvey's left hand prodding was so accurate and consistent that, in spite of a very strong finish by the Londoner, the points verdict went against him at the finish of a fine contest. 'Len Harvey, of Devonport, is going to make a noise in the fly-weight division,' said one observer of Humphries' second defeat.

Len returned to Kensington a month later, but had a much easier task. A match against Matt George, from Portsmouth, scheduled for twenty rounds, terminated in the third; the referee stopped the bout because George had sustained severe damage to his left ear. This contest seemed likely to end quickly in any event, as just before the bell sounded to end the opening round, the Portsmouth lad clipped his rival on the chin with a right hook and Len was put down, probably for the first time in his boxing life. He made a good recovery in the interval, fighting off Matt's strenuous efforts to put over a 'finisher'. But a stinging right burst open his 'cauliflowered' ear, and as his seconds could not stop this from bleeding, a halt was called soon after the start of the third round. Harvey's weight for this contest was announced as 8 st. dead, while his opponent was $2\frac{1}{2}$ lbs. heavier.

CHAPTER 2

'The Ring' at Blackfriars

In a series of articles published in a Sunday newspaper in 1954, Dan Sullivan claimed that he first caught sight of Len Harvey 'when he came up to London to take part in a minor scrap at Kensington Baths. He won and I carefully noted the natural skill of the boy.' It seems, however, that Daniel's memory had slipped after the passage of thirty years, for the simple reason that both of Young Harvey's appearances at Kensington took place on a Monday evening when 'The Ring' enjoyed its most important night of the week, and it was least likely that he would leave the premises over which he ruled so dictatorially to watch a 'minor scrap' at a newly-opened promotion on the other side of the River Thames. Also, as we have noticed, Len 'topped the bill' on each occasion.

What is more likely, if Sullivan did pass the rule over Harvey before taking control of the boy, is that it was at the National Sporting Club charity show, which took place on a Tuesday and on an occasion when the general public was admitted, it not being a Members' Night. Actually their initial acquaintance occurred the morning after the defeat of Matt George when Harvey Senior took his son to beard Sullivan in his den at 'The Ring' itself. Having paid out the train fare for two from Plymouth, Len's father took the opportunity of making the rounds of the leading matchmakers in London in an effort to find additional work for Len, and discovered Sullivan ready to proposition them into an arrangement from which he would gain most benefit.

'Sign the lad to me, do as I tell you, don't interfere and I'll make him a champion,' he promised them. 'My terms will be a quarter of Len's earnings in this country and a third if he ever goes to America. I will guarantee him at least twelve fights a year and build him into becoming a big money-earner.' These terms must have been acceptable to Len's dad, as before they left Sullivan's office, he had signed his son away for seven years, knowing that it was in Dan's interest to match him with discretion and so bring him along by easy stages. They were instructed not to accept any more engagements at the Cosmopolitan Gymnasium for the time being and be prepared for Len to make his first appearance at 'The Ring' in a month's time.

Situated in the Blackfriars Road, at the junction with Union Street, 'The Ring' had been built as a chapel for the Reverend Rowland Hill in the early nineteenth century; it was circular in design so there should be no corners in which the Devil could lurk. How long it served as a place of worship is not known, but in 1906 it became one of the first places in London to show moving pictures. The advent of larger and better designed cinemas brought it into disuse until in 1910 Dick Burge, a former lightweight champion of England, formed a syndicate calling itself the Blackfriars Athletic Club and took over the premises. They converted it into a boxing hall which became very popular in South London, having two, sometimes three, shows a week, on Mondays, Thursdays and Saturdays. Appropriately they called it 'The Ring', because its shape was ideal for watching boxing contests. When Burge died in 1918, his wife, Bella, took over the proprietorship, and Sullivan, who had been Dick's right-hand man, was appointed manager and matchmaker.

It had therefore been a fight arena for nearly fourteen years when Len Harvey made his first appearance in the chief supporting contest of fifteen two-minute rounds on Saturday evening, 12th April 1924, his opponent being the same Bill Riley, from Bethnal Green, who had given him plenty to think about four and a half months earlier in Plymouth. This time, however, Harvey employed his long left with persistency and precision to win an undisputable points victory.

With Len assured of a regular income that would automatically increase with time all the while he remained a professional boxer and continued to make progress, there was no sense in the family remaining in Devonport, so it was decided to move to London where a house was found at Chalk Farm near Camden Town. Besides the young boxer and his parents, there was his sister Vera, now aged seventeen, and also one-year-old Olive. The two elder boys, Ted and Wilfred, were in the army, while Winnifred had left home and married. The father being now wholly concerned with boxing, Len became the principal bread-winner, although he was not yet seventeen.

Sullivan kept his word about regular employment, as it was in his interests to do so; or perhaps it would be more correct to say that

Young Len assured this by winning consistently. There were thirteen appearances at 'The Ring' in the remaining nine months of 1924, the majority being over fifteen rounds, while four were reduced to twelve, but all of two minutes' duration. Harvey won them all with one exception, being held to a draw by Young Dando from Hednesford, a decision that was described as an 'injustice' to the boy from Plymouth. In a return bout sixteen days later, Harvey won on the referee's intervention in the fourth round after he had floored his opponent three times.

At first Harvey had to be content with appearing at the Thursday and Saturday performances, but when he met Ernie Jarvis, the Millwall flyweight who some years later was to box for the world title, Len had his first Monday night showing. He was too tall for the stocky Londoner, and was at an advantage in reach. A snappy left hook had Ernie down for 'nine' in the first round and long after he had retired from the ring Jarvis always maintained it was the hardest punch he had ever felt. Even so, he got up and battled on bravely to the final bell when the verdict rightly went to Harvey, who scored another good points win nineteen days later by defeating Young Freddie Welsh, from Pontypridd, about whom his fellow-countrymen thought quite a lot.

What the 'Ring' fans liked about Harvey, apart from his copybook boxing, was the way he could produce a knockdown punch when the opening presented itself. He knocked out Wal Jordan, from Peckham, with a left hook and following right to the chin halfway through the opening round, the two final punches coming with dazzling speed. Tim Rowley, of Camberwell, was another who did not last long, the contest being stopped at the end of the second round after Rowley had been put down from a neatly timed left hook to the jaw and then dropped again. He was in such a bad way when the bell sounded that the referee applied the closure in Harvey's favour.

Albert Hicks, from Stepney, put up a spirited battle against the slim, tall youth from Plymouth, but was never allowed to get to close-quarters, the place that best suited his style of two-fisted fighting. Aggressive in every round, Albert could not avoid Len's long left and had been well outpointed at the finish. Billy Streets of Plymouth was another forceful fighter who kept Len at full stretch for the first half of their contest, but once Len had got the range, he punished his rival with accurately-placed straight punches that not only kept his determined opponent at bay, but gave Harvey a well-deserved verdict over a great little loser.

When Bert Saunders, from Paddington, was beaten, it was noted that

'Harvey continues his winning way', while Sid Cannon, who came with a big reputation from Paddington, had his chances ruined by a neat right cross to the chin that toppled him over, and he was well behind at the end of a twelve-rounds contest. Harvey again gave 'a very polished performance that was very pleasing to the fans'. So far Sullivan had been giving his protégé opponents noted for their two-fisted tearaway tactics, who were made for Len with his long reach and straight punching, while his superb footwork kept him out of trouble from the hooks and swings that were vainly tossed in his direction.

Len engaged in sixteen contests during 1925, all but two at 'The Ring', his manager loaning him out to the National Sporting Club, where he provided a tit-bit to a championship fight, and at Harvey's special request, to Johnny Williams, former manager of the Devonport and Devonia Boxing Club, who was trying his hand at promoting in Plymouth, and wanted Harvey's help to get away to a good start. New Year's Day was celebrated with a five-rounds win over Seaman Harrod, from Chatham, who could never surmount his disadvantage in reach and after being punished methodically decided not to come up for the sixth round. It had been scheduled for twelve, but the fans were happy at having a reduced ration by the pleasing way Harvey performed. As one critic remarked: 'He is a wonder for a boy of his build.'

Over fifteen 'twos' on a Monday night, Harry Kent, from Tonbridge, was Len's next victim, although he tore into Harvey with such vigour in the opening round that the fans wondered if there was going to be a sensational upset. But by the second, the tall Plymouth lad had got his measure and, shooting out straight lefts and the occasional right cross, steadily robbed his energetic rival of a lot of his confidence. Even when Kent managed to slip in close he was surprised to find that Harvey could meet him on even terms with short punches from either hand. By the fourth round the Tonbridge boy was at the end of his tether and an easy target for whatever his opponent aimed at him. After Kent was dropped by a stiff left to the jaw and a following right to the ribs, the referee said: 'That will do.'

For his last twelve-rounder at 'The Ring', Len was due to meet Charlie Wright, from Stoke Newington, but instead met a substitute in Laurie Guard, a useful fighter from Greenwich, though no match for his rival's clean-cut punching. After being put down in the third and twice in the fourth, he was knocked off his feet again in the next round by a swift 'one-two' to the chin, whereupon the bout was rightly concluded by the referee.

Johnny Curley, from Lambeth, who was fond of the Plymouth boy and had given him a lot of encouragement, was challenging George McKenzie, of Leith, for the British featherweight title and Lonsdale Belt at the National Sporting Club. The Londoner and the Scot had already met twice in catchweight contests with a win apiece and all South London was hopeful that Curley would bring the championship back from Covent Garden. Young Harvey was keen to see his friend make his title attempt, but there was no way of getting in to see it, the audience being strictly limited to members. 'I suppose you couldn't get me a fight on the same programme?', Len asked his manager, who said he would see what he could do. There was no trouble at all as 'Peggy' Bettinson was interested in seeing the Plymouth boy about whom he had heard so much, and gave him a ten-rounds bout against Walter Malone, from Oldham.

In his anxiety to get to the dressing-room and change so that he could stand at the back of the stage and watch the championship fight, Len was very short with his Lancashire opponent, who was on the canvas before the contest was half a minute old. He took a count of eight seconds, was dropped again, this time for 'nine', and then put down for the full count with Harvey's next punch. It was over far too quickly for the NSC manager to take his look at Len. He had asked someone to tell him when Harvey was 'on' and was on his way to his ringside seat when he met Len hurrying away from it, having completed his night's work. Then he stood and watched for an hour and twenty minutes while Curley won the nine-stone championship after twenty very close rounds.

I do not know what prompted Len to win his next contest just as rapidly. Opposed to Johnny Thomas, of Clerkenwell, over fifteen 'twos' he deprived the 'Ring' patrons of half an hour's entertainment by planting a left hook on his rival's jaw in the opening minute that had 'knock-out' written all over it. So Dan Sullivan had to find some tougher opposition. By now Harvey was growing into a lightweight and none of the London managers who had promising boys at this poundage were keen to make stepping-stones of them. Consequently, continental boxers had to be brought over and the first of these was Karel Veldt, from Holland, who, at 9 st. 8 lbs. was 2 lbs. heavier than his seventeen-year-old opponent from Plymouth.

To justify this additional cost, because he had to pay the Dutchman's travelling expenses, the 'Ring' matchmaker exalted his boxer to the top-of-the-bill position for the first time and also extended the time of each round to three minutes. So Len was giving away 2 lbs., called upon to fight forty-five minutes instead of his usual thirty, and opposed to an unknown quantity. It was a tough assignment for any young boxer, but Sullivan was confident that Len would adjust himself to the occasion with his usual phlegmatic calm.

When the Harveys arrived for this important step in Len's career, his father told Sullivan that his son was suffering from tonsillitis and was under medical attention for it. 'But he insists on boxing,' he added. 'In that case,' replied Dan, 'I'll have it announced from the ring so that the customers will know that he isn't as fit as he might be.' And that is as far as Len's health interests were considered. The manager had confidence that his pet boxer could take care of himself and his opponent, tonsillitis or no tonsillitis, while Harvey Senior did not want to do anything that might hamper his son's career, being a mild man who would prefer the easy way out of a situation rather than to assert his authority.

Once again Len found himself opposed by a very aggressive fighter, but he was well used to this state of affairs by now and settled down to keep the Dutchman on the end of a long left as much as possible, while using his clever footwork and evasiveness to stay out of danger when Veldt managed to break through. Soon the bout settled down to as clean an exhibition of scientific boxing as anyone could wish to see, tense interest being maintained for round after round as Veldt tried his utmost to batter down his frail-looking rival. Bursts of applause kept coming from the fans as Harvey brought all his skills into play, jabbing away until his rival's face was smeared with blood, and cracking him on the chin with perfect rights after drawing him into making a fierce attack. Len was so much in control that in some rounds the Dutchman did not land a glove on him and at the end there was no need to name the winner. But the loser was well applauded for his plucky efforts against a master boxer, who might have won inside the distance had he been more fit.

A fortnight later, Paul Leukemanns was imported from Belgium to face Harvey in the main contest. This time Len was in good health again and demonstrated the fact by clipping his rival on the jaw with a snappy right that put him down for a short count. As soon as he was on his feet, Harvey drew him into another right to the jaw and the Belgian was down again. He showed courage by getting up and keeping at a distance to last out the round. He boxed on the defensive after this, trying hard to keep Len's left out of his face, but was down in the third for six seconds from another flashing right to the chin and, although catching one or two nasty rights in each round thereafter, managed to avoid any further knockdowns.

Leukemanns attacked the body in the middle rounds and when he went in to use both hands was met by keen opposition from the Plymouth boy, who showed he could shorten his punches when necessary; they had several sharp rallies from which the Belgian was glad to break off. It developed into a contest of skill and speed versus strength and stamina and Harvey's proficiency had him well ahead at the finish when the verdict in his favour was greeted with loud enthusiasm. Both men, it should be noted, weighed 9 st. 8 lbs., so Len was still growing.

Going the European rounds, Sullivan engaged Peter Bianchi, from Italy, to oppose Harvey in his next outing. Again it was obvious that Dan was carefully selecting Len's rivals, for here was another strong fighter, eager for battle, but having nothing to offer against a boxer of class. The Plymouth boy took a round or two in which to sum up the opposition, carefully blocking the strong attacks that Bianchi made on his slim body. When he cut loose in the fifth round, Harvey hit his man at will and in the next, after luring the Italian into making a wild attack, shot over a long right that landed flush on the jaw to score a decisive knockout victory.

Eight days later Len was elevated to a Monday night main event when taking on Fred Bullions, a stocky, determined fighter from Deptford, who was a favourite among 'Ring' fans because of his courage and tenacity. It was the same old story, Bullions attacking and Harvey fencing him off. Fred tried desperately to crowd his lean rival against the ropes, or force him into a corner, but Len was like an eel, twisting and turning, very often leaving Fred to stare into the crowd, while Len was behind him in the middle of the ring waiting for the next move.

In the fifth and sixth rounds Harvey repeatedly stabbed out his tantalising left, but in the next he suddenly put over a neat right that shook the recipient so badly that he dropped his hands, whereupon another right had him down for a count, the bell coming to his rescue. Len was punching so crisply and accurately that it was now a question of how much longer Bullions could last. He was down twice in the eighth round, three times in the ninth and had taken three more tumbles in the tenth when the referee answered the crowd's shouts of 'stop it'.

Terry Donlan, claiming the lightweight championship of Ireland, was the next victim, Len summing him up in half a round and then proceeding to deal with him promptly and cleanly. A stinging left to the face, followed by a swift right to the chin had Donlan down for a short count and he was floored twice more before the end of the first round. Soon after the start of round two, Harvey banged over a right that was meant to finish the one-sided affair, but the game Irishman just beat the count, only to be floored again, whereupon the referee signalled that he had seen enough and Harvey had won another quick victory.

It was becoming increasingly difficult to find worthy opponents for the clever Plymouth lad without putting him among the very top-flight boxers, so Paul Leukemanns was brought in again. Mindful of the fact that the Belgian had given Harvey a keen fight, if well outpointed, on the first occasion, Sullivan made this another Monday night offering and was rewarded with a packed arena, the locals anxious to see if Len could stop his tough rival this time, having put him down for three counts on the last occasion. Again it was a case of a superlative boxer versus a dour fighter, but it was obvious that Leukemanns had learnt his lesson and now advanced with a sound cover for his face and jaw with his gloves and crossed forearms. The Belgian took Len's leads and swung to the body in retaliation, having made up his mind that to attempt to box with the Englishman was next to hopeless.

He had to wait until the sixth round before he met with any success and then received a caution from referee Jim Kenrick* for landing a blow that seemed suspiciously low. Aiming higher, his blows dropped short as Len beat him to the punch with straight lefts, but in the eighth he managed to get through with a stiff left to the lower ribs that almost bent the Plymouth boy in two. His seconds appealed loudly that a foul had been struck, but this was ignored by the official who was now in the ring. Len had to back off and move around while the Belgian, sensing that he had hurt his opponent, tried hard to land another damaging punch to the body.

Harvey was scoring all the time, but had to be very wary of the pile-drivers that Leukemanns kept trying and towards the end of the ninth Paul got in another solid smash that drove Len back into the ropes, where he had to use all his cleverness to escape disaster as the Belgian swung away with both fists at the midsection. The Plymouth lad kept amazingly cool under this torrid attack, having another rough passage in the eleventh round when his determined rival got through with another swing to the ribs. The crowd applauded Len as he extricated himself from danger and he thrilled them by keeping the boxing at long range during the

* Former 8-st. Champion of England from Hackney, who boxed for the world's bantamweight title in 1910.

final four rounds to romp home a clear winner at the finish of a stirring fifteen-rounder.

Harry Gent, from Chorley, with thirty successive wins to his credit, was the next man to try out the youngster who was still unbeaten at 'The Ring'. The shorter but stockier of the two, Gent was clearly anxious to make this a close-quarter affair, but Harvey moved around, tapped the face with the left, but, unable to penetrate his rival's defence effectively, drew a lead and countered with a right to the chin that had Gent badly shaken. He pulled himself together, but had no way of coping with Harvey's stiff punching to the face and the rights that came over to thud on his chin. One of these, perfectly timed and fully powered, caught Harry as he came charging in and he went down flat on his back to be counted out.

There was a tremendous reception for Len when he appeared at the Plymouth Drill Hall to start off the promoting venture for his old friend Johnny Williams. The huge place was packed to capacity, most people marvelling at the appearance of the one-time boy boxer who had now grown into a full-blown lightweight. His rival over fifteen rounds was Bill Handley, an experienced warrior from Hackney, who tried hard to punch his way to victory, but was caught so effectively by Len's snappy punches to the head, two stiff lefts, then a solidly connecting right which dropped the Londoner for a count in the third round. Bill got up and continued to try and smash his way through Harvey's brilliant long-range boxing, but by the eighth round he had been punched to a standstill and was tottering about when the bell sounded. He was so badly used up that no one was surprised when his retirement was announced in the interval.

Back at Blackfriars, opposition to Harvey was supplied by Glyn Davies from Barnsley, but the Yorkshire lad did not last long. There was a big crowd for this Saturday night show and they saw a brief but sparkling display of fine boxing and shrewd hitting. Davies started confidently enough and was surprised to find himself down on one knee midway through the opening round. He got up and took a right on the chin that almost knocked him out of the ring, but the ropes saved him and he rested for a count of 'four'. The second round was only a few seconds old when the Barnsley boy was down again for four seconds. Then he leapt up and rushed at his rival, only to be met by a sweetly-timed right that he stopped with his jaw.

The blow did not seem tremendously hard, but it was so perfect in its timing that Davies spun right round and fell flat on his face. The referee immediately signalled that the fight was over. The Yorkshire lad's seconds came rushing in, carried him to his corner and worked over him for a long time, while Len looked on anxiously. As Davies did not respond to treatment, he was carried unconscious to the dressing-room; Len followed greatly concerned. He stood by in his fighting kit until Davies recovered and was pronounced fit to go home. Not until then did Harvey take a shower and get dressed.

By now Len's fame was spreading far beyond the bounds of Blackfriars and when he was matched with Henri Dupont, another Belgian, in the top-line contest it was looked upon as such a severe trial for the Plymouth youngster that 'The Ring' was greatly over-crowded: many ticket-holders and lady guests were brought into the press box on the east side of the gallery, and forms placed for standing on outside. Usually the middle of the week show had the leanest attendance, but Harvey's appearance was sufficient to fill the place on any night. Len's weight was announced as 9 st. 12 lbs., his heaviest yet, and this gave him a pound advantage over his opponent.

Dupont attacked from the start, coming in under a decided crouch, his arms held low with the object of swinging each in turn to the body. Len's sparse frame seemed an obvious target for concentrating upon; the difficulty was to get past the barrier of its owner's long reach and straight hitting. Harvey was soon peppering his rival's face, and even when Dupont managed to connect with a right swing to the ribs, he received in return a left hook to the chin, followed by a lightning right on the other side of his jaw that made his whole body tremble. Having let him see what to expect, Len now proceeded to reduce the Belgian's stamina with a variety of shots from long range, making it look so simple and artistic that the big crowd applauded him enthusiastically as the bell sent them to their corners.

Not having laid a glove on the Englishman during the last minute of the first round and having taken plenty of punishment as well, Dupont came out in sheer desperation to try and do something on his own account. By sheer force he got inside with the intention of hammering away two-fistedly, but Harvey seemed to have arms and gloves everywhere to block the blows or lessen their impact, while he possessed a powerful grip in each hand that enabled him to push his rival back into long range again.

There were two brisk rallies, with Harvey coming off best; then he banged in a slightly-swerving left with full force to the point of Dupont's chin and down he went flat on his back. Although badly shaken, the sturdy Belgian scrambled up very hurriedly, but he had not the wits to put up a guard and another left smote his chin to put him again on the canvas. This time he turned towards his corner to get the signal to rise from his seconds. He got up at 'eight', but immediately took a measuring left from Len, then a right hook to the jaw that bowled him over for the third time. Once again he took eight seconds to get to his feet, but was so far gone that it needed only a tap from the Englishman to knock him off his feet, whereupon the towel came in from the corner and it was all over in barely five minutes.

Harvey had not turned a hair and left the ring as he entered it – to a great round of applause. He had not put a foot or a hand wrong and his display was so impressive that the spectators went home feeling sure they had seen a certain champion of the future in action, as modest and level-headed as he was clever. As for his victim, Dupont paid a great tribute to Len when in the dressing-room he said that he had never before met an opponent as clever as Harvey, or one who hit as hard. 'I did not see the punch that put me down the first time,' he said. 'I did not know I had been hit until I found myself on the floor.'

To end a triumphant year, Harvey had a Frenchman, Edouard Baudry, to face on 19th November, another Thursday showing. The foreigner's style was too stiff and cramped to be attractive, his crouching attitude, with chin tucked behind shoulder, and his crab-like action, being in striking contrast to the upstanding boxing, speedy footwork and versatile hitting of his young opponent. It looked like being another quick win for Harvey when he put his rival down momentarily in the first round with two rapid rights to the jaw, but the Frenchman was extremely strong and retreated under his elaborate cover until the end of the round.

When Baudry was not backing away, he tried to land heavy swings on Len's body as he advanced trying to pick holes in the Frenchman's defence. As far as points scoring went, there was only one man in it, but the English boy was clearly puzzled as to how to make an impression on his rival's unorthodox style. Twice in the fourth round Harvey shook his man up with a swift left and following right and in the fifth he repeated this move to have Baudry badly hurt. But this grand opportunity went astray when the referee stopped the action and cautioned the Frenchman for a low delivery.

Thereafter Len had his man in trouble in almost every round, but could not get in a clean shot to end the affair. In the fourteenth he brought the foreigner to his knees with a powerful punch to the solar plexus, but again Baudry's toughness enabled him to get up and carry on, defying all Len's efforts to put him away. At the finish no one needed telling that Harvey was the winner by a wide margin of points. Afterwards his father announced that his son had fought his last fight as a light-weight. In future he would not box at less than ten stones and it would not be long before he was in the welterweight* class.

Len had now engaged in twenty-nine contests since coming under Dan Sullivan's management, and had won them all with the exception of the disputed 'draw' with Young Dando. Of his victories, six had been clean-cut knockout wins, nine had ended inside the distance and thirteen had been points verdicts. He was unbeaten since first coming to London three years earlier and now there was every justification for him being billed as 'Britain's Wonder Boxer'.

* 10 st. 7 lbs. (147 lbs.)

CHAPTER 3

Britain's Wonder Boxer

When Dan Sullivan announced that Harvey's next opponent would be the formidable Alf Mancini it was obvious that he considered that Len's apprenticeship had come to an end. He had been tried out over fifteen rounds, first of two-minutes duration and for the last eight months over the three-minutes course. Now he was to be given his first twenty-rounder, a severe test in itself, but all the more so because of the high reputation of his opponent. No doubt the manager considered it high time that the Plymouth lad was groomed for a championship chance, and that would have to be in the welterweight division. At the moment the title was in the hands of Harry Mason, who was also the reigning lightweight king. As he could still make the lightweight limit, it was reasonable to expect that the winner of a contest between Harvey and Mancini at 10 st. would provide a logical challenge to Mason for his heavier crown.

Mancini was looked after by Ted Broadribb, one of the shrewdest managers in the business, and he considered he had made a good match for Alf in pairing him with the Plymouth youth. Mancini was a mature twenty-three, whereas Harvey was only eighteen and a half. The Notting Hill Italian was a pocket Hercules in appearance and more than once had been a sculptor's model. He had been boxing for six years, latterly in good company, and was a notably strong puncher, his speciality being a left hook which had won him many contests. To pit him against a teenager, even if he was regarded by his friends as something of a phenomenon, seemed to be taking a big chance, but Sullivan was confident and Len's father saw nothing untoward in the match. As for Len himself, he regarded it as a further opportunity to gain experience. 'You get nowhere fighting mugs,' was his only comment.

That it was an attraction of the highest magnitude was demonstrated by the size of the crowd that packed into 'The Ring' on this particular night and the fact that many had to be content to wait outside and have the progress of the battle relayed to them from those standing nearest the doorway. More than half of Mancini's seventy-four contests to date had taken place at the Blackfriars arena and he had rarely been beaten there. He got as big a reception as did the local hero, who looked a mere slip of a lad against the compact, beautifully muscled man from Notting Hill. Alf was one of those who never stood on ceremony and paid no heed to reputations. There were no preliminaries when he left his corner, he went straight into action like a well-oiled fighting machine.

Harvey, taller by a couple of inches and looking as cool as a cucumber, met his rival's initial rush with a neat left to the face and was then knocked clean off his feet by Alf's speciality, a wicked left hook to the chin. Down went the Pride of Plymouth, and it seemed to be all over. Dan Sullivan's face went as white as a sheet, Harvey's seconds were shocked into silence, Mancini's supporters raised the roof. But Len got up immediately, before the timekeeper could start a count, and Mancini, who had imagined that it was all over and had trotted across to a neutral corner, now had to turn about and try to do it again.

This time Harvey stabbed him with two immaculate lefts to the face in quick succession, rocking Alf back on his heels and leaving him open for a right that came sizzling across to crack home on his chin. That was a hard clean punch and it was a good thing for Alf that he possessed a tough jaw. He shook his head and plunged in again, but Len moved gracefully about the ring, shooting out his left, flashing over his right and competently keeping his resolute rival at bay.

If Harvey had been shaken up in that opening round, he looked fully recovered in the next and now the fans saw the art of boxing at its very best. They whistled with astonishment as Len made Alf miss with his big punches by the merest inch and the perfect manner in which he sent in crisp countering blows. Mancini was not perturbed. He was determined to catch the youngster again and it looked as if he might in the third round, when Len dropped to one knee momentarily. But it was only a slip and he was soon back into his stride, hands, feet, body and brain working in complete co-ordination, making it all look ridiculously easy. In contrast, Alf's efforts seemed crude and laborious, although in fact Mancini was no mere slugger. The Notting Hill warrior carried plenty of craft, but he was foiled at practically every point, although he never once eased up in his attempt to bring the frail-looking youngster down for the full count.

At the end of the sixth round Harvey came back to his corner to be told by his Dad: 'Good boy, Len. You've got him where you want him. Keep it up and the fight's yours.' 'Think so,' answered his son. 'Well, he very nearly got me in that round. I don't know how I got through it.'

'What are you talking about?' said Harvey Senior. 'That was in the first round, this is the seventh coming up. You've been boxing beautifully ever since; you're well ahead on points.' 'Am I?' asked Len. 'Then I must have been fighting unconsciously for the last six rounds.' 'Well, now you can go out and lick him.'

In the next four rounds Mancini changed his tactics, and had a great deal more success. Instead of throwing himself forward and lashing out with big swings, he darted under Harvey's long left and set to work on the body. It was clear that he knew more about infighting than the boy from Plymouth, who was forced to resort to some holding, for which he received a caution. He also received a few butts under the chin as the energetic Alf jumped in to bang away at the ribs. Now he was beginning to slow Harvey down and Len found it a lot less easy to keep him at the end of his long arms. In the eleventh it looked as though sheer strength and pertinacity would prevail. Mancini dug deep into his rival's slim body and hooked viciously at the head. It seemed that he might batter the youngster down, but somehow Harvey managed to weather the storm and, finally getting away, peppered his rival with rapid left jabs and shook him up with some telling rights.

In the fourteenth Harvey was sent reeling back into the ropes and had to hustle along the hemp in order to avoid Alf's fierce follow-up. He showed great coolness under this persistent bombardment and the excited fans applauded again and again as his brilliant boxing saved him from disaster. Undoubtedly this Plymouth youngster was a ring marvel. Even when hard pressed by the energetic Alf, he never lost his head or became wild in his punching. Indeed, it seemed as though he was expanding his repertoire at Mancini's expense, sending in the occasional uppercut, first from one hand and then the other, turning straight punches into hooks, whipping in combinations.

At the three-quarter mark Harvey was definitely in front, but could he last out five more rounds against his strong and determined rival? Harvey's father had no need to hand out any advice, his young son was quite capable of looking after himself. Mancini, as dangerous as ever, fought with renewed vigour during those remaining rounds and no fighter has ever been called upon to use his wits to keep in a contest and at the same time maintain his scoring, more than Harvey was that night.

Yet he not only avoided all Alf's furious attempts to put him on the canvas, but gave back as good as he received, plus some extra. The Notting Hill boxer's face was now bearing signs of Len's sharp-shooting fists and more than once he was knocked off balance by a swift right to the chin.

The fighting was so tense that the rounds slipped by and then the bell rang out to start the twentieth session. The fans had cheered both men to their corners, roared all through the interval and were now urging each to go all out for a decisive win. Neither Harvey nor Mancini needed any encouragement. Alf went in to do or die, but to his amazement, and the delight of the onlookers, Len met him halfway and they had a battle royal in mid-ring. Eager to swap punches, Mancini bundled in with great vigour, putting his remaining strength and stamina into one last burst of two-fisted action. It was left hook for left hook, right for right, with chins as the targets. Harvey's seconds were yelling at him to move and keep moving, but Len knew what he was doing. A lot of the pep had gone out of Alf's blows, he was flat-footed now and show-ing all the signs of weariness. Harvey, too, was on his last resources, but he stayed just that little bit better and towards the end of the round took complete charge of the exchanges and Mancini was beaten back step by step as he took punches from all angles. The cheers for Len were deafening, but Mancini was far too tough to be put down, even though he seemed thankful when the timekeeper clanged the bell loud and long to make sure it was heard.

Back went the boxers to their corners. It looked as though the 'Wonder Boxer' had snatched a tremendous victory, but referee Moss Deyong decided otherwise. Beckoning both men to the centre of the ring, he grabbed Harvey's right arm and Mancini's left and held them aloft, indicating that his verdict was a 'draw'. Alf's army of supporters gave out a mighty boo and Len's followers tried their hardest to drown them. Then the whole audience stood up and cheered in unison, cheered and did not stop cheering until both men had left the ring and disappeared down the aisle that led to the dressing-room. What a fight it had been, clean, sporting and fought at tip-top speed. Only the result was dis-appointing, for a match such as this had been deserved a winner – and in the minds of most of the critics the victory should have gone to Harvey.

Perhaps the Editor of *Boxing* summed up the whole matter with these remarks: 'It was a great battle that was ruined by the verdict. How Moss Deyong arrived at the conclusion that the two contestants had divided the points we are at a loss to imagine. Nevertheless, if one had to judge by the volume of cheering that greeted the announcement, one would have to admit that the "finding" was a popular one. This, however, did not prevent the majority of the critics, and even of the ordinary public, from expressing their agreement with our view that Harvey had not only won, but had won well.'

A month later manager Sullivan released Len to box the highly-respected Billy Bird, of Chelsea, in the main contest at Lime Grove Baths, Shepherd's Bush. They were matched to box the best of fifteen rounds at 10 st. 6 lbs., and Harvey was the heavier by three pounds. For once he was fighting a stand-up boxer like himself, a master at long range work, who could ply a straight left as well as anyone in the business. He also had a rock-like defence which was very difficult to penetrate and Len could make little impression on the wily Bird in the opening round. Billy's defence was such that it was Harvey who was called upon to force the pace and do most of the attacking. He tried to catch his elusive rival with a right every so often, but it was not until the third that he met with any success and then it was a crisp left hook to the chin that put the Chelsea man down.

He got up at 'eight' and thwarted all Len's efforts to add to his advantage, and for the next three rounds it was a question of Bird's defence against Harvey's attack. By the seventh round Len decided to switch his offensive to the body, getting into close range and hurting Billy with some powerful punches to the ribs. The Chelsea man responded with two hard rights to the head that were too high to prove damaging, then Len threatened a right and drew his rival into a well-timed left hook that thudded against Billy's jaw and put him down. He rose to one knee midway through the count, but remained there, too dazed to rise, and was counted out.

While Harvey's popularity was growing steadily in London, his rise to fame was being followed assiduously elsewhere, notably in Plymouth where it had started, but also around his birth-place in Cornwall. His cousin, Ruth Pascoe, has happy memories of Len, whom she first saw when he was only a few days old. She enjoyed his company on his frequent visits to see his relations, especially his grandmother, who lived at Golberdon. While living in Devonport, he spent some of his school holidays there and she remembers him playing cricket with her brother and other village lads.

When he went to London and began to make the sporting headlines the Cornish people would wait impatiently for the postman to bring the

Western Morning News to the local Post Office, where they could find
out how Harvey had 'got on' the night before. They would come away
telling everyone they met that 'Young Len has done it again'. Later,
with the arrival of wireless, and with only a couple of sets in the village,
all were invited to listen in when his fights were broadcast and the whole
place thrilled with excitement when it was announced that he had gained
another victory.

When his grandmother first heard that he had taken up boxing at
such an early age, she was most anxious about him, being afraid that
he would get hurt. But he always assured her that he would be all right.
'Don't worry, grandma. You'll see my name in the paper like Carpentier's* one day.' Later on, when Len had won his first British title, the
old lady went about Golberdon telling everyone: 'That's my boy.' When
she was widowed at the age of thirty-three, she was left with five children and had to work to keep the home going, being caretaker at South
Hill School, where Harvey had his early education. He was very fond
of her, and Mrs Pascoe recalls him bringing his wife and son to see his
old friends and relatives on a number of occasions.

For Len's next contest a month after the defeat of Bird, he was engaged in a 'special' of twenty rounds, Johnny Sullivan, from Covent
Garden, being selected as his opponent. He was thirty-six days older
than Harvey, had been boxing professionally since the age of fourteen
and in forty-nine bouts had been beaten only five times. Three years
earlier, when undefeated in twenty-seven bouts, he had attracted the
attention of Francois Descamps, the wily manager to Georges Carpentier, who took the boy under his wing after seeing him act as a
sparring-partner to the famous Frenchman who was training for his
second fight with Joe Beckett. Descamps took Johnny to France where
he was given special tuition and fought several contests, all of which
he won. But Sullivan did not fit into the French scene and returned
home, where he fought among the leading welters with considerable success.

For the fight with Harvey he was considered as severe a test as
Mancini had been and once again the Blackfriars arena enjoyed a full
house. The match was made at 10 st. 4 lbs. and both men were half
a pound inside that poundage at the afternoon weigh-in ceremony. They
were pretty well matched in physique, about equal in height and reach,

*Famous Frenchman who became world's light-heavyweight champion and
fought Jack Dempsey for the world heavyweight title. He was the scourge of
British heavyweights.

although the lad from Plymouth was the more upstanding of the two. The referee was Joe Palmer, who had officiated at one of Len's earlier fights at Plymouth.

After some sparring, Sullivan was the first to score with a left to the body. He tried a left then a right 'downstairs', but received two hard blows to the head in return and was driven back against the ropes. Harvey was boxing in his usual cool manner, taking his time, picking his shots and getting through with some neat left jabs, although when he tried the right he was unsuccessful as Johnny came just inside them so that they passed round his neck. There were plenty of supporters for the Covent Garden man and they cheered whenever he got in a rangy left or right to the body, although he was equally applauded for those shots of his that were blocked or parried by the clever Cornishman. Sullivan did get home one long-range right to the head that Harvey did well to ride.

Johnny would duck under a straight lead, then go into a clinch where, regretfully, he was careless with his head and used it as a third fist under Len's chin. Frequently Harvey's head was tilted back by these illegal thrusts, but the referee took no notice and Len had to grab Johnny by the shoulders and shove him off, for which action he received a warning finger from the Third Man. A lovely left hook to the jaw shook Sullivan up and doubtless Len had his own reasons for not pressing his advantage. Sullivan consistently went for the body, then got in close, put his head on Harvey's chest and was again guilty of butting. It was not until the sixth round that Harvey gained a distinct advantage. Suddenly he started a brisk attack then, as his rival came forward, caught him under the chin with a sharp right uppercut. Sullivan staggered backwards, grabbed Len as he came in and there was some wrestling until the bell came to the Londoner's rescue. He had been badly hurt and showed it. Two rounds later Harvey repeated the process, but once again it was too near the end of the round for him to win decisively over a rocking rival.

It was not an exciting contest to watch, save for the skill which Harvey exhibited by drawing a lead from Sullivan and beating him to the punch with some perfect straight lefts. Several times Johnny tried the old dodge of going back suddenly into the ropes and then bounding off them to launch an attack. But not once did he surprise Harvey, who watched him go through his acrobatics without batting an eyelid, standing off until he had drawn Sullivan back into the middle of the ring where he could outbox him at long range.

With Harvey not taking any chances against a man who knew all the tricks of the trade, and Sullivan more eager to make a close-quarter job of it, the bout lost some of the anticipated sparkle, but there was a tense atmosphere in this battle of wits in which Harvey was the more controlled and generally the master of each situation as it appeared. On the other hand, Sullivan was in trouble at least three times in the last half of the contest and had to take drinks from a special bottle provided by manager Ted Broadribb, who was very voluble in his addresses to someone in the ring or on the other side of it and at times looked mentally distressed, especially when he heard one ringside bookmaker offering to lay a hundred to eight on Harvey.

On several occasions it seemed as though Len would send over a winning punch during the closing stages of the fight, but he was taking no chances. He knew he was well ahead, that if he kept breaking up Sullivan's attacks and kept him at arm's length, he could win without running any risk of being caught by a 'sucker' punch. During each interval his father told him he was doing all that was necessary and manager Sullivan, standing nearby, notified his boxer, quite unnecessarily, that it was 'in the bag'. In the final round, Harvey produced that little extra zip to win the session by a clear margin.

The final bell and the majority of the spectators were expecting Mr Palmer to walk across to Harvey's corner and raise his hand. Instead, to the dumb amazement of everyone, he went in the opposite direction. Sullivan himself was so astonished that he did not lift his gloved hands out of his lap, so the referee had to grab one and hold it aloft. Then the storm broke. The absurdity of the decision took a moment to sink in, then a thunderous roar of disapproval came from all parts of the arena, the ringsiders, the boys at the back and those in the gallery. Programmes, hats and other miscellaneous items were thrown into the ring and the announcer was not allowed to make himself heard. The longer the uproar lasted the worse it became. The referee had not dared to leave the ring and now from all sides men were clambering up to get at him.

Undoubtedly he owed his life to Mrs Burge, the proprietress. She called him to the side of the ring and urged him to slip to the floor. 'Stay right beside me,' she ordered and put her arm through his. 'Whatever happens,' she warned. 'Don't take any notice. Just keep on walking, I'm making straight for the dressing-room.' The disappearance of the referee did not stop the disturbance which had now developed into a near riot. Fights broke out in various parts of the building, seats were overturned and finally the police had to be brought in. Even then the din continued and although the next pair of boxers were hustled into the ring, the irate spectators refused to be quietened and no one could hear the announcement of their respective names. Palmer had to remain in the dressing-room guarded by a few stalwart boxers who happened to be on hand, and it was not until midnight that it was safe for him to emerge and go home. Both Johnny Sullivan and Harvey had long since departed and Len was cheered to the echo by hundreds waiting outside 'The Ring' until a taxi was hailed to drive him and his father home.

CHAPTER 4

Championship Chance at Eighteen

Although the adverse verdict in the Sullivan fight destroyed Harvey's unbeaten record in London rings, which was something of a setback, it was, in fact, about the finest piece of publicity that the young Cornishman could receive at this point in his career. While his growing army of supporters howled for the referee's blood and the press, almost *en bloc*, continued to upbraid the discredited official, Len himself was not bothered. He just shrugged his shoulders and remarked that we all make mistakes and as the rules state that a referee's decision is final, there was no sense in making a song and dance about it.

A letter signed by Dan Sullivan appeared the following week in *Boxing* in which he demanded that Mr Palmer should 'give his reasons for making Sullivan the winner' when the majority of those who saw the contest were of the strong opinion that Harvey had won by the proverbial mile. He argued that such an undeserved defeat might have the effect of undermining Len's confidence and thus bring him down to the level of an ordinary fighter, while it was very 'disheartening to a boy like Harvey who has ambitions to become a champion'.

All very commendable and the right thing to do in his boxer's interests. There was no hope, however, of having the verdict reversed, although the eight column inches the letter occupied was cheap advertising. Whether this, following the outpourings of the sporting press, was responsible for the self-appointed Board of Control to summon Mr Palmer to its presence and withdraw his referee's licence after a hearing, can only be surmised. It was strong administrative action and if it appeased the Harvey fans as 'true justice', Len felt it unnecessary and too severe a sentence.

While fully convinced that he had beaten Sullivan, he regarded Palmer as an experienced and trustworthy official and when his supporters exclaimed that the offending referee had got his deserts, Harvey did not agree. 'I got what I thought were adverse verdicts during my early days in Plymouth,' he told them. 'I was disappointed, but soon learnt that it was something you had to expect now and again. Who knows, one of these days I might be declared the winner of a fight I thought I'd lost.' As it happens his long record shows that he never received a verdict that, in the opinion of press and public, he had not well and truly won.

One close observer of the Sullivan/Harvey controversy was Harry Jacobs, at that time London's foremost promoter who staged mammoth shows at the Royal Albert Hall. He had presented weekly boxing tournaments at 'Wonderland' in London's East End from 1899, watched the place burn down twelve years later, and then converted a nearby warehouse into 'Premierland', where he continued as a fistic maestro until the opportunity came to move into the resplendent West Kensington concert hall, ideally constructed for the watching of fistic contests, even if the original planners had far loftier ideas for its use.

Here Jacobs, a talented matchmaker, was in his element. He revelled in pairing men in contests of tremendous public appeal and gave his patrons the biggest value for money it was possible to provide: several title fights on one programme, offering up to a hundred rounds of boxing in a single evening, many of his shows going on until past midnight.

Although the prevailing Board of Control claimed the sole right to make title fights, because it had the monopoly of the Lord Lonsdale Challenge Belts and the backing of the National Sporting Club, its power held no terrors for Jacobs, who made his own championship matches and could do so with total disregard of the ruling body, simply because he paid so well that all the top-line fighters clamoured to appear on his bills.

One of his favourite performers was Harry Mason, whom he had made British welterweight champion five months previously. Born in the East End, but raised in Leeds, where he had been taken because of the Zeppelin raids in the First World War, Mason possessed a natural bent for boxing and had become a champion in the Jewish Lad's Brigade before turning professional at the age of seventeen.

A brainy, confident boxer, he bore a cocky air that made him liked by some and disliked by others; but there was no question about his skill, which was of the highest order. Mason's ringcraft and fistic brilliance was a joy to watch, while his nimble footwork and defensive ability made him an elusive and tantalising target. A 'box of tricks' in the ring, he was a lively person out of it, never at a loss for words and with a chirpy zest for repartee.

Always smartly dressed and immaculate in both his fighting and civilian clothes, Harry had jet black hair which he anointed with oil and brushed back from his forehead, leaving a neat parting down the middle which he defied any opponent to disturb, it being his proud boast that he could travel twenty rounds and come out of the ring without a hair out of place. Undoubtedly he was one of the wiliest boxers ever to pull on a pair of gloves and they called him 'The Little Fiddler', not solely because he had taught himself to play the violin, an instrument that formed part of his training equipment.

Mason had been British lightweight champion in 1923 and after defending his title went to America, where he stayed for seven months and lost three out of eight bouts, mostly against welterweights. In his absence the Board of Control declared that he had forfeited his title and installed Ernie Izzard as lightweight champion. But on returning home, Harry scored a sensational victory to regain his laurels and then went on to become a dual title-holder by defeating Johnny Brown, of Hamilton, for the British welter crown.

Now promoter Jacobs thought it time for Mason to defend his heavier honours. Who better as challenger than Len Harvey, the youngster whose name had been so prominently in the news of late? It was a match that fired the imagination of the fans and proved a sell-out for the astute promoter. It meant a severe test for the lad from Plymouth who, although having the advantage in height and reach, lacked the top-class experience of the champion – already a veteran of eighty-four bouts, including six title fights, plus that American venture.

Harvey could boast almost as many contests, but many of these he had fought as a mere boy, almost a child, and were confined to six rounds of two-minutes duration, whereas Mason had started profession-ally as a ten-rounds boxer. There was also the big difference in age, Len being three months short of his nineteenth birthday, while Harry would have just celebrated his twenty-third – the difference between a youth and a man.

For all this, Harvey's father and Dan Sullivan must have felt confi-dent that young Len was quite capable of looking after himself and pre-sumably Jacobs was making the proposition financially worthwhile. There is no printed record of what he paid for the match, but one must presume that it was not less than £1,000, with Mason receiving the recog-nised champion's share of sixty per cent.

In any event it probably represented Len's highest purse to date and prompted his manager to send him to the Norfolk Arms at Wembley for several weeks of special preparation for his first championship chance. The training-quarters here were a complete change of atmosphere, and one which suited the quiet, reserved character of the challenger. A week prior to the fight Len gave a private try-out before a large crowd, including many members of the press, one of whom wrote: 'Harvey is the best piece of fighting material on view anywhere in this country today', and went on to say: 'He will be a better man at 10 st. 7 lbs. until he grows into a fully-fledged middleweight, than he has been at 10 st. or 10st. 4 lbs. and whether he wins or loses against Mason, he will have been shown quite a few of the finer points of the boxing game and be an improved craftsman as a result.'

As sparring-partners, Len had the assistance of Reggie Caswell, Bill Softley and a Belgian named Frank Rabosse. It was noticed that he was very 'merciful' to them: they did not have to take the rough treatment that was the usual lot of the hired spar-mate when their employer is reaching his peak of fitness and nervous tension.

Mason trained at Brighton under Alec Goodman, whom he regarded as without equal as a conditioner and counsellor. Harry, who had let himself balloon up to 11 st. 4 lb. before starting his preparation, was confident that he would know far too much for his youthful challenger. He even confided as much to Len when they met for the weighing-in ceremony, adding that he had the finest trainer in the world. 'But it's you I'm boxing, not your trainer,' quietly replied Len. 'You're in for a boxing lesson,' retorted Harry, whereupon Harvey remarked: 'I dare say I could do with one, I've still got a lot to learn.' He was coolness itself.

Some of the critics wondered if Harvey would be oppressed by his surroundings in the large Albert Hall, a place far bigger than 'The Ring' or any other arena in which Len had so far appeared. Nor had he ever boxed before a very large crowd. But there was no need to be apprehensive on the young Cornishman's account: to him a ring was a ring wherever it might be and he was oblivious to spectators during the course of a contest. His brain was ice-cold when he left the dressing-room and mounted the carpeted stairs that led into the big, circular auditorium.

The place was packed from the floor to the highest gallery and Len received a tremendous welcome from the multitude of his supporters who had crossed Blackfriars Bridge and made their way by bus, underground and car to cheer him on to victory in the most important contest of his life so far. Mason, too, enjoyed a thunderous reception, and Harry Jacobs had every reason to be extremely pleased with himself.

The buzz of excitement that had pervaded the arena from the time of the arrival of the two principals in the main event, died to a hush as the Master of Ceremonies announced that they would be fighting twenty three-minute rounds for the welterweight championship of Great Britain and that both men were inside the stipulated weight of 10 st. 7 lbs. Referee C. H. Douglas, who was seated at the ringside to officiate, called the pair up to the ropes for a brief lecture, they returned to their corners, the bell clanged and Harvey came out for the first of the twenty-one championship contests in which he was to participate during his long and meritorious career.

There was some cautious sparring, with Mason dancing round on his toes and Harvey more flat-footed, moving slightly, expectant. Harry darted in with a left lead that Len blocked, then tried a left hook that was parried out of danger. When he made another attack, he was met with a straight left to the mouth that made him hang on to the challenger, but Harvey, as cool as a cucumber, pushed him off, shot in another stiff left, then whipped in a right to the head and – the champion was down!

Sensation in the opening minute and the crowd roared. For a moment it looked as if Harvey was about to win the championship in the first round, but Len's right had landed a little too high for a knockout and Mason bounced up almost immediately, disdaining to take a count if only to show that he was unhurt. Now he had to use the ring to prevent Len from following up his advantage and in the last minute attacked briskly with both hands. But it was the challenger's round.

Now the crowd had to settle down and enjoy a battle of wits and skill. The fireworks were over for the time being, but the beautiful boxing displayed by these two masters of the fistic art held the fans spellbound. Mason's extra experience was matched by Harvey's superior hitting – he never wasted a punch. Harry used every trick and artifice at his command, but nothing that he tried could upset the calm equilibrium of his youthful opponent. Mason did get the better of the infighting, in which he excelled, but he was inclined to hit and hold and the clinches became prolonged, causing the referee to caution them both at the end of the third round. Len was pacing himself nicely, but inclined to let his nimble rival do most of the attacking, ready to catch him as he did in the fourth round, a right clip to the chin bringing the champion to his knees. Harry looked hurt, but Len did not follow up, no doubt thinking that Mason might be 'foxing'.

The champion took advantage of his rival's careful tactics by continually darting in and out with brisk two-handed light punches or running into holds where he proved the better at infighting. But he was caught by some good counters and there never seemed any likelihood of him scoring with a damaging punch. Yet his fast, snappy work began to win him the middle rounds by slight margins and at the end of the fifteenth Sullivan visited his boxer's corner to administer advice.

This proved ineffective, because Mason took the next two rounds by comfortable margins. Try as he might, Harvey just could not keep the smaller man at long range and his followers became anxious, feeling that he was tiring and Mason might sneak a verdict at the finish.

They need not have worried. At the start of the eighteenth Harvey set up a strong attack that had Harry on the retreat and forced him to fight at a distance. Pressing the champion hard, Len jolted in left leads to the face and at the right moment cracked home a right to the jaw. Mason staggered back under the impact and, following up, Len let him have a left and right to the chin and Harry was on the canvas again.

He had been badly shaken and took a count of eight resting on one knee. He looked very apprehensive when he got to his feet and was at once driven into the ropes by his determined challenger. The Harvey fans yelled encouragement, but Mason did the right thing in such circumstances and fought back two-fistedly to prevent Len getting through with a decisive blow. It was exciting stuff, and Harry had to thank his experience for keeping him out of further trouble until the bell.

Harvey was all set to establish victory in the last two rounds, but Mason was equally determined, and they exchanged fast punches to the delight of the fans. Len was hitting the harder and was more on the target, but Harry defied him with sudden bursts or by going in and tying his man up at close range, tactics that brought the referee into the ring to break up what might have been prolonged clinches.

Harvey's fine finish, together with his good start, seemed to have earned him the verdict and the title, but Mr Douglas found he could not separate them and declared a 'draw'. This result divided the house and if Len's supporters were disappointed, Mason's followers must have been relieved. As for Harvey, he was smiling when he went over to Harry and touched gloves. 'You were lucky,' said the champion cheekily, but Len patted him on his sleek head and went back to his corner without replying.

How prophetically true was Mason's pert remark, though in a way he did not intend. Had Harvey been named as the winner it would have meant keeping his weight down to the welter limit, a very dangerous thing for a boy in his 'teens. Without a doubt he would have been called upon to defend his title – perhaps several times – whereas he had almost grown into a middleweight before the year was out. So it was in the nature of a lucky defeat. Even so, an attempt was made to keep him in the welterweight division, but it was soon realised how much more important it was not to restrict his growth but to allow him to develop naturally.

CHAPTER 5

Florence the Faithful

Very generously, Sullivan gave Len a rest of forty-six days following the title fight with Mason. In view of the way managers exploited their boxers in those days, it was surprisingly long. Apart from a slight swelling near his left eye, Harvey was unmarked after an hour's combat with a champion. It had been the Cornish lad's third twenty-rounder to go the full distance in the space of four months and no doubt his father, if not Dan, considered that a respite was necessary.

This freedom did not entice Len to go off on the spree. He was not that type, a fact of which his mentors were well aware. They knew he would put in a training spell at Fred Duffett's gym every day and also be in attendance at 'The Ring' for the thrice-weekly shows on Monday, Thursday and Saturday, for Len was always ready to learn, and closely studied the styles and moves of the top-line boxers who performed at Blackfriars. He had several friends outside the boxing fraternity, but these were young men of quiet disposition – not tearaways – who took their pleasures modestly, but nevertheless enjoyably. They respected Harvey and his chosen profession and guarded his interests in the recreations in which he took part. They played games of billiards and darts, watched football matches and other similar pursuits. Len was also a great reader and was never without a book to occupy that small part of the day not given over entirely to boxing.

His next opponent was to be Nol Steenhorst, a tough Dutchman who had fought several times in England. He could not be termed a talented boxer, but possessed great staying power and, of course, was always dangerous. They were matched to fight fifteen rounds at 10 st. 8 lbs. on 14th June, but Steenhorst met with an accident and Billy Mattick, from Castleford, was brought in as a substitute. The Yorkshireman came with a first-class reputation and had fought the best at his weight, although his record was not entirely without blemish. Unable to make the stipulated poundage, it was agreed that they should box at catchweights, which gave the visitor the advantage of several pounds.

Mattick needed more than that to contain Harvey, who looked 'fit to fight for a kingdom' and from the start appeared a certain winner. Mattick was strong and knew how to punch, but was well short of Len's class. He set about his task with zeal and confidence until, midway through the opening round, the 'Ring' favourite drove in a well-timed right to the jaw that shook Billy down to his toes.

He fought back valiantly enough, but that one punch was sufficient to give the onlookers the key to the situation. With an advantage in height and reach, Harvey outboxed his sturdy and aggressive rival until the seventh, when he made the opening for another stunning right-hander that struck the Yorkshireman's chin at full force and sent him down and completely out for the count.

Steenhorst notified the 'Ring' management that he would be ready to fulfil his contract with Harvey on Sunday, 4th July – Independence Day in America, but, as will be seen, an equally important day in Len's life. This gave him a break of nearly three weeks. His closest friend, George Coote, who worked for his father as a cabinet-maker in Theberton Street, Islington, and had been granted a week's holiday, persuaded Len to go with him to Cliftonville, the stylish part of Margate. Up to that point Len had never had a real vacation – a complete change from the boxing routine that had governed his life for the past six and a half years. He thought it a good idea, especially when George pointed out that there was racing at Folkestone that week, which would fill in the time. Len liked horses and had a shrewd way of picking winners on a course.

He was also good at picking winners in another aspect. One day, finding little to interest them in their hotel in Gibson Square, they were walking along the promenade when the sound of a party of young people noisily enjoying themselves caused Len and George to look down on the sands where an apparently exciting game of cricket was taking place between, as it turned out, the boys and girls of one boarding house playing those of another.

A blonde was batting and George was surprised to get a nudge from his companion. 'Take a look at that girl at the wicket. What a stunner!' But at that moment she was given 'out' as having been stumped, a decision with which she did not agree. A fierce argument blew up between herself and the umpire. 'Listen to her,' chuckled Len. 'Just like a girl, but isn't she lovely!'

George could not believe his own ears, especially when his friend remarked that he would give anything to meet her. So far the young boxer had shown no interest in girls and no doubt had been warned off them by both his manager and his father. Now it seemed a case of love at first sight. That evening, either by design or accident, the two boys found themselves in the Cliff Cafe watching the dancing, and there was Harvey's heart-throb. 'Go and ask her for a dance,' urged George, anxious to make his friend happy, but Len was reluctant. 'I don't know her and she might think I'm taking a liberty,' he said. 'Well, you won't ever get to know her if you take that attitude,' replied George. 'Go and ask her – she can only say "no".' But this brilliant ring warrior, who feared no one, was too shy. The opportunity was lost and they went home. The truth was that Len had never been to a dance and did not know what to do. His footwork in the ring might be classical, but on a slippery dance floor, with a beautiful girl in his arms – the thought was terrifying.

A day or so later, when they were out walking along with George McKenzie, who was staying in the same hotel, Len spotted two girls coming towards them. 'That's her,' he whispered to Coote, and would have walked past, eyes averted, had not McKenzie stopped and spoken to one of them, whom he seemed to know.

'This is Florence,' he said indicating the blonde. 'And this is my friend Doris,' she replied. McKenzie introduced his friends as Len and another George and then asked the girls where they were going. 'Only for a walk,' said Florence. 'We are going home today unfortunately. Our bags are packed and we are catching the two o'clock train.'

'What about coming on the beach?' suggested McKenzie, who having heard of Len's interest in one of the girls, was anxious to make the most of this chance meeting. 'We are not dressed for the beach,' said Florence, indicating their every-day clothes, but they were not allowed to escape. 'What about clock golf, then?', and when it was pointed out that there were five of them, McKenzie suddenly remembered a pressing engagement elsewhere and made off, leaving the others to pair up. Remembering the disaster at the dance, Coote was quick to act and commandeered Doris as his partner. That left Len and Florence to play together. They did so in comparative silence until she broke through his shy reserve by asking him what he did for a living.

'I'm a boxer,' he admitted, and if he expected her to be surprised he was mistaken. 'So is my brother,' she said. 'His name is Dick, but he boxes as "Bert Laws" – do you know him?' Surely all boxers knew one another, she thought – all four thousand of them – so she was quite unperturbed when he told her that they had used the same gymnasium in Delancy Street, Camden Town. 'My name is Harvey,' he explained.

'I've heard Dick talk of you,' said Florence. 'In fact, if I remember rightly, he held a good opinion of your boxing abilities and said that you would be a certain champion one day.' 'Well, not yet,' Len told her. 'But isn't it strange that we should both have an interest in Boxing?' 'It is the long arm of coincidence,' she replied with all her eighteen-year-old philosophy, and they were to discover that their meeting could almost be termed providential.

Florence Law's parents both came from County Tyrone in Ireland, her father, Hiram George Law, being a journeyman printer, who was averse to settling in one place and had London as his ultimate destination. He was twenty-seven when he married Anne Maude Mellin, who was ten years his junior and quite content to follow him wherever his work took him and rear a family on the way.

Their eldest was Herbert Richard, who was known as Dick – he was born at Gloucester in 1905. Then at St Albans came Florence, born on 4th August 1907, just twenty-one days after the young boxer she had met at Cliftonville came into the world.* When her father eventually reached his goal and was working in Gray's Inn Road, London, she was seven, the same age that Len Harvey was when his family moved from Polhilsa to Devonport. Another amazing coincidence is that among the work that Hiram Law undertook was the collating of *Boxing* – which boasted of being 'the only paper in the world solely devoted to the Sport', and which was being published at that time at Windsor House in nearby Kingsway.

Florence thought the world of her brother Dick. Although of small stature he could play all games well, and excelled at football, cricket and swimming. As soon as he left school he was apprenticed to a firm of printers, it being his father's firm belief that to become a craftsman was the only way to reach success in life. One evening Dick went along to the Stanley Hall at Kentish Town where a 7 st.-6 lb. novices' boxing competition was being held. He watched one or two bouts, then asked if he could 'have a go' and finished up by winning a silver cup.

Immediately he took an immense liking to the Noble Art and proved so good at it that it was not long before he was fighting professionally at most of the London halls. But all without his father's knowledge, who would have banned such a hazardous business as being highly detri-

---

*Later on there was another son, Lowery Cole, who became known as 'Larry' and a second daughter named Constance.

mental to his son's printing career. So Dick adopted the name of 'Bert Laws' to hide the fact that he was a prominent boxer; and to further cover up his clandestine activities, he sought the assistance of his sister. On the nights that he was boxing, she would creep downstairs and let him in. 'How do I look?' he would ask anxiously and she would inspect his features before rendering the first aid necessary to make him presentable at the breakfast table the following morning. For her part in the deception she received the princely sum of half-a-crown a week.

Truth will out, however. Dick's employer became suspicious when his young apprentice turned up for work with a black eye, a swollen nose or a split lip. He was boxing regularly now, sometimes twice or three times a week and despite his skill, it was not always possible to avoid the marks of his additional trade. So Law Senior was consulted and the subterfuge revealed. The son was ordered by his father to drop professional boxing immediately, Dick begged to be allowed to continue as he was doing so well, and eventually it was agreed that he would be allowed to break his indentures and become a full-time fighter. It was then that he got to know the sixteen-year-old Harvey and realised his potential talent, telling his sister about the 'wonder boy' from Plymouth and foretelling a brilliant future for him. He took a liking to Len and more than once gave him his bus fare back to Hornsey where the youngster was living with his parents at that time.

Dick went to America where his talents were appreciated and then on to Australia, a country he liked very much and where he could have found plenty of employment as a printer had he cared to remain there. But his mother begged him to come home and when he did, the edict was laid down. 'No more boxing,' ordered his father, so back into the print trade went the son, leaving 'Bert Laws' as just a name in the record books. But in 1926 that name forged a link between his sister and Len Harvey, a link that was to grow into a life-long bond.

So two young people – miles apart in their origins and way of life – were brought together in simple but nevertheless unique circumstances. Florence was a shorthand typist in the famous advertising agency of Sir Charles Higham – he was in championship class as a boxer, a fact that she found difficult to believe. How could this slim-built, pale-faced young man possibly be engaged in such a tough and rough sport?

There was more talking than playing in that epic game of clock golf at Cliftonville in the summer of 1926, although Florence had to lead the conversation. But if Len was shy of asking questions, he was determined that this would not be merely a chance holiday meeting. Very curiously, because she later discovered that Len and his friend had return steamer tickets back to London two days later, it appeared that they were all travelling on the two o'clock train that afternoon, and so the friendship developed. Before they parted Florence had promised to go to 'The Ring' on the following Sunday afternoon when Len was due to have his postponed contest with Nol Steenhorst.

Florence told her parents that she and Doris were going to walk along the Serpentine in Hyde Park, a popular promenade for Londoners. Instead Len and George Coote met them with a taxi at the Elizabethan houses in High Holborn and took them to the famous Blackfriars arena. There was a crowd of men and boys pushing their way in and outside a trumpet player was appropriately rendering 'Two lovely black eyes'! It was all very colourful and exciting.

Len thrust three tickets into George's hands – he always bought tickets for his friends, even when at the height of his fame – saw them go up the stairs on the left of the building that led to the balcony, then went into 'The Ring' and through into the dressing-room. A portion of the balcony was partitioned off from the rest and in this secluded enclosure Mrs Dick Burge, the proprietress, would seat her guests and any VIPs who came along. The back row was reserved for the press, who, due to the sharp elevation of the balcony, enjoyed a clear and uninterrupted view of the ring. Here Florence and her friends found themselves.

Few women watched boxing at the small halls in those days, although they could have been seen at the ringside at classier places such as the Albert Hall, Olympia and Earls Court. It was pretty bold for two young and attractive girls to be seen at 'The Ring' and Doris was petrified. Florence, however, took it all very calmly. Her father had always refused to allow her to watch her brother fight, but now she was going to find out what it was all about.

To her surprise, Len made it look all so easy and she told him so afterwards when he asked her what she thought about it. 'It's not so easy as all that,' Len told her, but she remained unconvinced. 'No wonder my brother took it up,' she added, as they went back to Theberton Street when Mrs Coote entertained them to tea. But easy or not, once Florence had seen Len's superb athletic appearance and watched the skilful way he had outboxed the formidable looking Dutchman, she became an avid fight fan.

Steenhorst was not a skilled boxer, but his toughness, strength and powerful, if somewhat unorthodox punching, had carried him through a number of successes in British rings. This time he had met his master, however, and while he tried every move in his repertoire to batter down the Cornishman, he found he could not hurt Harvey, while he was unable to avoid Len's precisely delivered rights to the jaw.

The Dutchman was sent down seven times in all, but he would rise gamely, despite the fact, as he stated subsequently, that he had never before been sent to the canvas. He did force Harvey to box on the retreat in the sixth, seventh and eighth rounds, as well as once or twice later, but this was due more to his wild bursts of aggression than to any effective work. Once Len had his problem solved he opened out and freely punished Steenhorst with both hands to have him in such a defenceless state that the referee intervened in the fifteenth and final round to save a courageous man from further suffering.

There was an interval of ten weeks before Harvey's next contest and he spent the first part of this in a steady pursuit of the lovely Miss Law. Knowing that his manager would clamp down heavily on any adventures with the fair sex, Len kept her existence a secret, or tried to, because even if London's boxing fraternity did not at first know of the existence of Florence, they would recognise Harvey anywhere and Len could not have been surprised when Bill Dixon, an old-timer, asked, 'Didn't I see you going into *The Regent* at King's Cross with Bert Law's sister the other night?' Len urged him not to tell Sullivan, but Dan was to find out before long, in fact, Harvey was to betray himself during the course of his next contest.

Although it seemed fairly obvious to most observers that the now nineteen-year-old Harvey was growing fast, his manager seemed determined that he should have another crack at the welterweight crown. To this end he matched him with Johnny Brown from Hamilton, who had won over and lost to Harry Mason in title bouts and who regarded himself as a leading championship contender. The Scotsman willingly accepted an offer to box Harvey over twenty rounds at the welter limit of 147 lbs. and agreed to put up a side-stake of £100, whereupon Sullivan told the press that the winner would challenge Jack Hood, who had just taken the title from Mason.

Apparently neither Len nor his father could find fault with this piece of short-sighted matchmaking for the boxer went to Hampstead for special training three weeks prior to the bout which was due to take place on 13th September. *Boxing*, however, had this comment to make: 'That Len Harvey is shaping in the direction of middleweight is the opinion of more than a few competent judges and, if he matures to that weight, great things may confidently be expected of him. He is "built for Boxing" and his technique leaves little to be desired. Temperamentally he is cool-headed and alert in the most trying circumstances, and he has a punch, delivered unerringly with the knuckles, that is as effective as it is good to behold.'

Such an observation made the proposed match with Brown (at welterweight) appear an error of judgment, to say the least, and it proved a sad disappointment to the Blackfriars fans who filled 'The Ring' to capacity, most of them ardent Harvey supporters. Len came in at 10 st. 6¾ lbs., 12 oz. heavier than his opponent, but whereas Brown appeared strong at the weight, the same could not be said for Harvey, who, apart from having weakened himself in the process of making the required poundage, did not seem to have his full mind on the job at hand.

Sullivan, no doubt having backed his boxer to the hilt as usual, was more than perturbed when he saw that for round after round Harvey was content to let the Scotsman do all the attacking and seemed ready to indulge in prolonged clinches, negative work that he usually declined to be drawn into. Then the real truth dawned on Dan. Suddenly he noticed that whenever the pair went into holds, Len would look up towards the press box and wink at someone seated there. Who? He followed the line of his boxer's eye. A girl – it couldn't be. A blonde – heaven forbid. He gnashed his teeth and going to Harvey's corner at the end of the round, let it be known that Len's secret had been discovered and that he had better pull his socks up and forget the gallery if he wanted to win. It never occurred to the manager to question his judgment in making the match, but the records show that Len was never again asked to make the welterweight limit, in fact, within three more contests he was fighting at 11 st. 6 lb., even though he was well short of that weight.

Sullivan's pep talk had the desired effect and Brown was made to realise that he had a fight on his hands. By the eleventh round Len had practically closed his opponent's left eye with some well-timed rights while his attacks were being broken up by vigorous counter-punching. Harvey was fast making up leeway, and the Scot had to exert himself to the full in order to try and maintain the slight lead he had gained in the earlier rounds of the contest. Going all out for a decisive win in the nineteenth round, Len jarred his opponent back on his heels with some perfectly delivered left leads to the face, crossed the right superbly to the jaw, spinning Brown round in a half circle, and also scored with some telling uppercuts when Johnny came tearing in to try and retaliate.

The best round of the bout was the last, in which both men went all out for victory. Who had won? Many thought Brown, because he had done the bulk of the forcing in the first half of the bout and held his own in the second, while Harvey's supporters claimed that his storming finish had enabled him to snatch the verdict. Referee Sam Russell did not leave them long in doubt. He spread his arms wide to indicate a 'draw' and the majority went home satisfied.

The decision had saved Dan's money, but it cost him his temper. After the fight he gave Len the telling off of a lifetime. 'Are you mad?' he asked. 'In an important fight and looking up at a girl in the gallery. One of these days you won't know what's hit you if you go on doing that.' 'All right, Dan,' said Len in his quiet way. 'I promise you that I'll never look at her again while I'm in the ring.'

'That's not good enough,' snapped his manager. 'You're nearly ready for your big chance. Cut her out. I've seen this happen to fine fighters before. Give her up. Forget her. She'll ruin you.'

'I can't do that,' said Len. 'This girl is different. She knows all about Boxing – her brother is a fighter. She won't interfere with my career, in fact, I'm sure she will help it.'

'She may know the Fight Game,' answered the irate Sullivan. 'But only from a woman's angle. Maybe she is different in your eyes, but not mine. When love is kicking around they're all the same.'

'You haven't met her yet,' Harvey reminded him. 'Then go find her and bring her to me,' answered Dan. 'I'll give her a piece of my mind.'

Len brought Florence into the managerial office. 'All I've got to say to you, young lady, is if you're really interested in this lad, let him alone. He's only eighteen and girls can be ruinous to boys at that age. Boxing and women don't mix. I want you to promise that you'll never come again to see him box.'

'Rubbish,' said Florence sweetly, and walked out; but Len made it clear to her that Sullivan had a point and in future she must not expect the kind of attention she had received that evening. He also laid down a few laws she would have to observe if she wanted to watch him box. 'No matter what happens,' he said, 'you must promise not to show your feelings either in word or action. Keep all your thoughts until after the fight.'

Florence promised and kept her word for the rest of Len's career, except for one solitary occasion ten years later when she left her ring-side seat at Wembley Arena, when he was fighting for the world title, to go to his corner during one of the later intervals and tell him that he should try and take more of the initiative in order to make sure of winning the contest.

CHAPTER 6

Long Trail to the Top

Sullivan could never accept Florence and did his utmost to break the friendship which he emphatically considered would prove disastrous to his boxer's bright prospects. He was suspicious of Miss Law and would like to have barred her from coming to 'The Ring' but as Len always bought the tickets, he could not refuse her admission. In fact, she never missed one of his fights there, indeed saw all his London bouts to the end of his boxing life with the exception of those at the National Sporting Club in Covent Garden, and then only because women were barred from going there.

Harvey fought a return contest with Nol Steenhorst in his next engagement, mainly because the Dutchman was of the opinion that he would have gone the full distance in their first meeting had the referee not called a halt in the last minute of the contest. He also claimed that he had been called upon to make too low a poundage and requested that this time the stipulated weight should be increased to 11 st. 2 lbs. His faith in himself seemed justified in that he did last until the final bell at the second time of asking, but only after he had been compelled again to take a good deal of punishment.

Some of the boxing reporters criticised Len for allowing Steenhorst to stay the full fifteen rounds. They argued that the Dutchman could have been knocked out or stopped at any time after the fifth round, overlooking the great humane streak in the Cornishman's character. Harvey was to prove over and over again, in fact, had already proved many times, that he could be a 'killer' when the occasion demanded. But it gave him no satisfaction to destroy a game opponent over whom he had demonstrated his mastery. It was up to the referee to decide when a man had taken enough and if a bout was allowed to continue when it was obvious to Len that his rival had no hope of winning, he was prepared to be lenient. Besides it was against his nature to go berserk after scoring a knockdown, for he knew that very often a hurt boxer can be extremely dangerous when he gets up, while a spate of wild hitting in an attempt to knock a rival unconscious was a sure way of risking damage to the hands, to say nothing of a waste of energy if the other man survived what was intended to be a decisive finish.

As it happened. Steenhorst started the proceedings in businesslike fashion by swinging a powerful left at the Cornishman's chin. Harvey avoided this with ease, side-stepped a rush that was intended to sweep him into the ropes, and caught the oncoming Dutchman with a picture punch right to the chin that crumpled up the recipient on the canvas. It took him eight seconds to get to his feet and the fans yelled to Harvey to step in and finish him off. But Len never listened to the crowd, probably never heard them. He remained his cool and collected self and proceeded to fulfil his professional requirements. In other words, he was there to win a boxing contest, not a fight.

He closed his opponent's eye in the second round, shook him down to his toes with a right to the jaw in the fifth and knocked him off his feet again in the thirteenth. He took the honours in every round and the unhesitating decision of the referee at the finish. Not once was Len asked for anything more by that official and if any of the spectators who filled the one-time chapel to capacity went home feeling they had been deprived of a bloodbath, at least they had seen an exhibition of the finer points in the art of self defence.

Harvey had weighed 11 st. dead and looked to be stronger and fitter than ever before. Twenty days later he was back in the same ring, this time weighing 10 st. 13 lb., 12 oz. lighter than Andrew Newton, from Marylebone, who came to contest the best of fifteen rounds. While the Londoner was not renowned for his science, he boasted a long and creditable record that fairly bristled with inside-the-distance wins. He was six years older than Harvey and had been boxing professionally for almost ten years.

An aggressive fighter with a knockdown punch in each fist, he seemed to be the very man to test Len's defences to the utmost and it was no surprise to find 'The Ring' filled to overflowing for this Monday night tit-bit. There was not a single vacant seat and barely a square foot of standing room when the principal pair climbed into the ring. The fans anticipated action from the start, for Newton was always in a hurry to establish his superiority and came from his corner looking very warlike, his gloves held low, ready to be sent over in devastating arcs to his rival's anatomy.

With his first blow, a smart straight left to the face, Harvey warned him that guards should be kept up. Andy tried a big swing, but Len ducked beneath it, moved lightly around, shot in a few more lefts and was then bustled into the ropes and almost over them. Referee Sam Russell ordered Newton to step back; the boxer obliged and then charged in again. This time he was caught by a left hook to the chin, a peach of a punch, well-judged, solid, and with all the Cornishman's bodyweight behind it.

Down went Newton and it looked all over, in fact, the blow was hard enough to have knocked out most men. But at 'nine' Andy managed to get up and for the rest of the round had to retreat and cover up in order to remain in the fight, while Len peppered him at will. Newton recovered sufficiently in the interval and came forth full of fight for the second round, forcing the pace and chasing after his opponent, who moved like a ballet dancer, making Andy miss by inches, but meanwhile picking up the points with his straight and timely hitting.

The Marylebone man was concentrating on heavy swings to the body and one that got through shook up Harvey, forcing him to go into a clinch and recover. This single success proved to be Newton's downfall. It produced the fighting spirit that Len kept for special occasions. That blow to the body had hurt and he set about his rival with gusto, another magnificent right to the chin putting Newton down again; but this time the bell sounded to interrupt the count.

Andy did not have a chance after that. He tried hard to land his big swings, but was out-generalled and outboxed. At the start of the sixth, Harvey darted across the ring and caught his opponent with a straight left to the chin that dropped Newton to his haunches. He rose at 'three', but was in trouble throughout the round, being put down for the fourth time before the bell brought him a little relief. Gallantly he came up for more, but after he had been punished severely and had paid further visits to the canvas, the referee stopped the contest midway through the eighth round.

Harvey had scored a great and decisive victory and the fans stood up to applaud him when he was named the winner and this continued until he had left the ring. They had seen him at his very best. He had shown championship form, placing every ounce of weight behind his punches, wasted no opportunities, got up on his toes and, both in his offensive and defensive tactics, left nothing to be desired. Afterwards, in the dressing-room, when I complimented him on his superb performance, he replied: 'Well, it takes a real good man to make one fight at one's best,' a remark that must have been some consolation to Andy Newton in his hour of defeat.

Next day the boxing writers were cogitating whether the nineteen-and-a-half-year-old Cornishman was ready to challenge Tommy Milligan for his British and European middleweight titles. The hard-hitting Scot had just stopped both George West and Ted Moore and outpointed the reigning light-heavyweight champion, Tom Berry. He was due to give Moore a second chance at winning his titles, so for the time being Len would have to wait. Meanwhile, there was one outstanding middleweight of championship class, victory over whom would make Harvey an outstanding contender. This was Len Johnson, from Manchester, barred from fighting for the British title because he was coloured, but considered in the North as the uncrowned champion because of his undoubted boxing ability and distinguished record.

Johnson was nearly five years older than Harvey and had been boxing professionally since 1921. He had spent the early part of 1926 in Australia where he had fought six twenty-round bouts, losing only one of them. An upstanding boxer, who made the fullest use of his long reach, the majority of Johnson's bouts went the full distance. Like Harvey, he preferred to let his opponents come to him, when he would pick them off with nicely-timed straight lefts or check their attacks with fine counter-punching. He had made himself a favourite at 'The Ring' by putting up a brilliant twenty-rounds contest with Jack Hood, a bout specially requested by the Prince of Wales (Edward VIII).

Because of their similarities in style, many of the critics imagined that the bout between the two Lens would not be wildly exciting, but all agreed that if Harvey could win over the clever Mancunian it would be a distinct feather in his cap, while a points setback would not be calamitous. In any event the young Cornishman, who was now living with his parents in Barnsbury in the Borough of Islington, would learn a lot from this battle of wits with Johnson.

Harvey chose a new training venue for this twenty-rounder, setting up camp at the *Black Bull* at Whetstone in Essex, where he was to return several times and which was to prove a lucky place, probably because in rummaging round one of the outbuildings he came across a horseshoe which had been made many years previously by Bob Fitzsimmons, his boyhood hero. Len nailed it up in the 'lucky' position and never parted with it until long after he had retired from the ring.

As soon as he realised that neither argument nor threat would keep Len and his girl friend apart, Dan Sullivan appointed trainer Archie

Watson as chaperon, his job being to see that the young couple were never left alone. As soon as they met he would shadow them with all the zeal of a private eye, follow them on their walks, into a cinema and, if they took a bus ride, and they were very fond of travelling on top, there he would be sitting a few seats behind.

While Len was at Whetstone, Florence would dash away from the advertising office where she worked and catch a bus to the *Black Bull*. As soon as she arrived, there was dear old Archie hovering around, and when they went into the bar parlour for a quiet chat, in he would come to keep an eye on them. She made these trips not only because she enjoyed Len's company, but she felt that after an intensive day's training in the sole company of men, he needed another interest, someone who could take his mind off the Fight Game that had so far dominated his whole life and prevented him from taking part in the recreational pursuits enjoyed by ordinary young people in the mid-1920s.

Harvey and Johnson were matched over twenty rounds at the middleweight limit of 11 st. 6 lbs., the Manchester man at 11 st. 2½ lbs. being the heavier by four pounds. Their meeting stirred the imagination of the fight fraternity and once again Rowland Hill's old chapel was bursting at the seams by the time the two Lens left their dressing-rooms. No one expected sensations, but these ardent connoisseurs of the fistic art anticipated an exhibition of Boxing at its highest level. They were not disappointed, although those who supported Harvey – and they were in the vast majority – knew that, good as was their favourite, the more experienced Johnson would be a difficult man to beat.

Both were reluctant to carry the attack to the other and after a cautious start in which the men were frequently in holds, referee Sam Russell found it necessary to climb into the ring and break up the innumerable clinches mostly brought about by the Manchester man's determination to limit his younger opponent's efforts to pick up any points. After a round or two of negative warfare, Harvey realised that this would not do and if Johnson was content to take a purely defensive role, it was up to him to take the initiative, even if it meant playing into the Mancunian's hands.

So, to the loud encouragement of the bulk of the spectators, Harvey set about making a fight of it, only to find he was trying to penetrate an almost insuperable defence while having to risk exposing himself to clever counter-shots that matched any of his own successes. There was one moment in the sixth round when the hopes of the Cornishman's supporters rose to excitement pitch. Drawing a lead he stepped back and as Johnson moved forward, so Harvey landed a solid right to the head, just a fraction too high to score a knockdown, but sufficient to shake up the coloured man and cause him to claim his opponent and hang on until parted by the referee. Urged on by the crowd, Harvey got in another hard right that caused Johnson to smash his own dexter hand to the body. This was on the low side and earned a reproachful glance from the Cornishman and caused Sam Russell to shake his head in reproof.

The bout livened up considerably after that, with Harvey the more enterprising, but much of his work was negatived by Johnson, who would come back with sudden spurts that enabled him to gather points before going on the defensive again. It was a battle of wits between two stylists, with Len from Manchester just keeping his nose in front. He had to survive several hard rights that Harvey got through, especially in the fourteenth, but by the time the final round came up the majority of those who had backed the local man were ready to acknowledge that Harvey was in arrears in the point scoring.

No one knew that better than Len, and he went all out in the last three minutes to try and bring off a decisive win. But his rival merely baulked all his efforts and when the concluding bell sounded the referee pointed to Johnson and left the ring, leaving MC George Harris to announce that the coloured man had gained a points victory. It was a close thing, but there was no disapproval from the fans, who went home feeling that any deficiencies their local favourite might have in his fistic abilities, these had been exposed by his more experienced opponent. Afterwards it was stated that Len's nose had been broken as early as the second round and this had proved a serious handicap during the course of this marathon contest.

The injury was sufficient to keep Harvey out of action for the next seventy days. But there was another reason why he was not in a hurry to get back into the ring. In February his mother died and her loss was a bitter blow to Len. Although she could never bring herself to watch him box, she gave him all the care and comforts that a child needs, saw that he had the right diet as a youth and young man to aid his arduous occupation, rejoiced in his triumphs and made light of his few setbacks. She took a liking to Florence when she was invited home to tea and was glad that Len had found a girl who suited him so well and understood his quiet temperament and the special demands of his hazardous profession. His mother's death broke up the family, for most of the children had left home, leaving only Len, his father and the youngest daughter, Olive, then no more than five years old. She was sent to relations in Dorset, his Dad remained in Barnsbury and Len went to stay with his friend George Coote, who lived with his mother in Theberton Street, Islington.

The adverse Johnson result was not a serious setback and all the critics agreed that there was plenty of time for the young Cornishman yet to fulfil all his expectations and promises. He had now to demonstrate his superiority over all prevailing middleweights as fast and as competently as possible. The Johnson fight had taken place on 3rd January 1927 and during the rest of the year Harvey was engaged in eleven more bouts, all of which he won, and all but one of which took place at 'The Ring'. To keep his boxer fully employed it was necessary for Sullivan to provide him with no less than eight continental opponents.

First came Maurice Prunier, a thirty-two-year-old Frenchman, who had been middleweight champion of his own country and who knew enough to be able to stay the full fifteen rounds although he had to pay two visits to the canvas, one for nine seconds in the third round from a whipping left hook to the chin after Harvey had threatened with a right, and the other nine rounds later when a left drive to the 'mark' sat Prunier down with a gasp for another long count. It was Len's first bout for ten weeks and he gave himself a nice work-out to win by a wide margin of points.

Three weeks later he was back again, this time facing Joe Bloomfield, middleweight brother of Jack, the former light-heavyweight champion. Joe, who had a 4 lbs. advantage at 11 st. 4½ lb., was a rough-and-ready fighter with a penchant for making a special target of the mid-section. He had built up an impressive record, with many more wins than defeats, although twice recently he had been ruled out of contests he seemed likely to win because of erratic body punching.

Bloomfield liked to come in under a crouch and swing his big fists into an opponent's ribs. Many folded up under his persistent thumps and Len, like others before him, found the Islington boxer hard to pin-point with straight lefts, while it was a hazardous business to try and catch him with a right for fear of breaking a hand on his bobbing cranium. Joe liked nothing better than coming in close to maul away until ordered apart by the referee. These were rough-house methods that Harvey disliked intensely, but he had to contend with them in order to avoid being butted. The Harvey fans urged their idol to uppercut his uncouth opponent, but Len was not chancing his arm in order to oblige them and endeavoured to outbox Joe on orthodox lines.

Things went on in this fashion until the twelfth round when Bloomfield swung a heavy left to the body that was aimed at the solar plexus,
but landed considerably lower. Len gasped, clutched his abdomen and
went down. As he was falling Joe cuffed him with a left hook to the
face followed by a right to the side of the head. This last blow was sufficient in itself to justify disqualification, but it was the body smash that
the referee adjudged as being foul. While his seconds came in to take
the stricken Harvey to his corner for attention, Bloomfield walked round
the ring protesting his innocence. But the booing showed that the onlookers thought the referee was right and his word was final anyway.

It took them half-an-hour to get Harvey on his feet again and when
he went into Sullivan's office, his pain was relieved when he heard that
the National Sporting Club was staging a big show at Holland Park Rink
at Shepherd's Bush. He had been matched in a fifteen-rounds contest
at the middleweight limit with Joe Rolfe which would be regarded
officially as an eliminator for the British title and Lonsdale Belt.*

This promised to be the kind of fight that produces thrills, for whilst
Harvey was a classical boxer, his opponent was a natural fighter, strong
and aggressive, with plenty of knockout wins to his credit. Rolfe was
an iron man, hard to hurt and difficult to stop, and it can be stated
beyond dispute that the majority of the many fans who crowded into
the one-time skating rink came to see if Harvey could stand up to
Rolfe's heavy onslaughts, or if he would be clever enough to box the
Bermondsey man to a standstill.

Florence had no doubts as to the outcome and was keen to watch
Len score another victory. So, too, was her young brother, Larry, himself
a keen amateur boxer. Tickets were bought for them both, it being
arranged that they would be picked up at Holborn Town Hall as Len
was on his way to the arena. When Sullivan heard about this, he instructed Archie Watson to tell the taxi-driver not to stop until they
reached the boxing hall and to Len's anger and his girl-friend's amazement, the cab flashed by them and she and her brother were left stranded.
She was so indignant at what she wrongly concluded was forgetfulness
on Len's part, that they went home, Florence in a temper and her brother
almost in tears with disappointment. Their father, who had always had
a strong aversion to Boxing because of Dick's escapades, and was not
pleased with his daughter's involvement, surprisingly produced a pound
note and told them to be off.

*Top of the bill was Tom Berry defending his British light-heavyweight
title against Gipsy Daniels.

When they got out of the taxi at Holland Park Rink, Florence was amazed to find herself claimed by Lionel Bettinson, who had taken over from his celebrated father* as manager of the National Sporting Club. 'Thank God you've come,' he said. 'You must come to the dressing-room at once, because Len is refusing to get ready for his fight.' He took her arm and they pushed their way through the milling fans and found Len, still in his civilian clothes and seething with anger at the way his plans had been thwarted by his manager. Dan was trying to excuse his duplicity, Archie was looking on helplessly, and Florence had never seen Len so angry, as it was not in his nature to be upset by anything.

'Here she is,' announced Lionel triumphantly. Len's face lost its black look immediately and he gave Florence a big smile. 'Okay,' he said, 'you and Larry get into your seats and I'll see you afterwards.' He was taking his coat off as they departed and promoter, manager and trainer breathed sighs of relief.

There was no further reproach from the boxer, who changed into his fighting gear in cold silence. But all three knew that Harvey, young as he was, was not the person with whom to take a liberty. On the way back, after the contest, Florence asked what would have happened if she had decided to stay at home. 'Would you have refused to fight?' she asked. 'Of course not,' Len assured her. 'I have a duty to the public and would not have let them down, nor would I have deprived Joe Rolfe of his purse money. But I would have made Dan stew in his own juice for as long as possible and given him the scare of his life for interfering with my personal affairs. I hope it's taught him a lesson.'

* Arthur 'Peggy' Bettinson who had founded the National Sporting Club in 1891 and remained its efficient manager until his death in December 1926.

CHAPTER 7

Peak of Punching Power

The incident was a bad thing for Len's opponent, as Harvey was in a particularly belligerent mood, so unlike his normal sedate self, when he came from his corner to face Bermondsey Joe. It was generally expected that Rolfe would do all the attacking and he came at Harvey with his right hand cocked for devastating action. But neither he nor the fans expected the blistering counter-action that the Cornishman let loose as soon as Joe got into range.

Len was there to work off his irritation at his opponent's expense and shortened his punches to get in some telling shots to the head, blows that beat a tattoo on the tough South Londoner's jaw, causing him to swing both fists in lusty, if wild attempts to retaliate. He did get through with some of these haymakers, but they had lost their power by the time they landed and Harvey rode them well. He shook Joe with a solid left hook, then banged in two swift rights to the chin, the last of which sent Rolfe sprawling, but he scrambled up at 'five' to show plenty of fight although it was fast becoming obvious that the bout would not last the scheduled distance.

In the tenth round Joe fought so fiercely that Harvey was compelled to hit out forcibly in self-defence. Suddenly he drew back from a powerful swing, then sent a really beautiful punch to his rival's wide-open jaw. Rolfe was knocked flat and was so obviously 'out' that the referee did not bother to count. 'That will do,' said Mr Douglas and Len was named as the winner.

All through the contest young Larry had been beside himself with excitement, especially when it became clear that Harvey was on top. 'Come on Len, knock him out,' he yelled, jumping about in uncontrollable joy. 'Can't you keep him quiet,' asked a sad-looking man in the next seat. 'There are plenty of other people making a noise,' replied Florence, 'why shouldn't he give vent to his feelings – Harvey is his hero.' 'Not while he's sitting next to me,' said the aggrieved gentleman. 'And what is so special about you?' demanded Florence. 'I'm Joe Rolfe's manager,' was the answer.

Although he had won his 'eliminator' most conclusively, Harvey was not to get his title chance for a long while. Champion Tommy Milligan was meeting Mickey Walker for the world crown at Olympia and although Alex Ireland had publicly challenged Harvey, and been accepted as an opponent, the contest had not matured and to keep Len in fighting trim it was again necessary to feed him with a few foreigners. First to try his luck against the 'Wonder Boxer' was Piet Brand, but after he had been showered with precise punches in the opening round and returned to his corner with a wavering gait, he lost all sense of direction with his punching and after being twice cautioned for low hitting, was ruled out for this offence in the sixth round.

Next to toe the line against Len was Emil Egrel, from France, who took enough punishment to satisfy an army one Sunday afternoon, but kept coming up for more until Harvey got tired of hitting a tough and courageous opponent and midway through the thirteenth round gave the referee an appealing glance, whereupon the one-sided bout was stopped.

A month later Harvey achieved a workmanlike success by disposing of Charles Screve, another Frenchman, in a round and a half, with a short right to the chin followed by a wicked left hook to the body. Billy Farmer, a middleweight from Rotherham, also found Len in devastating form three weeks later, being put down and 'out' halfway through round two. Up to that point Harvey had been placing his punches freely and accurately against a forceful opponent, then suddenly it was all over. Stepping in, Len thudded home a left hook to the solar plexus, and immediately whipped the same hand to his rival's chin with lightning speed. The last was a master-stroke and the Yorkshireman was knocked flat on his back for the full count.

This conclusive victory earned Len a front page photograph on *Boxing*, showing his superb physical development and extraordinary long reach for a young man who had just celebrated his twentieth birthday. The caption to this picture read: 'Len Harvey, of Plymouth and Barnsbury, our ostensibly "best bet" for the world's middleweight title.' But whatever the 'Bible' thought, and its Editor was apt to change his mind occasionally, it was to be some time before the Cornish youth was to get his big chance.

Milligan was slaughtered by Walker and did not box again for nearly five months. Meanwhile, it was assumed that the Scotsman had retired, whereupon Frank Moody outpointed Roland Todd, a former British middleweight champion, under title conditions and was acclaimed as champion in some areas, particularly Wales. So Len had to continue to add to his reputation and there were four more contests at 'The Ring' before 1927 was out.

Primo Ubaldo, a sturdy Italian middle, who had boxed with great success in British rings during the year, ventured to Blackfriars one Thursday evening to fight the best of fifteen rounds with the local favourite. A rushing, tearing fighter of the gamest order, he had the large crowd in an excited state as he tried to break through Harvey's immaculate defence. Len, poker-faced and ice cool, kept him at bay during the first round while he schemed out a way to get in a solid blow.

The Italian's awkward stance and bobbing head made him a difficult target to hit, but in the last minute of the second round Len made the opening he was seeking. One of his pet left hooks to the body caused Ubaldo to lurch forward and that was it. Like lightning, Harvey cracked home a short right to the chin that had 'KO' written all over it. Down went the Italian and he did not stir while being counted out and was still incapable of rising when his seconds came in to carry him to his corner.

Len's next opponent was an old acquaintance in the person of Piet Brand, the tough-as-teak Dutchman. They had met four months earlier when Brand went astray with his punching and was ruled out in consequence. He had begged for another chance ever since and it was not in Harvey's nature to refuse anyone anything if it was in his power to oblige. So on a Sunday afternoon they met again over fifteen rounds with 'The Ring' packed tighter than ever before, not solely because Len could always attract a 'full house', but because the ever-popular Ted (Kid) Lewis happened to be boxing to a sell-out at 'Premierland' and the over-flow of fans who could not get in hastened from the East End across Blackfriars Bridge to force their way into an already well-filled arena.

They saw a tremendous contest, with the Dutchman intent on pounding his way to victory and Harvey just as determined to check his ambitions. For round after round Len gave a classical illustration of how to deal with a strong and energetic attacker, with the 'foreigners' from around Petticoat Lane loudly urging Brand to knock his rival into the middle of next week. This unexpected and, so far as 'The Ring' habitués were concerned, unwarranted advice to the Dutchman could not be tolerated and strained tempers suddenly erupted between two of the 'standing' patrons, fists flew, the crowd parted to give them elbow room and the glove fight they had come to see was totally ignored.

Sensing the sudden change of atmosphere outside the ring, Len calmly held up a gloved hand to halt Brand in his advance, indicated the disturbance and, putting his left arm round the Dutchman's shoulders, led him over to the ropes. Then resting on the top strand they both watched the bare-fisticuffs with great enjoyment and remained there vastly amused until order was at last restored, whereupon Harvey led his foe back into the centre of the ring, they touched gloves and resumed their conflict.

Unfortunately the person responsible for recording the number of rounds became somewhat confused. He mistakenly assumed that a new round had been started and hastily changed his cards from 'eight' to 'nine', which meant that when the timekeeper rang the bell for the end of the contest, only fourteen of the scheduled fifteen rounds had been fought, a fact that was not discovered until the referee studied his score card. Not that it mattered so far as the result was concerned for Harvey had won practically every round with his superior boxing skill and it was only a formality to announce him as the winner on points. When, in the dressing-room, they were informed of what had happened, Piet looked enquiringly at Len as if wondering if they were expected to go back for another three minutes. 'Not likely,' said Harvey. 'They've had their money's worth and anyway, I've got tired of hitting you,' adding, 'It isn't often you get paid for something you haven't done, so put on your clothes and let's go home.'

Ted Moore, that fine Plymouth middle, who had gone fifteen rounds with redoubtable Harry Greb for the world crown and had twice been unsuccessful in taking the British and European titles from Tommy Milligan, now came out with a challenge to Harvey, offering to wager £300 to Len's £200 on the result, but stipulating that the match should not take place at 'The Ring'. Harvey responded by saying that he would prefer to fight at the National Sporting Club where it might receive recognition as a championship eliminator, and offering to put up a sidestake of £500 on the outcome. For some reason this alternative proposal fell on deaf ears, which was a pity, because a match between someone born in Plymouth and another brought up there would have had tremendous drawing power.

Instead Len took on Jack Etienne, a hard-hitting Belgian middle, who had lost only one of five previous bouts in London, that being a points defeat by Jack Hood. He was a fearless opponent for anyone and set about Len with great gusto, forcing the Englishman to bring out every move in his classical repertoire to contain his rival's determined and continuous assaults. The Monday night crowd thoroughly enjoyed this battle between brain and brawn, admiring the way the Belgian walked through Len's precision punches and the manner in which Harvey remained unflustered under the barrage of blows that were thrown at him from all angles.

Nothing that struck Etienne's chin seemed to check his advance, his body appeared to bear armoured plating, his courage was unfaltering, his stamina inexhaustible. The contest was action-packed and thrilling. Would the Belgian be able to batter down the Britisher; would Harvey be able to produce the one punch that would pay for all? The fight appeared likely to go the full distance until the thirteenth round began, then the fans saw what a great champion Harvey promised to be.

A powerfully-placed straight left to the mouth sent the Belgian spinning into the ropes. He bounced off them to be caught by a crisp left hook that sent him to the boards for a count of 'eight'. Only sheer instinct enabled him to get on his feet, but he was finished. Those last two magnificent punches had knocked every vestige of fight from his limbs and brain. Harvey drove his beaten rival round the ring under a shower of lefts and rights until Etienne, void of all defence, suddenly held out an arm in token of full surrender.

Harvey's last contest in 1927 was with Marcel Thil, of France, who later was to become middleweight champion of his own country, of Europe, and also the world. Three years older than Len, he had been boxing professionally for only two years, but was coming along fast and had already boxed six times in London, beating Andrew Newton and Joe Bloomfield, but dropping decisions to Billy Farmer, Bloomfield in a return match and Jack Hood. He had also secured a drawn verdict with George West. The Frenchman was fundamentally a close-range fighter, who bulled his way in by sheer force and strength to assail the body and head with hooks from both fists, but with a weakness for holding with one hand while he thumped away with the other.

His style did not permit of attractive boxing. He was a rough customer for anyone and although Harvey could outpoint him easily enough at long range, it was difficult to keep him at arm's length. Whenever Thil managed to slip a lead and indulge in some mauling infighting, his methods caused frequent clinches, so much so, that in the ninth round little Jim Kenrick, who was officiating outside the ropes, was impelled to get into the ring in an effort to keep the men apart.

When it came to sheer boxing there was only one man in it and he was not of French origin, but though Len got in some crisp punches at long range and rocked his opponent more than once, the fact that Thil kept his head well down when making his rushes made it difficult to pinpoint him with a decisive blow. One round was very much like another until the twelfth, when Harvey managed to get to work with a stinging left to the face that shook the Frenchman. But when Len attempted to add to this advantage with some clean two-fisted work, Thil hung on like grim death and refused to 'have a go'. Well ahead on points, Len went all out in the last two rounds, standing off and punching briskly with both hands, jarring Marcel considerably, but unable to put him down. After the verdict had gone the only way possible it was announced that Harvey's next opponent would be Kid Nitram, the French middleweight champion, at the Albert Hall on 19th January.

Before that important date, however, there was to be a great change in Len's life. The past year had been an eventful one domestically, in addition to his ring exploits. There had been the untimely death of his mother which had affected his fistic performances for a month or two; there had been the managerial upset over the Rolfe fight; while later on, his father, who did not always see eye to eye with Dan Sullivan over the way he was conducting Len's affairs, decided to opt out and confine himself to seconding his son in future.

If his manager felt he now had sole control over his highly-ranked boxer, he was in for a shock. Len and Florence had become engaged during the year and while he was quite comfortable and happy with the Coote family, Harvey wanted a home of his own and the companionship of a wife in whom he could confide and with whom he could plan for the future. When he proposed an early marriage, Florence was willing enough, but there was stolid objection from her father, who was still resolutely opposed to his daughter marrying into the boxing business, and was all for delaying such a step by refusing to give his consent, pointing out that they were both under age and far too young to take on the responsibility of marriage.

Neither of them would be twenty-one until the following July and neither of them wanted to wait that long. 'We can elope,' suggested Len. 'We can give false ages and be married at a registrar's office.' 'That won't do,' answered Florence. 'We could get into all sorts of trouble. My father is the only real problem and I think I know how to get round him.' That night she told her Dad that they were determined to get wed, with or without his consent. 'We'll go to Marlborough Street Court and seek permission of a magistrate,' she threatened. 'Don't be so foolish,' he replied. 'Go to bed and forget it.' But next morning, after he had gone to work, Florence found an envelope on the mantelpiece addressed to herself. All was well – she had called his bluff and won.

They fixed 1st January as the date and everyone was pleased – except manager Sullivan. 'Are you mad?' he exploded when Len broke the news. 'You're fighting Nitram on the nineteenth. He's the best middleweight in France. He's got a fine record. You can't afford to lose this fight. It's at the Albert Hall and you'll be boxing before six thousand people. I can't call it off.'

'I don't want you to,' said Len. 'By getting married first, I will go into the ring unworried and perfectly relaxed. I will be at my best because I shall be fighting for someone else besides myself.' 'Postpone it until after the Nitram fight,' pleaded Dan. But Harvey was adamant. A few days later his manager told him that most of the critics thought he was mad in getting married so soon before such an important match. 'They say it will be the finish of you,' added his manager. 'It will be the finish of me if I don't,' snapped Len and there was no further argument.

They were married at St Albans, Holborn, the sole witness being Ted Harvey. Others present were his youngest daughter, Olive, Len's oldest brother Ted, just back from army service in Egypt, and Aunt Mabel, plus faithful George Coote and his mother, and Mr and Mrs Law. There was a reception at an Italian restaurant at King's Cross where the party was joined by Mrs Bella Burge and Dan Sullivan, and a number of Len's ardent supporters who came after the Sunday matinée show at 'The Ring'. In all there were about one hundred and fifty guests.

The couple were to have only two days' honeymoon, to be spent at – well, of course, where they had first met – Cliftonville. 'Make sure you have him back at the *Black Bull* by Tuesday night,' Sullivan ordered Florence. 'And mind you look after him,' he added. 'Shouldn't it be the other way round?' enquired the mother of the bride. They stayed at the Surrey Court Hotel and as soon as they got into their room, Len opened the wardrobe and peered in. 'Whatever are you looking for?' demanded his young wife. 'Just making sure Old Archie isn't lurking in there,' he replied, his face as solemn as a judge, although there was a merry twinkle in his eye.

CHAPTER 8

Triumph in the Law Courts

Mrs Len Harvey kept her word and her husband of two days was delivered safely into trainer Watson's hands at Whetstone right on time. She visited the *Black Bull* twice weekly during the ensuing two weeks, but was never left alone with Len, the faithful Archie always hovering around, and if they went for a walk they would find themselves shadowed by one of the three sparring partners; Gipsy Daniels, Billy Bird or Joe Bloomfield.

The coming fight with Nitram (his real name was Martin, but he spelt it backwards to provide a *nom du ring*) was of such importance that *Boxing* produced a photogravure plate of Harvey which was presented free to its readers the week before the scheduled date of the contest. With it was a pen picture, somewhat inaccurate, but nevertheless giving full credit for Len's performances to date that had brought him within reach of titular honours.

It also gave the following description of the Cornishman's physical endowments:

> Physically, Harvey has reached perfection for his profession. Above the average height (he is 5 ft. 11 ins.), long in the limbs, light in the leg, and full in the arm, he yet has that broad, muscular torso necessary to the speedy and effective hitter. Facially the Devonian is somewhat different from the general conception of a pugilist. His features are finely chiselled, his eyes bright and keen, his hair dark and 'wavy', with his head well set upon a neck which is neither thin or 'scraggy'. His complexion is pale – too pale one might judge at first sight – but his pallor is a healthy one, as we can testify who have seen him frequently stripped and in 'close ups'.

The newly-weds had set up home in Turle Road, off Tollington Park,

Islington, and there they spent the day until it was time to go to the fight. Len went off to the weigh-in and returned accompanied by Archie Watson, sent specially by Dan Sullivan to ensure that Florence did not give her husband too many cups of tea. She had been given a ringside seat and was determined to use it, so when Len and Archie started off for the big event, she accompanied them and found herself seated next to Mrs Burge, who, apart from being proprietress of 'The Ring', had been married to the former lightweight champion of England, so she knew a good deal more about Boxing than her young companion.

There was not a single vacant seat in the Albert Hall from floor to dome when the two principals in the main contest of the evening came into their corners. Harvey was resplendent in a brand new red silk dressing-gown and when he took this off he was seen to be wearing a pair of red trunks, edged in black, with his initials on the left leg and, at the bottom of the right leg, a small square depicting the badge of Cornwall, fifteen gold bezants on a black background, which had been presented to him at a dinner in Plymouth.

Obviously there was some wifely influence at work here: Florence had noticed with dismay that whereas continental boxers always looked spruce and neatly dressed in the ring, many English boxers appeared very scruffy by comparison. She wanted her husband to be as immaculate in his dress as he was in his boxing, and soon there came a marked change in the ring attire of British boxers, one of the first to copy the idea of initials on the trunks being Ted Broadribb, who at that time managed a large stable of prominent fighters. Florence also provided Len with a pair of slippers for use when he stepped on the scales at a weighing-in ceremony, thinking it unnecessary and unhygienic to walk about in bare feet, besides being a safeguard against dangerous objects, such as pins or tin-tacks that might be trodden on by accident.

Referee Sam Russell had a few words to say before sending them back to their corners to await the starting bell. The 'house' hushed down and the bell clanged, but as Len came to the centre, Nitram was still chatting to his seconds, his back towards his opponent. Harvey would have been within his rights if he had dashed over and clouted the French champion on the chin; instead Len looked at the referee and was on the point of tapping the Kid on the shoulder, when Nitram's seconds realised that the fight had started and turned him round to face the Englishman.

Harvey landed the first punch, a left to the face. He moved round as the Frenchman advanced threateningly, sent in another left, then a right and looked calmly in charge of the situation. But there was a shock in store for the 'Wonder Boxer' and his army of supporters. Suddenly Nitram flashed over a right that clipped Harvey's chin and sent him down. All in the first half-minute; an astonished roar went up from the big crowd. But Len was up at once and in no way disturbed. A bookmaker behind Florence shouted, 'Twenty to one against Harvey', and quickly turning round, Mrs Burge said, 'I'll take that in pounds.' Remembering all that Len had told her about keeping self-control during his contests, Florence did nothing, although she regarded it as an insult that such long odds should be offered against her talented husband.

Throughout the remainder of the round Nitram tried hard to connect with another knockdown right, but Harvey had learnt his lesson and skilfully avoided the big punches as they swept over, although there were two near misses that had the fans gasping. Len had to use all his ring-craft to avoid disaster in the second round, but by the third he had summed up the strength and ability of his opponent and settled down to prove his own superiority with a wide range of moves and punches. At this period of the contest the Frenchman was punching the harder of the pair, but was throwing his blows at a cleverly retreating target. Frequently Len would beat him to the punch with a left to the face or a dig to the body and then withdraw to avoid Nitram's vicious counters.

There was real brain behind Harvey's work. Len had been going back, but he started to step forward in the fifth round and to send rights into the ribs – just long shots and a get-away. These hurt and Nitram, anxious to shield his midsection, kept his elbows down. Harvey was in no hurry. He kept digging at the Frenchman's rib-cage while the Kid swung back in retaliation – and missed. To try and put Len out of his stride, Nitram opened out fiercely in the sixth, but was met by uppercuts and a hard right to the head. Harvey was scoring three punches to one and those he took were usually on his elbows, whereas his own shots thudded against vulnerable flesh and bone.

Nitram was keeping his chun sunk into his chest, but Len was not concerned with making the head his target: he kept slamming at the body, and when the Frenchman dashed in to clinch and do some in-fighting, he was cautioned for the misuse of his head. A mix-up, a brief clinch, and a right to the head from the Kid on the break opened the eighth round, and he followed up with a fierce attack. Harvey backed off for a bit, then came back with a lovely left underneath and a jarring right to the head that put him back into the picture. He boxed beautifully to keep Nitram out and shook him up with a combination left and right to the head just before the bell.

So the duel went on between rugged fighter and master boxer, with one or the other getting in a good scoring shot, although generally it was Harvey who was gaining the majority of the points with his more accurate punching. The Frenchman swung and hooked, while the Englishman stabbed with his left and scored with straight rights, all the time making the body his main target. The rounds went by with Harvey adding slightly to his lead and then came the thirteenth with the superstitious among the spectators wondering if this would prove lucky for one and unlucky for the other. Their doubts were soon dispersed. Harvey had been working to a plan and the time for putting it into practice was at hand. Apart from the dramatic opening to the fight, thrills had come but occasionally, although the atmosphere had been extremely tense. Len was now satisfied that he knew all there was to be known about his opponent. He realised that he had sufficiently weakened Nitram with those continued body drives and the time had come to administer the finishing touches.

He was also out to show that those who had credited the French champion with the heavier punch were mistaken. He fancied that he would now be able to prove that this was in his possession and proceeded to do so. A whiplash left to the face, a right to the head, and a peach of a left hook to the jaw sent the Kid in an untidy heap on the boards. The Frenchman was badly shaken, got up at 'eight' and tried to smother, but Len was not allowing him any time to recover. Picking his punches with the utmost coolness, he thumped Nitram's ribs, brought down his guard, and then with a shower of hooks, sent him down again.

This time the Kid took the full allowance of time in which to regain his feet, arising at 'nine', but only to be driven helplessly across the ring. He was on the verge of being knocked out, but before Harvey could deliver the final blow the bell sounded to give the continental a brief respite. Nitram came up gallantly for the next round, but despite the feverish work of his seconds during the interval, he was still dazed and only able to offer the feeblest resistance.

With cold intent, Harvey measured him with his eye and then, with a right under the heart and a swift left hook to the jaw, once more sent his weakened rival to the canvas. Again Nitram was forced to take a count of 'nine' and when he got up it was plain to see that it was all over bar the shouting. Another right to the body and the Frenchman was floored for the fourth time. Again it was a struggle for him to reach his feet in time and as Len threatened to bang in a left to the solar plexus, the Frenchman dropped to his knees.

As he had fallen without having been struck, he was able to be up in two seconds but received a caution from the referee for this infringement of the rules. Sam Russell said, 'Box on,' and Harvey darted in. But before he could catch Nitram with another punch the Frenchman collapsed on the boards – and that was the end. The referee hoisted him to his feet and sent him to his corner, then left the ring to inform the Master of Ceremonies that the Frenchman had been disqualified.

It was a regrettable decision, if technically correct, and while the big crowd raised the roof at Harvey's great victory, many thought that the result should have been recorded as a stoppage by the referee to save a game fighter from unnecessary punishment. On paper it appeared anything but the crushing defeat that Len had imposed on his highly-rated opponent.

Undoubtedly it was Harvey's best performance to date and the Editor of *Boxing* was fully in agreement with this sentiment:

We went to the Albert Hall curious to discover whether the recent bridegroom would, or could, display form which would justify his claims to a meeting with Tommy Milligan for the British middle-weight title and Lonsdale Belt. We were fully satisfied on the initial point soon after the contest with Nitram had gone halfway. When it was over and we had leisure in which to sort out our impressions, we were asking ourselves whether Harvey could not be asked to dispute Mickey Walker's tenure of the world championship.

We shall adhere to that opinion unless Len himself makes us think differently. Not that we think he will meet with defeat, since we fail to detect any middleweight on this side of the Atlantic capable of beating him, but it will be some time before he can gain either of the honours that lie in his path and he could lose that peak of perfection that he has reached during the past two years. Milligan is out of action with an eye injury while Walker, who picked up a sizeable fortune when disposing so decisively of our champion,* is not likely to be tempted here again without a similar lucrative offer, or even a larger amount, and there is not a promoter around at the present time who can accommodate such demands. Meanwhile anything can happen.

*Walker knocked out Milligan in the tenth round of a world title defence at Olympia, London, on 10th June 1927.

It is worthwhile remembering these flattering remarks and to compare them with those expressed by the same pen later in the year.

On the way home Florence told her husband about the bookmaker who had offered twenty to one that he would be beaten after that knock-down in round one. Len grinned: 'Twenty to one? Well, didn't you take it?' 'Why, no Len,' she answered. 'Of course not. You told me never to bet on fights.' Harvey raised his arms in mock horror. 'But twenty to one – think of all the money we should have won!'

He was a great leg-puller in a quiet, mischievous way. One Sunday afternoon before they were married they were walking in Hyde Park and Florence was wearing a modish hat that was attached to her blonde head by a large ornamental hat-pin. Suddenly Len clapped his hand to his right eye and gasped: 'Your pin, you've stabbed me.' He was due to fight the next day and she was horrified at the damage that she might have caused, however inadvertently. 'We must go at once to St George's Hospital,' she announced, and set off as fast as she could run on her high heels, dragging Len behind her. They got out of the park and darted across the traffic-filled road to the hospital. Up the steps dashed the frenzied girl, but at the door Len stopped, uncovered his eye and said: 'Ever been had?'. Florence stared at him, slapped his face, ran down the steps and caught a bus home.

One day at Whetstone after a work-out, Len and trainer Watson were resting in the hotel lounge. Harvey always changed after a session in the gymnasium and was an entirely different person in an everyday suit to when he was in the throes of training. He was reading aloud from the *Morning Advertiser* and Archie, who was no great shakes at reading anything, was listening intently as Len picked out such tit-bits as he thought might interest him. 'Listen to this,' Harvey suddenly announced. 'Their boxing correspondent is saying that the sooner I get rid of Archie Watson, the better. That I'll never win the championship with you around.' 'He does, does he,' said the trainer, then lapsed into silence. Len chuckled to himself and promptly forgot the joke. But when they went to the weigh-in there was a sudden commotion among the attendant pressmen, one of whom was holding his nose. He was the *Morning Advertiser* representative and Archie had walked straight up to him and dotted him one without any explanation. It was up to Len to do the apologising and he did so with his natural charm and all was soon put right and the joke enjoyed by everyone, even the stricken boxing writer seeing the funny side of it.

Sullivan was so pleased with Len's decisive victory over the French champion that he decided the young couple deserved a holiday as their honeymoon had been so short. He had not got around to accepting Florence whole-heartedly, in fact, he never did forgive her for marrying his Wonder Boxer. But he sent them off for a month and Len decided that his wife should see something of the county in which he had been born. He showed her his birthplace, the small cottage in the equally tiny village of Stoke Climsland, and took her to see his grandmother. 'She has always been resolutely opposed to me taking up Boxing,' Len explained. 'So we won't talk about it.' Florence agreed, but on entering the old lady's home was surprised to see on one wall a 'Ring' poster with her husband's name blazoned across the top, together with his picture. His grandmother was obviously very proud of him.

It was back to 'The Ring' for Harvey's next bout, a fifteen rounds affair with Antoine Forr, another Frenchman, but as was to be found, not in the same class as Nitram, for after being completely outboxed and scientifically weakened by the Cornishman, he was put down for nine seconds in the seventh round from a stunning right hook to the chin and on rising as 'ten' was called, held out his hand in token of surrender.

When a tournament was staged at the National Sporting Club in aid of the West Norwood Orphanage and Len was asked to top the bill, he did not hesitate to show his willingness to appear, as he had given his services for charitable causes many times before and was to do so again during the remainder of his career and for ever afterwards. Opponent over fifteen rounds was Auguste Lengagne, a strong and durable Frenchman, who looked in the peak of physical fitness, as did all continental boxers, and did not appear in the least daunted by the Englishman's high reputation. He put up a determined, but losing battle against superior ringcraft until the tenth round when a stabbing left from Len badly lacerated his opponent's right eye, causing so severe a wound that the referee stopped the bout and declared Harvey to be the winner.

Meanwhile, Milligan had lost his titles to Alex Ireland on an alleged foul, so automatically Len and his manager turned their attention to the new champion. They would not have been surprised if Ireland had told them not to be impatient; that he required some while in which to get accustomed to his new role, while being entitled to the customary six months respite from a challenger. But the NSC, which had been launching out with big public promotions, was anxious to stage a middleweight title fight for a Derby Week tournament on 4th June with Harvey in the challenger's corner, an arrangement which had met with Ireland's full approval.

Then, out of the blue, came the news of a brand new promoting syndicate with plans to steal the NSC date and stage a mammoth tournament on the Chelsea Football Club's ground at Stamford Bridge, with the matchmaking in the capable hands of Dan Sullivan. It was to be a quadruple championship offering, for in addition to the Ireland v. Harvey affair, Johnny Hill would dispute the Flyweight Championship of (?) Europe with Newsboy Brown of America who claimed the world crown; Harry Corbett would meet Luigi Quadrini of Italy, for the European featherweight championship, while Gipsy Billy Daniels would defend his British light-heavyweight title against Frank Moody, a fellow Welshman. With a top price (including tax) of £2 15s 6d and seventy thousand unreserved seats as low as 2s 4d, the new McBarris Syndicate appeared to be on to a good thing.

So did the boxers concerned. All had been promised and signed contracts for highly satisfactory purses. Len was delighted at the prospect of being given another chance to win a British title, plus earning his biggest ring wages to date, something in the region of £4,000. Florence, too, was highly excited, as when she was invited to a luncheon at Romano's famous restaurant in the Strand for the purpose of publicising this ambitious project, one of the syndicate principals promised her a present of a magnificent diamond ring. At the function she had sat next to Mrs Jimmy Wilde, who showed her the bag of diamonds which her husband had won when defeating Joe Conn on the Stamford Bridge ground ten years previously and which she carried about in her handbag for 'safety'. 'Well, I'll be satisfied with one to start with,' said Florence happily, and she and Len thought this would be the turning point in his career.

Not yet! Harvey went off to Whetstone where his sparring partners reported in awe his dedicated work and his resolve to make the most of his big opportunity. All went well for a month and then rumours began to spread about the financial standing of the McBarris Syndicate. The two Scots were the first to break camp and go home, some of the others delayed their departure for a while until it was made plain that the much heralded Tournament of Champions was off – definitely. Only Harvey remained in training. He had taken legal advice and was informed that as long as he continued to prepare for his scheduled contest with Ireland, his contract would have to be honoured, or at least he would get his training expenses refunded.

So, despite the fact that his spar-mates had been dismissed, Len stayed on at the *Black Bull* and Mrs Harvey came to see him every day. They sat in the orchard and chatted over their disappointment, with Archie keeping watch in case a snooper appeared, when he would cry 'bogey' and Len would jump up and do some energetic shadow-boxing. On 4th June he went to the offices of the *Sporting Life* and weighed-in; in due course he took the absconding promoters to court and won his case.

It was all very disappointing, but Harvey had to keep in top fighting form and also earn his bread, so Dan Sullivan arranged for him to meet Emil Egrel in a return contest at 'The Ring'. The pair had met eight months earlier when the Frenchman had been stopped in thirteen rounds and if anyone wondered if this second appointment was necessary, let it be said that the Blackfriars establishment was sold out, the capacity crowd no doubt drawn by their loyal devotion to their local star. Egrel outweighed Len (11 st. 5½ lbs.) by over half a stone, but he kept his opponent waiting a long while before entering the ring and once there did little more than become an animated punch-bag.

Not that the fans minded. They had come to see Harvey demonstrate what the Noble Art was all about and they saw once again a classical exhibition by a master boxer. No doubt the poker-faced Cornishman could have ended matters any time he liked after the first few rounds, but he had no wish to unduly punish a game fighter or run the risk of knocking up a hand or sustaining a cut through endeavouring to destroy a tough and durable opponent for the sake of providing a Roman holiday. The fight went the full distance of fifteen rounds and Harvey won every one of them. He was criticised by some for allowing the bout to go the full distance, but everyone went home happy, with the exception, perhaps, of Egrel and his entourage.

George West came next, also at 'The Ring'. He was from Fulham and apart from being a rugged fighter, had all the toughness to go with it. He could hit hard, mainly to the body, and had gone fourteen rounds with Milligan for the British middleweight crown. An ex-guardsman, George was fancied by his friends to be the one person who might put a spoke in the Harvey wheel. The weight was fixed at the middleweight limit and whereas West just tipped the beam at that poundage, Len came to scale two pounds lighter.

There was the usual big attendance for a 'Harvey' night, the fans looking forward to an enthralling battle between men of completely different styles. But it fell far below expectations simply because West had but one objective, to get in close and then rough his rival up in every possible way. He rushed in, grabbed Harvey and then mauled about while Len did his utmost to extricate himself and get settled into some long range boxing. But George was not prepared to let his stylish opponent move into a smooth scoring stride and his holding and hugging brought referee Jimmy Bissell into the ring by the third round to administer a stern reprimand to the Londoner.

Whenever Len was able to get free there was only one man in it, but he could not get in more than a few straight lefts before West had bundled into him again to continue his rough-house methods despite anything the referee had to say to him. The official was very patient, but during the next round, after being pulled off Harvey, George jumped in again to grab and wrestle, whereupon Mr Bissell showed he had had enough by ordering West to his corner – disqualified. If George was disturbed at this 'black mark' on his record, Len was equally dissatisfied with the way the contest had ended. He liked to win conclusively and got no satisfaction when an opponent was ruled out for not observing the rules. Besides he preferred to send the fans home happy and with the feeling that they had received good value for their money.

A month later Dan Sullivan had his star boxer back at 'The Ring', this time engaged to fight Alf Peggazano, a twenty-five-year-old middle-weight from Marseilles, who had fought several times in London and was well thought of in Paris where he had enjoyed a number of successes. At the last moment, however, Alfred found himself unable to make the trip and Auguste Lengagne, who had boxed Harvey at the NSC nearly six months earlier, volunteered to take his place. The Frenchman felt he had been unlucky to lose on that occasion due to a badly cut eye, but now he came determined to do better this time. At 11 st. 5 lbs. he had the advantage of a single pound over the Englishman. As it turned out that was his sole point of superiority.

Having summed up the Frenchman's abilities at their first meeting, Len had no need to feel out his man, but started straight away to out-box him. Up on his toes and moving round smartly, he sent out long lefts to the face and body, easily evading the Frenchman's heavy return swings. Lengagne tried all he knew to get in and wreak damage on his rival's mid-section, but could never get past that unerring left hand, which kept sending him back on his heels.

Game and a great trier, the Frenchman persisted in his efforts to make a show, but it was really no race. Cool and confident as usual, Len let his strong opponent dissipate his strength while he helped the process with some well-timed and precise punches. By the eighth round Lengagne was almost at the end of his tether and a straight left jab to the mouth put him on the canvas for eight seconds. He lasted out the round, but had such a punishing time in the next that the referee visited his corner during the interval and then left the ring, informing the announcer that the Frenchman had elected to retire.

So Len had finished matters a round earlier than previously and once again stopped Lengagne inside the distance. He had done what he had been asked to do and done it competently and satisfactorily. It was therefore a shock to his friends to find a castigating and damaging report of the contest appear in *Boxing* two days later. As he never read the reports of his contests, this vitriolic account of the fight with Lengagne had to be brought to his notice and even then he was inclined to pass it off as just one of those things, excusing the Editor by suggesting that maybe he wasn't feeling so good that night, or perhaps had indulged in a glass too many. Dan Sullivan was furious, however, and sought advice from a solicitor. He in turn suggested taking counsel's opinion and as a result, proceedings were instituted against the editor, proprietors and printers of *Boxing* on the grounds of libel and defamation of character.

Here is the text of the offending report:

If Len is anything like the champion he has been cracked up to be, he would or could have terminated the affair inside a couple of rounds at the outside. As it was he allowed it to go on for nine dreary rounds, playing light, and only occasionally sending over even the imitation of a hard punch. This may have been business, but it certainly wasn't war, nor did it suggest that it would ever commence to look like war. Lengagne's face certainly did get mussed up a trifle, but he was not seriously hurt, save perhaps when he was sent off his feet by a straight left to the mouth. He was also thumped about the head and on the back of his shoulders a few times, but the exhaustion from which he was clearly suffering towards the close, that is prior to his retirement, must have been due to his over-exertions in swiping the atmosphere.

Why Harvey is being so continuously presented with these 'lemons' we are unable to guess, but we do have to say that he can by no possibility benefit from them. We have to suppose that Len feels some need for exercise, but, as this affair was going, a shadow boxing exhibition would have been fully as useful for that purpose. Len wasn't even trying to knock his opponent out. He would permit the Frenchman to hit him once or twice, but this was possibly because even the faithful Blackfriars crowd were commencing to get restive.

To our mind 'the madam' was too palpable, Len actually pulled his punches, bestowing 'love pats' on Lengagne, who either could not or would not infuse any suggestion of reality into the business. Lengagne would slap the ribs at intervals – long ones, and when Len sent one of his hard rights across, it would go to the shoulder blade, even although Lengagne had not ducked. And then Harvey would reach forward to lead with his right at full stretch to the ribs. In so doing he would expose himself, but yet Lengagne failed to connect with any counter.

The action came before Mr Justice McCardie in the Law Courts six months later and resulted in one of the most amusing sporting cases ever heard. The judge was noted for being witty and he caused a lot of humour with his remarks and questions. Looking at the offending report, he said to a boxer who was giving evidence: 'I see it is suggested that this Frenchman was a lemon. What is a lemon?' The witness groped for words and then answered: 'Well, it means he was dead easy.' Looking quite baffled, the judge asked: 'What does that mean?' He replied: 'I think they thought he was a mug.' '"A lemon, dead easy, a mug", well that doesn't get us very far, but I think I understand your meaning.'

When Harvey entered the witness box he displayed his customary coolness, as if he had been used to giving evidence all his life. After answering a few questions quietly but confidently, he was asked by Mr McCardie to leave the box and come and stand by his side. 'Do you know what "pulling a punch" means?', the judge enquired of the boxer. 'No, your worship,' said Len. 'Well, you know what "pulling a horse" means?' Len replied: 'I think a jockey does this if he wants to prevent his horse from winning.' 'Quite,' said Mr McCardie. 'Now does not that imply the same thing in Boxing?' 'I wouldn't know. There aren't any jockeys or horses in Boxing.'

'So you do not know what "pulling a punch" means. Now I want you to take a punch at me, but just before it lands, I want you to pull back your arm so that you do not strike me.' Everyone in the court looked on apprehensively. You could have heard a pin drop as they waited to see what Len would do. His answer came clearly and deliberately. 'Will I be responsible for the consequences?' he asked His Lordship. 'What consequences?' was the reply. 'Well,' said Len. 'I've never yet struck a blow without it landing with my full power behind it, but I'll try. Do you wish me to hit at you with my left or with my right?' The judge smiled and said: 'Neither, young man. You can go back to your seat. The court is adjourned for lunch.'

Harvey's shrewdness had won his case. During the recess, the newspaper's counsel realised that Len had made a decided impression on the judge and he offered to settle out of court. This was accepted and damages agreed, the costs being borne by the defendants. When the case was resumed the judge made known that agreement had been reached between the parties concerned, saying that the result of it had been 'to vindicate the honour, good faith, as well as the ability of Len Harvey'.

CHAPTER 9

'But 'Twas a Famous Victory'

Harvey's next opponent, following the return fight with Lengagne that had finished up in the Law Courts, was one he had wanted for a long while and which the British boxing public were equally keen to see – a return with Johnny Sullivan. It was thirty-two months since their first controversial meeting and they would have been brought together long before had not the Covent Garden boxer taken a trip to America, and on his return, been keeping himself busy while growing from a welter into a full-blown middleweight. The matchmaker at the National Sporting Club secured the contest and when they went on the scales it was seen that whereas Sullivan made 11 st. 5½ lbs., Harvey did not have to undress completely to make the same poundage. It was scheduled for fifteen rounds.

This was one of the fights that Florence did not see, firstly because women were barred from the famous Club, and secondly because she was expecting their first child. The baby was due on the very night of the Sullivan fight, so while Len was climbing into the ring to try and get revenge for his disputed defeat at 'The Ring', his wife was in a Maida Vale nursing home awaiting her happy event, with only the matron knowing that she was married to a boxer. For the past fortnight she had not seen her husband. He had been at the *Black Bull* at Whetstone while she was waiting at home. They wrote to each other every day and in the evening there would be long telephone conversations.

From the outset Harvey proved himself the master. He opened the proceedings in far more aggressive style than was usually the case, pumping in a stiff left to the face, followed by a right that just grazed his rival's jaw. Sullivan was slow by comparison. He seemed to have no defence for Len's rapid left leads and was forced to counter with shots to the body. He escaped disaster several times by just being able to get his head out of the way of Harvey's following rights. Johnny was well behind after three rounds and knew it. He put in a spirited attack in the fourth, a right to the ribs appearing to hurt his rival, and Sullivan followed up with a right to the jaw.

Harvey rode the punch and came back with a left hook to the chin that made Johnny bend at the knees. Before he could recover, another smart left hook to the jaw put him down and he was forced to remain on the canvas for eight seconds. On rising he was dropped again, more from a push to make him an easier target, than from a punch. He was soon up, but had to rush in and keep close to his opponent in order to last out the round.

In full command now, Harvey hit out with both hands, weakening his rival still further with crisp punches to the jaw. Sullivan tried gamely to fight back, but his defence had dropped and a perfect right hook to the chin had him on the canvas for another count of 'eight'. No sooner had he got to his feet than he was floored again and was still down when the bell ended the fifth round to give Johnny a welcome respite.

When Len reached his corner his seconds were beaming and one of them said: 'There's been a telegram for you. It's a boy! They're both all right, but you've got to get out of here quickly.' The minute rest seemed like an hour to Harvey, then he darted from his corner to bang over a right that dropped Sullivan flat on his face. By sheer instinct he got up just in time to beat the count. But he was finished and a light blow from Len put him down once more, whereupon the towel came in from his corner and it was all over.

Hardly waiting to hear himself announced the winner Harvey made all haste back to the dressing-room. Then his trainer said: 'There's no need for all the rush, Len. We wanted you to finish Sullivan off, so I had to think of something. But you ain't a father yet – maybe by the time you get to the nursing-home ...' But Harvey had gone – straight to a telephone box. Before going to the fight he had promised to let her know the result. 'You go and do your job,' she had said. 'I'll be here waiting to do mine.' She sat quietly reading until a nurse came, a puzzled look on her face: 'There's a telephone message for you,' she said. 'It's from your husband, but I can't make head nor tail of it. I do hope you can.' 'Please, what is the message?' asked Florence. 'Well, he says he stopped Sullivan in the sixth and sends his love. Does that mean anything?' 'Yes it does, nurse,' said Mrs Harvey. 'Thanks very much.' Actually the baby was not born until a fortnight later – but it *was* a boy and they named him Leonard Terence.

Just before Christmas Len took on two Belgian middles who could not have heard of his reputation, or they would not have dared to cross the Channel. The first, Leo Frick, was put down five times in the first round and, after taking one more punch at the start of the second, was rescued by referee Jim Kenrick. The second, Antoine Dubois, who wrongly claimed the championship of his country, stayed in the ring for an even shorter period. He met Harvey in a charity show in Birmingham, found the Cornishman in a brisk mood, and was sagging into the ropes in a helpless state when referee Eugene Corri stopped the proceedings after 104 seconds of the first round.

Whilst at the Birmingham show Len was introduced in the ring with Jack Hood by Jack Callaghan, a London promoter of experience and distinction, who told the onlookers that he had matched the pair to box in an official eliminating contest, the winner to be rewarded with a title fight with Alex Ireland. He represented a syndicate calling themselves British Boxing Enterprises who planned to stage the contest at the Empress Hall at Earls Court on 7th February 1929, and were putting up a purse of £3,000. Dan Sullivan, as Harvey's manager, and Ted Broadribb, as Hood's, were also presented and the news was received with acclamation by the Birmingham fans, for Hood was one of theirs and a great local favourite.

On the way home Len asked Dan how this had happened. 'I thought I was fighting for Harry Jacobs at the Albert Hall on 24th January for his purse and £500-a-side. Why the change?' Sullivan explained that an American promoter named Jeff Dickson, who was operating in Paris, had been trying to buy the Albert Hall lease from Jacobs in order to be able to stage a much-awaited heavyweight fight between the British champion, Phil Scott, and a young German, Ted Sandwina, who had been sweeping all before him. 'Harry didn't want Dickson over here, so he pinched the Scott/Sandwina fight for himself and has passed your fight on to Callaghan. Jack's found two fellows called Harris and Emanuel, and they are putting up the money for you and Hood. So it's all right, isn't it?' 'You might have told me,' answered Len. 'I don't like being sold like a bundle of firewood,' adding, 'I hope this isn't going to be another McBarris fiasco.'

In getting a match with Harvey for his boxer, Broadribb was making a very shrewd move. Hood was reigning welterweight king, so had nothing to lose by fighting Harvey at the middleweight limit, even if it meant giving away several pounds. Jack of Birmingham had not been finding it all that easy to find welterweight opponents or, in fact, to make that particular poundage himself. He would be far happier and stronger at over 11 st. On the other hand, apart from beating a champion, Len had everything to lose and nothing to gain. For even if he beat Hood conclusively it would be argued that victory had been obtained over a man smaller than himself. Defeat by the Birmingham boxer would put Len right out of the middleweight championship reckoning. He did not think his manager had done him a favour in agreeing to the contest. But, he would go through with it just the same.

As it happened he wasn't destined to fight Hood yet awhile. Nor was he to fight at Earls Court — ever! Suddenly the contest was switched to the Crystal Palace, a venue that had been used quite successfully by the Hulls family* in the past, but was generally considered to be too far out to attract a vast gathering of fans. But the new promoters had a ready-made winner with Harvey versus Hood — or had they? A week before the contest Mrs Harvey received an unexpected call from a close friend of her husband's, Eddie Tocock. He told her that Len was very worried and wanted her to come at once to Whetstone. Florence knew that it must be something of a very serious nature for Len to need her in such haste. She imagined that he must have met with an accident, but was assured that he was all right physically. He just wanted to see her urgently. She parked the three-months-old baby with her mother and she and Eddie broke all speed limits in getting to the *Black Bull* as quickly as possible. When she made her way into the lounge she found Len there, together with his manager, the Callaghan brothers, who were acting for the Syndicate, and Norman Hurst, the boxing writer.

When she wanted to know what it was all about, they informed her that Hood had broken his right thumb on a sparring-partner, heavyweight Bob Carvill, and had been forced to pull out of the fight. 'We want to put in Frank Moody as substitute, but Len's objecting,' Sullivan told her. 'But what are you doing here, anyway?' 'My husband has sent for me and that's good enough,' she replied. 'I am not surprised that he's objecting. Moody is British light-heavyweight champion, he will outweigh Len by at least a stone. Why should he be asked to fight a man who has had such vast experience and fought the best in America? If he loses my husband will be out of the championship status he has worked so hard to reach.' Then she asked Len outright if he wanted

*J. T. Hulls and his son, Sydney.

to go through with the fight. 'No, I don't,' he replied. 'And I don't have to either. My contract calls for a substitute of equal calibre, if one is necessary, and I don't regard Moody in that light.' 'That's that, then,' she said. 'Let's go upstairs and pack, there is no sense in staying here.'

In Harvey's bedroom they collected his things with righteous gloom. Then in came Sullivan. He pleaded with them both not to ruin the promotion by refusing to accept Moody as a substitute. 'Think of all the tickets that have been sold. Think of the other boxers engaged on the bill.' 'Think about my future, Dan,' answered Len. 'You should be safeguarding that, not putting me in a spot where I can come to more harm than good.' 'Why are you so keen on taking Moody?' asked Florence, and after some hesitation it came out that Dan was in some financial difficulty. He had sold a large number of tickets and lost the money at the races, now he was relying on Harvey fighting to put matters right. He implored them not to leave the *Black Bull*. If they did, he would be ruined.

Asked how he expected to raise the money he needed, Sullivan blandly replied: 'By betting heavily on Len, of course.' They both stared at him and Mrs Harvey could not conceal her disgust: 'Come on, Len, let's go home,' she said, but her husband hesitated: 'I know how you feel, but I can't let him down,' and after some further deliberation it was decided to go on with the fight. When they got downstairs the Callaghan boys were jubilant until they heard that it would cost the promoters an additional £500 that would have to be paid to Harvey as compensation. They hesitated until Len said: 'Do I go back into the gym to continue training – or not?' Then they succumbed and Mrs Harvey returned to her baby.

They were to fight fifteen rounds at catchweights and at the weigh-in Harvey scaled only 11 st. 3 lbs. Moody, who had received only three days' notice, was probably in the region of 12 st., being on the light side for a 'cruiser'.* But he was a champion of that division and had previously held the British middleweight title. In America he had fought such stalwarts as Harry Greb, Tiger Flowers, Lou Bogash and Jock Malone. He was a puncher, too, and not long before had knocked out Tommy Milligan in a single round with a mighty right to the chin.

---

*At this time the light-heavyweight division, 12 st. 7 lbs., was still called the 'cruiserweight' class in Great Britain.

Substituting Moody for Hood had no effect on the sale of tickets and over five thousand fans wended their way to Sydenham, fully anticipating a punch-up because the Welshman was renowned for his big hitting and durability. None of them realised how close they had come to not seeing the fight at all, nor were any of them aware that one of the principals had encountered the hardest difficulty in getting into the vast arena. When the Harveys, complete with friends, arrived at one of the public entrances, the doorman refused to let Len in. Boxers did not need tickets of admission in those days, but the man in charge was new to the job and obviously had never seen Harvey, either in the ring or out of it.

When Len explained who he was, he received a sarcastic reply: 'Oh yes. Well, you're the fifth Len Harvey I've had trying to get in here tonight and you look less like him than any of the others.' 'Well,' answered the boxer. 'If you don't let me through, there'll be no big fight tonight. So please yourself.' Florence thrust her ticket into her husband's hand. 'You go in and start getting ready. I'll wait here until you can find someone to let me in.' That was sufficient to convince the doorman that all was above board. Len kissed his wife and asked her to come to the dressing-room after the fight. She did not want any prompting and wished him luck as they parted. Of the pair it was natural that it was she who had the 'butterflies' in the tummy.

When he reached the dressing-room Len found another argument in process. Sullivan was insisting that they should wear 8-oz. gloves, feeling that as Moody was such a hard hitter, it would be in Harvey's interests to wear the larger size. The Welshman's manager wanted 6-oz., but as soon as Len knew what was going on, he said: 'Get the smallest you can find, Dan, 4-oz. if you like. I feel in the mood to do some punching myself tonight.' Sam Russell was referee. He had been a boxer himself, knew all there was to know about the rules, and was respected for it. His only observation was the necessity for going to a neutral corner in the event of a knockdown. He did not know it then, but he was in for a busy evening at counting.

Immediately they left their corners it was obvious that Moody was out to get it over as quickly as possible. He came in, head lowered, both fists cocked at chest height, his brow thrust forward as a tempting target. Possessed of a hard skull, he did not mind taking a few punches there when he would counter with his big swings and hooks as he closed in. Harvey used the ring and boxed brilliantly. He gave ground, but made the fullest use of his straight left, not only to make points, but to damage and weaken his heavier opponent. Len had his elbows tucked into his sides to take the edge off Frank's body smashes, while his step-by-step retreating ensured that his rival was unable to get home with full weight behind his blows.

Now and again Harvey whipped in a solid left hook that bounced off Moody's chin. Len also pounded the Welshman's jaw with full-blooded rights, but with the same result. Most of the time, however, he was chipping away at Frank with his resolute left, but having to skip back every so often to avoid being punched out of the ring. The first two rounds held the crowd spellbound as they watched the slim-built Harvey outbox his strong opponent, while Moody was pinning his hopes on one sleep-producing punch. The applause was deafening at the end of each round, both of which had to be credited to the Cornishman.

The Welshman came out as before, bent on business, but still without guarding his chin, and he ran into trouble almost immediately. He lashed out, but was caught by a telling right to the head which clearly shook him badly. He swung another big punch, but Harvey moved inside it and hooked his left to Frank's chin with such power that the heavier man was sent flying to the floor. That punch was a beauty and Moody had to rest for eight seconds before he could rise. He tried gamely to fight back, but was in a bad way and Len was not in the mood to let him recover.

A shower of blows fell on the unhappy Welshman, hooks, uppercuts, jabs and crosses. They came in a stream and Len made light of the body smashes with which Moody tried to keep him back. A sizzling right to the chin dropped the light-heavyweight champion for another count of 'eight'. A left hook, followed by another swift punch from the other hand, sent Frank sprawling and only his will-power enabled him to get to his feet on the eighth second. It looked like the finish and the crowd was frantic with excitement, keyed up for 'the kill'. Gamely Moody came forward to meet his tormentor, but was soon on the boards again from another wicked right, but only 'two' had been counted before the bell ended the round and his seconds darted in to help him to his stool. Harvey, himself, was not without trouble. During the third round his left boot had split asunder, making his foothold insecure and when he reached his corner, it had to be removed and he fought the rest of the contest wearing only a sock and hoping that his opponent would not tread on his unprotected toes.

Most men would have had enough after that disastrous third round, but the man from Pontypridd was made of stern stuff and wanted no urging off his stool to resume the battle. Len met him halfway, crashed home a neatly-timed right and once more Moody sank to the canvas. Again he rested for eight seconds before getting up, then came forward, a grim look in his eyes, as if he was determined to get something of his own back. His face was badly marked by now, his left eye swollen and nearly closed, yet he launched a powerful attack, lashing out with all his remaining strength, aiming a big swing at Harvey's head that missed by an inch as Len drew back.

Harvey was showing his customary coolness, prepared to let his opponent expend his remaining stamina by making him miss, while catching him with crisp punches from both hands, with the target well-picked, and carrying weakening power. Through the fourth and fifth rounds Frank refused to be kept at bay, marching through Len's precision barrage with amazing fortitude, striving to get in a really decisive blow and resolved to go down with flying colours. But he took a rather wavy course back to his corner, and his features were in something of a mess.

That he had shot his last bolt must have been obvious to Harvey as he wasted no time when they met for the sixth round. Two swift left stabs to the face, followed by a brace of hooks to the head and the Welshman was forced to give ground. He had been shaken by those four punches and before he could recover, a powerful right struck him just behind his left ear. Down crashed Moody and it seemed as though this must be the finishing touch. It wasn't, for miraculously Frank got up, only to be smashed down again from a similar destructive blow.

Yet once again this courageous man struggled to get up, his arms at his sides, defenceless. Even so, he took a step forward but was immediately struck by another tremendous right behind the ear that knocked him flat on his back and seemingly beyond all recall. But, to the amazement of the onlookers, his frame stirred, he raised his head, then put his arms behind him in an effort to push himself up and beat the count. Referee Russell did not propose to let him take another punch, however. When he had reached 'eight' and it looked as though Moody might yet get to his feet, Sam helped him to rise and led the reeling Welshman to his corner. It was all over and Harvey had gained a sensational win – the very best performance of his career so far.

Len was cheered to the echo as he was announced as the winner. The clapping, stamping and yelling continued as he went over to Moody, shook his hand and enquired if he was all right. When Frank got up to put on his dressing-gown he too was given a great ovation, the fans standing up to applaud both victor and vanquished as they left the ring. Mrs Harvey found her way out of the arena and hurried to the dressing-rooms. The first one she reached was Moody's and he came to the door. 'Are you Mrs Harvey?', he asked. She nodded and he said: 'Well, take care of that husband of yours. He's a great fighter and will go a long way. But he's a very cruel man.' 'Not to me,' she said, smiling. 'No, I don't suppose he is, but he is to his opponents.'

The next person she met was Sullivan. He was wearing a broad smile and said: 'What did I tell you, I knew there was no risk in Len taking on Moody.' 'No risk so far as you were concerned,' she retorted, then went on to congratulate Len. 'What price the Old Man now?' he asked, while he hurriedly changed into his outdoor clothes.

One might wonder what a husband has to say to his wife after such a tense experience for both of them. What would they talk about on the way home? Actually they spent most of the journey arguing over the wording of Robert Southey's poem *The Battle of Blenheim*, although they agreed on one line: 'But 'twas a famous victory',* which aptly summed up the events of the evening. There is a piece to add that gives a notable sidelight on Len's kindly character. As the car sped away from Sydenham to North London and they were nearing home, Harvey tapped the driver of the car on the shoulder and said: 'Stop on the next corner, will you. I want to pick someone up.' Whoever could that be? wondered his wife, but Len went on to explain. 'He's the fellow I always get my newspaper from and I told him I would be passing this way after the fight and that we'd give him a lift home.' Florence stared at him un-believingly. Here was a man who had come through a hard battle and won a tremendous victory, yet he hadn't forgotten a promise made to a street-corner newsboy. 'Well,' explained her husband, apologetically. 'You see, like me, he's a great supporter of the Arsenal.' So the car stopped, picked up an extra passenger, complete with unsold copies of his wares, and they proceeded to Tollington Park.

The next day all the boxing writers were of one accord. Without any doubt Harvey was the outstanding contender for the British middle-weight title and Alex Ireland was called upon to give the Cornishman an early opportunity to fight for the championship. The Scot, after taking the title from Milligan, had successfully defended it against Moody, but

---

* 'It was the English,' Kasper cried, 'Who put the French to rout, But what they fought each other for, I could not well make out. But everybody said,' quoth he. 'But 'twas a famous victory.'

neither of these contests had involved a Lonsdale Belt. Alex was keen to fight for one and so was Len, which meant that if such a match were made it would have to be under the auspices of the National Sporting Club.

CHAPTER 10

British Champion at Twenty-Two

More than one promoting body was anxious to stage a match between Alex Ireland and Len Harvey, which stood out as a 'natural' if ever there was one. It was only to be expected that Scotland would be in the running, because the champion came from Leith and had won his title and successfully defended it in Edinburgh. The London syndicate that had put on the Harvey *v.* Moody bout was eager to secure the obvious follow-up contest, while the NSC dangled the Lonsdale trophy as tempting bait. With it they offered a purse of £3,500, and while the other promoters could have gone above that figure, they had no Belt to offer as an additional award. So the famous Club booked Olympia, London's largest arena, for 12th May and made sure of a sell-out by adding two more British title bouts: Harry Corbett to defend his featherweight crown against Johnny Cuthbert, and Teddy Baldock and Alf (Kid) Pattenden, both of whom claimed the bantam championship, to settle the question of superiority.

Two other proposals had been put to Harvey. Efforts were made to induce Mickey Walker to return to England and defend his world title against Len of Barnsbury, but were dropped hurriedly when the famous Toy Bulldog demanded £20,000 for his services. As he had accepted £11,000 to fight Milligan, it must have seemed to Len's supporters that the American considered him a far greater risk, hence the raising of the price. The other suggestion was a return meeting with Marcel Thil, who had just become European middleweight champion. Len had scored a clear-cut points victory over the Frenchman and no one doubted that he could repeat the performance. But Thil was under contract to Jeff Dickson, who would have willingly staged a title match between the pair, but for the fact that so far he had been denied a licence to promote in Great Britain by the British Boxing Board of Control.

Len did not mind. He was intent on winning the British crown and the Belt that went with it. Ireland was entitled to sixty per cent of the gate, but those behind Harvey thought that he was the bigger attraction of the pair in view of his staggering win over Moody and were not content with the remaining forty per cent. Finally they settled on an adequate sum and Len went back to the *Black Bull* where he had the assistance of Joe Bloomfield, Billy Bird, Jack Marshall and Bill Dixon. At Whetstone he was always very happy and enjoyed the harsh training routine. The place had every facility for preparing for a fight and was ideally situated for road work. As the date came near his spar-mates were convinced that he was hitting harder than ever.

Ireland went to Shoeburyness near Southend-on-Sea to get into fighting trim, taking with him that prince of trainers, Jack Goodwin. The Scot was nearly six years older than his challenger, but his experience was longer. As an amateur he had engaged in over a hundred bouts of which he lost but seven. In 1920 he had reached the final of the welterweight class at the Antwerp Olympic Games in which he met Jack Schneider of Canada. After three rounds the judges were undecided as to the winner so ordered an extra round. Ireland won this beyond doubt, but the decision went to his opponent. The following year Alex won the ABA welter title and in March 1922 he turned professional, compiling a useful record over the next six years, even going to South Africa where he won all his four contests. He did not gain much acclaim, however, until he surprisingly defeated Tommy Milligan on a foul for the British middleweight title and then beat off a challenge by Frank Moody to keep his crown. That was eight months ago and he hadn't fought since.

Olympia was filled for the triple championship tournament, in fact, it housed the biggest assembly ever seen at a British promotion up to that date. The Club had made a real gala occasion of it; never had a big fight been staged in such brilliant surroundings. It was ablaze with glittering lights and the attendants were dressed as footmen in full livery and powdered wigs. Mrs Harvey was so impressed that she left her ringside seat and climbed up to the top of the arena, among the electricians, to look down on the thousands of people surrounding the tiny ring. She thought it all very wonderful. As he was leaving his dressing-room to go into the ring, Len passed Johnny Cuthbert, who was wearing a wide smile on his face and a glittering Lonsdale trophy round his waist. He had regained the title he had lost to Harry Corbett at the second attempt to get it back, their last meeting having ended in a 'draw'. 'Well done, Johnny,' said Harvey, then remarked to his seconds, 'That's one title that's changed hands tonight – it's a good omen.'

The fight was announced as being for the British and European middle-weight titles, in spite of Marcel Thil's recognition for this continental honour by the International Boxing Union. Milligan had won the title when beating Bruno Frattini, of Italy, and had not been dispossessed of it up to the time of his defeat by Ireland. Alex therefore was European champion by right of succession and the NSC were justified in giving a double heading to the fight between Len and Alex. Not that either of the contestants was unduly bothered and the same could be well said of the many fans who were there to see a good scrap, nothing else mattering.

The challenger stood up straight, taking every advantage of his extra height and reach, which were enhanced by the Scot adopting a crouching stance. Len did not seem to be in any particular hurry. He fiddled and feinted and then, when the champion shaped for a delivery, he was met by a jarring straight left to the face. The Scot rushed, but was checked by another left jab, then a hard left and right to the body. Alex came in again, this time getting through with a left to the face. There was a brisk exchange on the ropes, some more open sparring, then the bell sounded to end the first round that quite clearly had gone in the Cornishman's favour.

It was plain that Len had the faster pace as well as the advantage in reach. Ireland was smart in ducking and swerving, but he was slower in his deliveries and although getting to the body once or twice, was being jabbed and clipped with neat punches that had plenty of power behind them and were delivered almost at will by the calm, poker-faced challenger. In the third Harvey landed a left and then a right to the jaw that caused the champion to sag at the knees. He went in close to hold and indulge in some scrambling infighting and the referee, seated at the ringside, called out: 'Don't hold – either of you.'

Nothing dramatic occurred in the next two rounds, although Harvey did the bulk of the scoring and his punches were far more effective than those of his rival. Alex was warned to keep his body punches up, both were again told not to hold, whereupon Len pushed Alex off, then invited him to come in and fight. The champion rushed into another clinch, but on the break Harvey shook him up with hard jolts to the jaw and the Scot's return to his corner at the end of the fifth was none too steady. So far Harvey had won every round without exerting himself unduly.

Ireland came out warily, drew a lead from Len which he ducked, then put over a good right to the chin, followed by a left then a right to the body. It was his first lively piece of work, but he had to pay for it. Len was stung into retaliation and he opened out briskly. A left to the body almost doubled the champion in two, while a terrific right uppercut under the chin lifted him off his feet and sat him on the canvas. Ireland's face showed only too plainly that he was in pain and he had difficulty in getting up before 'nine' could be called. Then he had to bring all his experience and ringcraft into play to stay on his feet. Harvey followed him over the square, got in some good left stabs to the face as Alex retreated, but the full power was dissipated as the target was going back. When he felt his back to the ropes, Ireland darted forward for some close-quarter work and managed to avoid another damaging punch throughout the remainder of the round, which also went to Harvey.

At the start of the seventh, Ireland seemed to have made a full recovery. He looked strong and businesslike, while Harvey watched him intently. Alex sparred and moved, then darted in, but was met by a left that came with the speed and accuracy of an arrow. The champion was stopped in his tracks by this unerring blow and could not avoid the following right that crashed against his jaw or the left that came in a whipping arc to catch him under the ribs on his right side. It was a punch full of destruction and it not only put down the champion, but knocked every vestige of remaining wind and stamina out of his body. He sat up, his face distorted with suffering, and struggled manfully to get up in time to beat the count. But as he reached his feet so the 'out' was called and Len Harvey had reached his first goal and was a British titleholder at last, nine years after he had started off as a little boy on the championship trail.

The vast crowd cheered to the echo as Lord Lonsdale climbed into the ring and presented Harvey with the beautiful gold and enamel belt that was the emblem of British championships. Len shook hands with the famous sporting Earl who had given his name to these trophies, which were the envy of the world, then got out of the ring as quickly as he could and made for his dressing-room. Meeting Florence he told her that they were rushing home for a special reason. When they got there his mother-in-law asked them not to make a noise as it would waken the baby. 'I'm going to wake him all right,' said Len and he and his wife went to the cot that held their sleeping son. Len dangled the Belt over the child and the jiggling of the metal woke him up. He reached out a tiny hand and clutched the trophy. 'This is yours, son,' said the proud father. 'I'm going to win it outright for you as quickly as I can.'*

* When Harvey had made the Lonsdale Belt his own property in just over a year, he took it to Mappin & Webb's where an additional plaque was added, donating it to Terry and inscribing his name thereon.

Once again Harvey had scored a decisive victory that earned him the sporting headlines the following day and, of course, he was besieged with challengers. Len Johnson, pointing out that he held a victory over Harvey, was hoping that the Board of Control would lift its colour bar and allow him to fight for the British title. There were again talks of pairing the new champion with either Walker or Thil, but the same difficulties presented themselves as before: Charlie Rose, always a humorist, suggested that Phil Scott, whom he managed, would be willing to take on Harvey, to which challenge Len asked what else he was expected to give away besides the four stones difference in their weight, at the same time intimating that if a promoter could be found ready to pay him handsomely for the disadvantages in size and poundage, he would be quite willing to swap punches with the heavyweight champion.

Suddenly it seemed that the fight everyone wanted to see was the one between Harvey and Hood that had been arranged earlier in the year, but was called off by the welterweight champion when he broke his right thumb in training. It would now be a contest between champions, giving the Birmingham stylist a chance to win another title and Harvey the opportunity to gain a second notch on his Belt. Jack had already been presented with his, although he had fought only twice for it instead of the usual three times. But the rules provided that in the event of a recognised challenger not being forthcoming within three years, the trophy would become the absolute property of the holder. Hood had defended his title against Alf Mancini during that period of time, but the bout had not been granted official status, so it was not supposed to count. Anyway, Hood had one trophy and now had a chance to lay his hands on another one, while Len was eager to go a step further towards making true his promise to his young son.

Several promoters made bids for the match, Hood's manager, Ted Broadribb, being anxious to secure it for British Sporting Promotions, for whom he was acting as matchmaker, or for Jeff Dickson, who intended to promote in London despite the Board of Control's refusal to grant him a licence to do so, and with whom Broadribb had arranged to join forces. Jack Callaghan suggested £3,000 as a starting price, and Harry Jacobs came to the Harvey home to try and induce Len to box under his banner once again. Len told him that he had promised the NSC he would fight for the Club and was waiting to hear from them. 'But you haven't signed a contract,' said the promoter. 'I know,' came the reply: 'But I have given my word and, I'm sorry, but that's the end of it.' 'You are a very honourable young man,' responded Jacobs. 'I respect your attitude, because I know that is how you would behave with me.'

Another proposition came in the form of a cable from Tom O'Rourke, one of America's leading managers, urging Harvey to come at once to New York. 'You can earn far more money here than ever you can in England and I can steer you into a title fight with Walker,' was the gist of the message. But it had to be rejected as manager Sullivan was doubtful if he could qualify to enter the United States. Len could have gone on his own. He even discussed the prospect of his wife accompanying him. But their son was still only a baby and they thought it too early to leave him. 'America will have to wait,' said Len. 'I'm not dropping the substance for the shadow. Winning the Belt outright is my immediate objective.'

Such moves, to which the newspapers gave full publicity, undoubtedly spurred the National Sporting Club into positive action. A big offer was made with the Lonsdale Belt as an additional inducement, the idea being to stage another extravaganza at Olympia. Hood, who had everything to gain and nothing to lose, accepted what amounted to more, or as much as, he would have got elsewhere, while Harvey stuck out for the champion's share, which topped what his opponent would be getting. Then the Club found it impossible to find suitably attractive bouts to support the championship contest and fill out Olympia, and decided to switch the bout to the Holborn Stadium where they had moved after losing their long-established home in Covent Garden.

It meant jacking up the prices to a maximum of five guineas and the lowest at £2 7s, expensive in the currently lean years, but acceptable to the many who were prepared to pay anything for what they knew would prove a model boxing contest between the two best stylists in the country. Hood went off to his favourite training place, the *Nag's Head* in the Malvern Hills, under his regular trainer, Willie Weston, while Harvey returned to the *Black Bull*. Here he quickly settled down to prepare himself for the first defence of his title, just over five months after winning it, but was surprised one day to receive a visit from three of the stewards of the newly re-formed but self-constituted British Boxing Board of Control. They were Lord Decies, Sir Walter De Frece and Lieutenant-Colonel Myddleton, RE.

'No doubt you have heard of the newly re-formed Board of Control,' said their spokesman. 'And we are here to ask why you have not yet taken out a licence to box and to try and persuade you to do so. We gave full warning in the press that unless licences in all the branches of employment in professional Boxing were taken out by 31st May 1929, anyone without a licence would not be permitted to continue as a participant in the sport. You are the only British champion who has not fallen into line and applied for his licence and you are held in such regard by everyone connected with Boxing that we appeal to you to do so, not only for the good of the sport, but for your own good as well.'

Len, who had just finished a hard training stint, listened quietly and politely. 'Excuse me for enquiring, but do I understand that unless I buy one of your licences, you will stop me from earning my living? Because, if that is so you can save further argument by getting out of here. I am not joining any body that has set itself up to rule over my sport and then comes to me while I am training for an important fight and tries to blackmail me into becoming a member. I have never needed a licence up to now. I've got on very nicely without a Board of Control. I abide by the recognised rules of my sport and do not require anyone to see that I do so. You offer nothing, but expect me to sign myself away into your keeping. I'm sorry, gentlemen, but I'm tired and sweaty and want a bath. Good-day to you.' And he went off, leaving the trio to stare at one another and then depart.

It would have been interesting to see what would have happened if the matter had ended there. Harvey had a legal contract to box Hood and no one could have prevented that from happening without paying full compensation for so doing. And what would have been the public response had the practically unknown Board of Control suddenly declared that a British Champion had been barred from boxing because of his failure to buy a five shilling licence? Foolishly the NSC had taken out membership with the Board of Control without considering whether any of the boxers contracted to fight on its next promotion were themselves holders of BBB of C licences. Had Harvey been prevented from boxing, the Club would have been in an invidious position, being liable for Len's purse and legal costs had he taken them to court.

At the same time the Board could not afford to take 'no' for an answer. They sent Lionel Bettinson and Sam Russell to the Harvey home and asked Florence for her help. 'This is not a matter for me to decide,' she told them. 'It is up to Len and if he doesn't want to join, then he won't, and nothing I say will alter his decision.'

'You could go to his training camp and persuade him to see reason,' they prompted. 'You must realise that Boxing is in need of a controlling body, it should have had one years ago, and it can only do good for the sport. It is not in Len's interest to stand aside. If he joins everyone will join and all will benefit in the long run.' 'Why can't you wait until after the Hood fight?' asked Florence. 'If you had any sense you would know that when a man is in intense training and is reaching his peak of fitness, he gets very edgy and to approach him on such a small matter as taking out a licence could not be at a worse time.' 'We want Len in the ring as a properly licensed boxer,' said Sam. 'We want him as an example to the others – not as the one man out. The success of the Board depends on men of repute like your husband.'

'Very well,' replied Mrs Harvey. 'I will go out to Whetstone this afternoon and do what I can. Easy-going as Len may be, he has the typical Cornishman's obstinacy and will not be bullied by anybody. But I will try to talk him into joining on one condition. That I am allowed to go to the Holborn Stadium on the night of the fight.' 'That's utterly impossible,' exclaimed Bettinson. 'You know it is a long-standing and unbreakable rule of the NSC that women are not allowed inside its premises, certainly not to watch the boxing.' 'All I am asking is that I am allowed to be in the building so that I can hear the result immediately it is announced. I promise not to go anywhere near the ring.' 'If you give me your solemn oath not to attempt to go into the hall and watch, I'll arrange for you to be there,' said the NSC manager. 'Just let me in, that's all,' replied Florence – and so it was arranged.

Persuading her husband was another kettle of fish altogether. First of all he was angry because they had gone behind his back to get her support. 'What good did they think that would do?', he demanded. 'I'm sure I don't know,' she replied. 'But now I'm here, what are you going to do about it? The way I see it is that Boxing has never been legalised in this country as it has in others, and the authorities of law and order here are quite prepared to let a controlling body of reputable men, such as members of the National Sporting Club, take over the responsibility of governing the sport in this country. That gives them a great deal of power and I am afraid that if you stick out against them, it could be that you will never box again. Normally you wouldn't think of letting them down or the public by not fighting, but if you have to, because you will not take out this licence, it could be the last nail in your coffin as a professional boxer. All the years and hard work you have put in would be wasted. Still, it is your decision and whatever you do, I will never criticise you afterwards.'

'It goes very much against my principles to be forced into doing something I don't approve of,' declared Harvey. 'They've got me in a cleft stick, but I can't let my pride interfere with our plans for the future. I'll join. They left a form here when they called, so I'll fill it in and send it off. You can tell them of my decision if they get in touch with you again. But tell them not to come here.'

Florence did not dare tell him of her plan to be at the Holborn Stadium on the night of the fight, but a day or so later she was told to be at the back entrance to the hall at a certain time when she would be admitted. All went as arranged. She waited at the appointed place and soon a member of the Stadium staff let her in and she was put in a small room on her own. She could hear in the distance the noise of the fans who were watching a preliminary contest and was asked to remain where she was until the man returned and told her the result of the contest.

She now discovered that she was next to one of the dressing-rooms and after a time she heard someone say: 'Harvey is on.' Then her immediate surroundings were plunged into silence and she walked up and down like a caged lioness. She looked at her watch. It was 10.15 p.m., a late start to enable those who had gone to the Motor Show to be back in time for the big fight. At last she could bear it no longer and, opening the door, went out into a passage that led into the arena. She paced this short corridor a number of times, then heard the crowd working up into a noisy and continuous roar. A row of high screens prevented her from seeing anything, but she noticed a gap between them, high up and apparently intended as a place for a long-range camera. No photographer was in sight, so she darted back to the room, seized a chair and putting it against the screens just managed to peer through the opening. To her delight she had a perfect view of the ring and the two boxers in action and watched Hood and her husband put up a marvellous exhibition of scientific boxing. To her they seemed very evenly matched in fighting skill and it was only natural that she should think that Len was just that much better than his opponent.

Suddenly she heard someone say: 'And what do you think you are doing up there, young lady? You've no right to be here, it is against the rules for women to be in the arena.' 'I'm not in the arena,' answered Florence. 'So I haven't broken any rules. Len Harvey is my husband. He doesn't know I'm in the building. I intend to watch the contest right through, so please go away as I don't want to miss any of it.' She didn't know it then, but her questioner was Lord Decies, who, when he got back to the ringside told C. H. (Pickles) Douglas, one of the NSC referees that, believe it or not, young Mrs Harvey was watching the contest. When it was over and she returned to her place of captivity, she was allowed to visit a triumphant Len in his dressing-room. 'Len has won,' a reporter told her. 'I know,' she replied gaily. 'I saw him win.' Next day the papers had headlines that read: 'Harvey keeps title. Wife watches fight'; 'Wife breaks Club ban and watches Harvey win'; and so on.

Harvey's points victory after fifteen tense rounds had been due to his exceedingly clean punching and to his greater show of aggressiveness. Boxing with clocklike precision, he watched every move made or threatened by the welter champion and directed his punches with perfect timing and direction. There was scarcely a punch of which he did not make use, but the favourite weapon was a deadly right uppercut. This item of his armoury he used whenever opportunity offered and it said much for Hood's fine condition and stamina that he was able to remain upright against this punch that kept colliding against his chin. One of these uppercuts, delivered midway through the tenth round, would have put most welters away for the night.

Hood's display was a study of elusiveness and a cameo of extremely clever ringcraft. Facing a man whose coolness and hard hitting had become renowned, Jack refused to falter or to lose his control. He knew that to break ground at an inopportune moment or to rush in wildly when Len adopted the 'come into the parlour' attitude would be to court disaster, and this he resolutely would not do. Once or twice the middleweight champion did manage to lure Hood into the ropes, but after Jack had received a heavy clip to the jaw as a result of following his man, he stayed wisely at home. For him it was once bitten twice shy.

The challenger's eyes were for ever watching Harvey's deadly right hand and although Len connected quite frequently with it, a less highly-skilled opponent than Hood would have succumbed early in the fight. Their left hand work was pretty evenly matched, although Harvey had a slightly longer reach, therefore his leads carried that little extra sting. They fought cleanly and openly and referee Sam Russell, who was in the ring the whole time, was given the easiest of tasks because of the strict adherence to the rules shown by both men. Not once did he find it necessary to go between them. When he asked them to 'break' they did so immediately. Their exemplary conduct was fully appreciated by the fans who applauded them generously at the end of each round.

At the halfway stage Harvey must have been ahead in the points scoring, but in the eighth, Hood, who so far had made very sparing use of his right, no doubt because of the once-broken thumb, suddenly flashed over a solid punch to Harvey's cheekbone that caused a slight swelling to rise under Len's left eye. But this did not bother the middle-weight champion, nor did it get any worse, although Jack tried his hardest to increase the damage. Harvey took full command in the tenth, aiming at the body with the object of weakening the lighter man. Heavy hooks from Len, right smashes to the ribs and those devastating uppercuts had Hood in real trouble, but he brought all his defensive powers into action and weathered the storm, although it was a tired challenger who went to his corner at the end of the round.

The betting was now two to one on Harvey which gave a good indication of how the fight was going. But Hood was still there and now the exchanges became more exciting as they both abandoned caution and sought and made openings for scoring punches. Hood had to be admired for the way he took the best Len could give him and still remained a danger. In fact he put up a grandstand finish in an effort to snatch the fight out of the fire. But his punches did not carry the power to do Harvey any harm, whereas a number of Len's blows had marked effect. The final session had the fans in an uproar as each boxer tried hard to bring off a decisive finish. But when the referee added up his score card after the final bell, he walked unhesitatingly over to Harvey and raised his right hand. Len had defended his title and Belt like a real champion and was good value for the verdict, even if those who came from the Midlands or had backed Hood, felt somewhat grieved. As for the rest of the fans they 'brought the house down' in their recognition of a masterly win by the middleweight champion.

CHAPTER 11

Winning the Lonsdale Belt Outright

So that was notch number two and when almost immediately the NSC proposed a return match with Hood within two months' time, Harvey could not sign his contract quick enough. Other promoters made bids up to £5,000 for the contest, but by taking Olympia again, and this time not having to bother about an expensive supporting card, the Club was able to offer terms that were acceptable to both men. To Len it meant more than just another chance to prove his superiority over the welter king; he saw it as an opportunity for setting up a record time for winning a Lonsdale Belt outright. The previous quickest of eleven months and eight days had been achieved by bantamweight champion, Jim Higgins, of Scotland, in 1920–1. Now Harvey had an opportunity to reduce this to the almost unbeatable time of six months and eighteen days. It was a target he felt was quite within his compass.

As always, Harvey would go to any length to confer a favour on a friend. George Harris, who had been Master of Ceremonies at 'The Ring' for a great many years and must have introduced Len more times than he could remember, had just become licensee of the *Bell and Sun* at Ware. He wanted all the publicity he could secure to get away to a good start and asked Harvey if he would train there for the return fight with Hood. Now it is well known in the Fight Game that to change your training-quarters is to risk changing your luck, but Harvey was not superstitious about such things and even if he was, a request for aid from someone like George – whom he had heard so many times say, 'And in this corner...', and whom, at the end of a contest, he had seen climb into the ring, point to where the referee had nodded and merely say, 'The winner – so-and-so' – was a request not to be refused. So Len and his helpers left the *Black Bull* where every fight he had trained for had been a winning one, and went off to Hertfordshire. Perhaps the fact that he neglected to pack the Fitzsimmons Horseshoe may have had something to do with what followed.

There was a gap of fifty-eight days between the two Harvey *v.* Hood fights, the second taking place exactly a week before Christmas Day. At the weigh-in, for which Harvey was late owing to dense fog outside London, the middleweight champion scaled way below the stipulated poundage at 11 st. 3 lbs. which gave him only a five pounds advantage over his opponent. He was also $2\frac{1}{2}$ ins. taller, a factor of which he made the utmost use once again. Sam Russell was appointed referee and once more he had an easy task for the pair put up one of the cleanest, most open, and truly scientific contests ever seen anywhere. On the whole it was even a faster-fought encounter than the one at Holborn. True there were no sensations, but they were not expected. When Harvey and Hood came from their corners they were watching each other like a pair of cats and the same vigilance was maintained throughout the contest, so that the scoring achieved had to be of the most skilful quality. The big crowd sat in silence throughout the rounds and applauded generously each time the men went back to their corners.

At the start Harvey showed marked superiority and won the first six rounds in a row. He meant business and took the initiative in each of these sessions and inside a minute had opened a cut close to Hood's left eye. In the fifth he caught his challenger with a left hook that opened a cut near Jack's right eye that bled freely. It was patched up in the interval, but was opened again in the next round at which point you could not put a bet on the middleweight champion and Hood's prospects seemed rather dim. Then the Birmingham man seemed to wake up to the fact that he was being steadily outpointed and surprised his rival by stepping up the pace considerably and getting in first with his straight lefts at long range, while he punched away briskly at close-quarters.

No doubt Harvey was content to let the lighter man expend his energy, for having sampled the best Jack could put over with his left and having little to fear from his right, Len allowed his challenger a little rope for the next three rounds. Finding that Hood was as strong as ever, Harvey took over again and the exchanges were fairly level for the next two rounds. But Len shone in the twelfth when a hard right hook to the head spun the challenger round and he had to keep his wits about him to avoid further trouble.

It was still a tremendous duel between two outstanding boxers and Hood, no doubt acting under orders from his corner, made an even more determined attempt to get on top in the thirteenth round. He worked his left rapidly into Len's face and although the champion was taking advantage of every opportunity to score, he had slightly the worst of the round. But he was still nicely in front in the opinion of most of the spectators and with only two more rounds to go it seemed pretty certain that he would now pull out all the stops to make certain of victory.

There was very nearly an extra fight thrown in during the interval. Dan Sullivan, who had taken up his stand in Harvey's corner from the start, seemed to fancy that Ted Broadribb, who was doctoring Hood's damaged eyes each time Jack came back, might be putting some special, and perhaps illegal, concoction on the wounds. He began to shout excitedly, even raced round to Hood's corner to emphasise some protest he had to make. For a moment or two it looked very much as though Dan and Ted might exchange blows, but the starting bell for the fourteenth round checked any extraneous fisticuffs and as the referee paid no attention to Sullivan's protests, order re-established itself.

Harvey was on his mettle now. He was out to prove himself the winner beyond doubt. He had Hood on the defensive under a determined barrage of picked punches. Jack tried to come back at him and they swapped blows toe-to-toe in a manner that thrilled the fans. It was obvious that the middleweight champion was putting more power into his efforts, but he could not get through with a punch to put Hood down, although he tried hard enough. The crowd cheered the lighter man for his game fight, but the honours of the round had to go to Harvey.

They both came forth to do or die, Hood in particular looking very grim and earnest, but he could scarcely have been satisfied that he had victory safely in his grasp. Harvey was just as determined and the exchanges were as fast as the men could make them. The challenger was still pinning his faith on an unerring left to the face, but Len would not be checked by this and advanced with some very fierce and heavy double-handed hitting. He was fighting as fresh as when he started and was making his extra weight tell as he had Jack going back under the blazing fire of his attack. In the last thirty seconds Hood set up a furious counter blast, but Harvey matched him punch for punch and they were still exchanging shots when the bell sounded the end of the bout.

There was a moment of hushed tenseness. Then the MC climbed into the ring. Holding up his hand to quiet down the last vestige of sound, he announced: 'Ladies and gentlemen, the referee's decision is "A Draw".' At once came a storm of resentment and even if those who supported Hood breathed a sigh of relief, they were completely outnumbered by Harvey's faithful supporters, plus the majority of the spectators who could be classed as 'neutral'. Among the many pressmen present only

one was in agreement with the verdict and it was wondered if Mr Russell
had not made a miscalculation on his score card. But no, he had failed
to separate the two boxers, although most of the ringside reporters
felt, as did *Boxing*, that Harvey had won seven clear rounds, with three
even, thus leaving five in Hood's favour. Their fight at the Holborn
Stadium had been closer than the return bout, yet the same referee had
given it to Len. The bulk of the spectators went away feeling that Harvey
had been most unlucky in not making the Lonsdale Belt his own property,
while Len went home in silence, keeping his thoughts to himself, even
if Florence shared his misfortune. Perhaps the only happy people over
the result were the members of the committee of the National Sporting
Club. For the time being at least, they had been spared the expense
of providing a new trophy.

The fact that Jack Hood had allegedly held Harvey to a drawn verdict did not in any way lessen the demand for Len's services. He was
still wanted in American rings, there were overtures from European
promoters, while at home there were suggestions that he should fight
Hood for the third time. Several middleweights were put forward as
opponents, including Len Johnson, the sole conqueror of Harvey since
his arrival in London, apart from Johnny Sullivan, whom Len had since
removed as a possible contender.

To fill in time, the Cornishman returned to 'The Ring', after an absence of fifteen months, his opponent being the newly-crowned Belgian
middleweight champion, François Stevens, who came to scale half a
pound inside the stipulated weight of 11 st. 8 lbs., with Harvey weighing
11 st. 4 lbs. Stevens had wins over Joe Bloomfield and Billy Adair in
London engagements, so seemed likely to put up more resistance than
some of his fellow-countrymen who had traded punches with the
Britisher. But after an opening round in which Len was feeling out the
calibre of his opponent, the action started in a big way.

Halfway through the second round a Harvey 'special' in the shape
of a long right smote the Belgian on the left cheek, a little too high to
have damaging effect, but enough to make the recipient go on the retreat and tuck his chin well behind his left shoulder. This caution
availed him nothing, however, as Harvey jerked his head back repeatedly
with a straight left and punished the continental while scarcely taking
a blow in return. In the third a left swing to the jaw had Stevens
staggering across the ring to fall in a neutral corner. He was up without
taking a count, only to catch a swift and powerful left hook to the chin
that knocked him unconscious before he hit the canvas. He did not stir

while the full count was called and it was some time before he was fit enough to leave the ring.

Shortly after this Steve McCall, from Aberdeen, took the Scottish middleweight title from Alex Ireland and at once issued a challenge to the British champion. The National Sporting Club, fighting hard to stay in business against increasing competition from Jeff Dickson, seized on this situation to provide a top-of-the-bill contest for another big Olympia presentation. Their matchmaker had no difficulty in arranging terms with the Scot, who was keen to fight for the title with money as a second consideration, while if he expected it less easy to get the champion under contract, he was pleasantly surprised. Len had his mind set on an American adventure, but wanted first to take the Lonsdale Belt with him as his personal property. He suggested a fair price and got it without argument, the promoters being confident that his name would attract enough ticket buyers to fully justify the size of his purse.

In support of the middleweight championship bout there was a feather-weight title contest with Johnny Cuthbert defending his laurels against Dom Volante, from Liverpool; an Empire bantamweight affair of fifteen rounds between Willie Smith, from South Africa, and Dick Corbett, from Bethnal Green; plus another fifteen rounds heavyweight contest featuring Don Shortland, of Sheffield, and Charlie Smith, from Deptford. With prices ranging from 8s 6d to £3 10s, the Club felt it was entitled to a 'full house'. That this was achieved was due compensation for its enterprise; what is more, each of the four bouts was full of interest from start to finish, while the main event ended sensationally.

Harvey, who had trained at Fred Dyer's gymnasium in the Strand for his fight with the Belgian champion, now moved to new quarters at the *Star and Garter Hotel* at Windsor, where the licensee, George Godfrey, was a staunch supporter of Boxing.

Here Len made a complete change of sparring-partners, choosing three smart welterweights in Alec Thake (Canning Town), Archie Sexton (Bethnal Green) and Jack Griffiths (Hastings) to keep him at top speed, with the local heavyweight, Jim Brooks, to take the hard punching. McCall trained in Glasgow under his trainer-manager, Billy Aitchinson.

That the British middleweight champion meant business from the start was shown by the way he banged in his first punch almost before the Scot had got his hands up. It was a powerful left to the jaw that spun the challenger round and sent him reeling into the ropes. Most of the onlookers expected to see the challenger go down from that devastating punch, as no doubt did Harvey, as he did not follow up immediately.

McCall had been hurt and he showed it by flinging back a mighty right, a punch that Len evaded, also a right aimed at his body. They went into a clinch where Len busied himself until the Scot was glad to break away. He fought back, endeavouring to give blow for blow. But he had been severely shaken up by that first punch and was being wildly heroic. Len contented himself by adding to his score with well chosen shots and won the first round by a wide margin of points.

McCall had realised by now that to stand off and let Harvey dictate the fight would be fatal. He was shorter in the reach and could not trade left leads, so he had to leap in with his punches, then try to dodge the swift and severe counters that were unleashed against him. He also had to try and avoid being beaten to the punch, so it was an uphill battle for the Scot, but he kept at his task with great determination and courage. Sometimes he got in a left to the face, on several occasions he put over a right to the head or body, but he did not seem able to hurt the champion or disturb his calm equilibrium.

Meanwhile, Len was allowing his man a lot of rope, containing his persistent attacks and, at the same time, chipping away at his resistance with a variety of well-picked punches. To the onlookers, especially those in the seats furthest from the ring, it may have seemed that McCall was not only holding his own in these early rounds, but perhaps winning them by a shade. He was displaying more energy than the champion, but those who understood Harvey's fighting style and appreciated its science, knew that Len never wasted a move or a punch if he could help it. When occasionally made to miss, he was never off balance, and kept amazing control over his emotions even when caught by a good delivery as sometimes happened.

The challenger's supporters were quite pleased at the way things were going until the eighth round began. Then it seemed that Harvey had completed his homework and was about to start and finish his essay. A left feint to the face caused McCall to raise his guard and, swift as an arrow, a stiff left went into his ribs, immediately followed by a right under the heart. Then the same hand came over the top to land on the Scotsman's jaw and cause his whole frame to shudder. Now the barrage began and he was beaten back under a rapid fire of jabs, hooks, crosses and uppercuts.

The fans applauded as McCall brought all his defensive skills into play, ducking, parrying, smothering and seeking close-quarters to try and nullify as much of the bombardment as he could. He was so occupied in avoiding a damaging punch that he was quite unable to make any counter attacks. But he did avoid disaster and received a prolonged cheer for his tenacity as he returned to his corner. He had totally lost the round, but the champion did not appear to have inflicted much damage for the energy he had expended.

Or had he? Steve was off his stool very smartly for the start of the ninth round. His success in evading decisive defeat had given him increased confidence, while no doubt his seconds had urged him to try and get some of his own back. Whatever was in his mind when he left his corner, he came out in an almost reckless manner, a fatal thing to do against a superlative boxer like Harvey. Len waited for him to come into range and then hooked his chin hard with the left, a wicked blow, so well timed that the challenger met it full blast and dropped as if he had been shot.

It took him eight seconds to reach his feet but he was wide open to a smart right to the jaw that bowled him over for another 'eight' count. It was a weary, completely beaten challenger who struggled to rise this time. But he did, more by instinct than anything else, and as soon as he shaped up, Len walked up, humanely tapped him on the chin with his right and as McCall sank down for the third time two towels came in from his seconds and referee Douglas waved his hands to indicate that it was all over. Harvey watched as they picked up the semi-conscious Scottish champion, then walked over to ensure he was all right.

Len was announced the winner and the Lonsdale Belt which he had now won outright, was put round his waist to the enthusiastic applause from the big crowd. He again went across to the now fully-recovered McCall and they exchanged good wishes. 'Sorry, chum,' said Harvey as they shook hands, and Steve replied: 'It's not so bad when you're beaten by a great champion like you.' No hard feelings! Eight years later when Len went to Glasgow to fight Manuel Abrew, who should meet him on the platform with a band of other local boxing enthusiasts, but Steve McCall, who saw his old opponent to his hotel, waited on him and accompanied him to his dressing-room at Shawfield Park before watching the master boxer display his skill at someone else's expense.

Having disposed of his sole recognised contender, Harvey next switched his attention to the light-heavyweights and a challenge was issued to Harry Crossley who held the British title. Len was so confident of beating the stylish Yorkshireman that he suggested a side-bet of any-thing up to £200. It had been his boyhood dream to be able to emulate his fistic hero, Cornish-born Bob Fitzsimmons, and win three titles, middle, light-heavy and heavy, and having achieved the first leg of this bold plan, he was anxious to start on the second. But the National Sporting Club had no more tournaments in mind for the time being and Jeff Dickson was more keen to match Harvey with Dave Shade, a high-ranking American middleweight, in a match that could be advertised as an eliminating contest for the world crown.

As soon as he heard this, Jack Kearns, manager to Mickey Walker, whom everyone thought had relinquished his title, cabled to suggest a meeting with Harvey and Dickson, who had just staged a sell-out show at Wimbledon Greyhound Stadium when Young Stribling had demolished Phil Scott, was fully prepared to put on a Walker/Harvey match there. Kearns suggested a modest £15,000 for his champion, while Len asked for £5,000 for himself. Dickson thought this far too much, whereupon the Cornishman replied that if Tommy Milligan had been considered to be worth £7,000 for fighting Walker, surely he was entitled to £5,000. There being no answer to that argument the idea was dropped.

So it was back to Dave Shade and Dickson announced that Harvey and the American would meet over fifteen rounds at the Albert Hall on 29th September, the press being informed that the winner would fight for the world title, either in London or New York. Both Shade and Harvey had agreed to box on a percentage of the 'gate' and Len went back to the *Star and Garter* at Windsor for his very first fight against an American opponent. Among his sparring-partners was Les Ward, a strong middleweight from Woking, who found his employer in a very determined frame of mind during his preparation.

Promoter Dickson, in a realistic attempt to stamp out the chances of a fight ending in disqualification because of low hitting, had brought back from New York a supposedly 'foul-proof' cup which he expected his boxers to use at his tournaments. He presented one to Len, who examined it and asked if it was really necessary. He was assured that Shade would wear one and that Harvey should do likewise. 'I don't see it,' said the Cornishman. 'Wearing one of these is only inviting your opponent to hit you below the belt. The rules say that if a man goes low with his punching, he is liable to pay the full penalty and lose the contest. If I hit a man low I expect to be disqualified and if my opponent fouls me I expect him to be treated similarly. I am not prepared to condone foul punching by wearing a protector which permits a man to foul me as much as he likes while I am expected to be made foul-proof. It is against all the highest principles of Boxing.' He handed it back. 'I'll try my luck without it,' he said. 'I've not been disqualified yet and I don't intend to be if I can help it.'*

While waiting for the Shade fight to mature, Len had made two brief appearances at 'Premierland'. He made his debut at this popular East End arena one hot Sunday afternoon in June, meeting Charlie McDonald, a coloured fighter from Sunderland, who had met the best at his weight – but not the very best. He was allowed to show his paces in the first round, but soon after the start of the next, Harvey parried a left lead by knocking it aside and then belted Charlie with a left swing to the body. McDonald gave a loud gasp and collapsed to be counted out.

Manny Lyttlestone, who made the matches at 'Premierland', did not feel that his patrons had seen enough of the Wonder Boxer from Blackfriars, so three weeks later he had Len back again, this time in opposition to Henri Vandevever, a light-heavyweight from Brussels, who suffered a similar fate, but on this occasion in the opening round. The contest was not fifteen seconds old when Harvey pushed aside a left lead to spin the Belgian round, whereupon a heavy left swing sank into his solar plexus. It looked as though the afternoon's sport was over, but Henri got up, not once, but four times after lengthy counts. Then referee Jack Hart put a stop to the slaughter.

Shade came originally from Vallejo in California. He was very close to his twenty-eighth birthday, had started boxing in four-rounds contests when he was sixteen, and had drawn with Jack Britton in a fifteen-rounds bout involving the welterweight championship of the world. In 1925 he had dropped a fifteen-rounds decision to Mickey Walker for the same title and when he came to London was unbeaten in his last seventeen bouts, one of which had been drawn and another being of the no-decision variety. He had fought all over America and in the Argentine and was noted for being almost a chain-smoker of cigars. He came to England under the managership of Walter Friedman, who, when asked what he thought of his boxer's chances said: 'Well, if Harvey beats him, I'll back Harvey with all I've got to beat Walker.' Shade stayed in London for his training, working-out at Fred Dyer's gymnasium and doing his roadwork in Regent's Park.

Against Shade, Harvey was meeting a very tricky opponent. Not in the Harry Mason sense, but in the way an old campaigner in American rings gets into the groove for spoiling the efforts of an upstanding boxer,

*Throughout the whole of his twenty-two years as an active boxer, Harvey never lost a contest through disqualification.

while doing what damage he can to weaken his rival's resistance. If Len had studied Shade's record, which is very much to be doubted as he was more interested in what a man could do than what he had done, he would have seen that the big majority of Dave's wins had been on points, which did not denote that he carried knockdown power in his punches. Nevertheless, he made the body his major target, swinging to the ribs as he came in and holding and hitting once he could get close enough.

To a boxer who cherished long-range boxing in the manner of a fencing master, Shade was an awkward customer to deal with. Harvey stood upright and used his long left as a measuring rod for his right. Shade ducked, bent low, swerved and drew back, making him one of the most difficult targets to hit. Consequently Len missed with his leads far more than he liked and it was not until after the halfway stage, when the American began to tire, that Harvey was able to dominate the fight with his straighter hitting. Up to then Len had been forced to be very economic in the use of his right, because to try and strike the American's low, bobbing head, meant hitting downwards with the risk of damaging a hand on his hard skull. So, if he was unable to do much damage to the British champion, Shade at least saved himself a lot of punishment.

Although the exchanges were interesting enough to hold the big crowd in silence, apart from the occasional shout from an enthusiast to "it 'im 'Arvey', there was a tense atmosphere as Shade threatened to do something damaging and one never knew when Harvey would manage to get in a really telling punch. The American incurred disapproval from the fans and several rebukes from referee Charlie Thomas for endeavouring to pull his opponent on to a punch in the clinches. Dave looked surprised at what in British rings is not permissible, but which was a common practice in his own country. He continued to do it, especially on the blind side of the official, but the onlookers were quick to spot the trick and Shade should have got wise to the fact that by so doing he was not scoring any points and at the same time not making himself popular, either with the fans or the referee.

As the gong started each round they would be up very smartly, Harvey to shoot out a left, Shade to wait and make it miss. He could do this twice out of every three times, but the one that got home made up for the misses. After drawing Len's lead, Dave would slam back at the body with all his power and it spoke volumes for the Cornishman's fitness that he was able to take these hefty swings without showing signs of distress. Some of the American's punches seemed to be with the inside of the glove, but Harvey, as always, was hitting with the knuckles, a fact of which Mr Thomas, one of the best referees of his day, was fully observant.

The two final rounds were the crucial ones. If Len was ahead at this point it could have been only by a small margin. He had been increasing the pace from the tenth when the American had first shown the signs of weariness, now the British champion was all set for a grandstand finish that would settle the issue beyond doubt. Shade was not making him miss as much and when he came in to maul, Harvey shook him off and kept far more of each round to long range work than he had been able to do previously. Len was looking the stronger of the two and on one occasion when he lashed out with both hands to stop his opponent from coming in to clinch, the American was seen to be bleeding slightly from a cut by the side of his right eye.

At the final bell there were a few shouts of 'draw' from those who had backed Shade, but the Welsh referee did not hesitate in raising Harvey's arm and the few boos were speedily drowned by an overwhelming applause in favour of the decision. It had been a hard, if not punishing, fight to win, but once again Len had demonstrated that the good old English style of stand-up boxing was superior to any other brand, and he left the ring unmarked. The next day Shade's manager was ready to wager a thousand pounds on a return contest, but Len was not interested. He disliked going over the same ground twice when it could be avoided. So Shade stayed on to meet Jack Hood a month later, this time being held to a 'draw' over twelve rounds.

If the followers of Boxing and the boxing writers wondered what would be Harvey's next move, they were not long kept in doubt. On paper headed 'Len Harvey Ltd.' was worded a letter to the press stating that the British middleweight champion barred no one at his weight and would tackle all the men who had been listed as likely opponents by the critics, one after the other at fortnightly intervals, providing promoters could be found willing to stage the bouts. Len added: 'I have had over three hundred fights and the best of them could not mark me. When I go to the States, they will find I am a worthy successor to my late fellow county and countryman, Bob Fitzsimmons, and I have every confidence that our American cousins will give me a fair deal.' This was not a boastful challenge, but merely to silence those who, for some reason or the other, thought Harvey was showing reluctance in meeting their own particular choice as a challenger.

Len planned to go to New York early in the New Year, but eleven days before Christmas he responded to an offer from Leeds promoter, Albert Heslop, and agreed to fight George Slack, who hailed from Doncaster. The fans packed into the Town Hall while hundreds jammed the streets and stopped the traffic. Everyone wanted to see the great Len Harvey and those who got in were eager to learn how he would cope with a heavyweight who outweighed him by two stones. They saw soon enough as Len opened the contest with a swift left to the body and a right clip to the head, shock tactics that put Slack in his place, after which the Cornishman was content to give them an exhibition of boxing at the Yorkshireman's expense.

The thick-set Slack gained confidence and set out to make a fight of it. He did all the attacking and the fans were continually applauding the clever way in which the lighter man kept out of danger while, at the same time picking up the points with a fine repertoire of picture punches. Just to show that he could hold his own at infighting, Len invited his opponent to come in and they swapped punches at close range. George took something of a liberty in the ninth when he landed two good lefts, but Harvey came back with a terrific right to the jaw that rocked Slack to his toes. The last three rounds were all in Len's favour as he kept the Yorkshireman on the defensive the whole time to finish a comfortable and popular points winner.

CHAPTER 12

Misadventures in America

The Harveys sailed for America on 18th December 1930, aboard the White Star Liner *Olympic*. Archie Watson accompanied them and travelling on the same boat also was Jack (Kid) Berg with his parents, and Johnny Peters, the rising young Battersea featherweight. Dan Sullivan did not make the trip, obviously having very good reasons for not wanting to venture into the United States, preferring to stay safely at home and collect his managerial cut without raising a finger. He had, however, arranged for Walter Friedman, Shade's manager, to represent him in New York, but this gentleman could not be expected to have Harvey's full interests at heart, apart from any monetary commission he might collect. Len and his wife were excited at seeing the Statue of Liberty. They did not realise then how glad they would be to see it disappearing behind them on the way home four months later.

It was Christmas Eve when they docked and Florence was astonished to see many wreaths hanging on doorways and shop fronts. 'Has the President died?' she asked innocently, but was assured that it was a seasonal custom in America. They drove down the Great White Way of Broadway to the Alamack Hotel where a suite of rooms had been booked for them. The next day Len went off to Orangeburg in New Jersey where he was to work out at Gus Wilson's famous training camp. Wilson was an Englishman who had been Georges Carpentier's trainer in the past. He took a liking to Harvey, admired his ring artistry and was most helpful and friendly.

Len's first New York bout was to be of twelve rounds at Madison Square Garden, his chosen opponent being Vince Dundee, born in Italy in 1904, but who had done all his boxing in America. Real name Vincente Lazzaro, he had been boxing professionally for over seven years, most of his contests being won on points decisions. The boxing scribes thought he would give the British champion a good try-out, but none of them tipped him to win, Len's victory over Shade making him very highly respected, in fact, *The Ring* magazine that month had Harvey rated second only to Mickey Walker, who was still regarded as the world champion. Len's Lonsdale Belt had been on view at the Garden since his arrival and caused great interest. It had also been necessary for him to put up a £500 bond with the American Customs to ensure that he did not sell it during his stay – as if that was likely. He had also put up a bond for his trainer for whom he was responsible whilst in the United States.

There were ten thousand fans to watch Harvey's debut and he was made favourite to win at eight to five. That these odds were justified seemed fully apparent in the opening round when, after the initial sizing up, Len drew a left swing from Dundee and then hooked a great left to the jaw that sent the American down heavily amidst a great roar of excitement. The referee sent the Englishman to a neutral corner before starting to count and this must have occupied several seconds that were fully appreciated by Dundee who managed to get up at 'nine', but looked very shaky. He tried to rush into holds, but was met by a left, a short right, and was then dropped again for another nine seconds by several crisp punches to the ribs and a neat clip to the chin. Somehow Dundee struggled to his feet again and then had to retreat and cover up as the British Champion tried his utmost to effect a sensational one round victory. But the cagey American was able to avoid a finishing punch and was there at the bell, hanging on and looking very distressed.

Dundee appeared none too happy when he came out for the second, clearly very wary of Harvey's straight left. He waited for Len to lead and then jumped in close to hold and hit and generally rough things up. He did this so frequently and without reprimand from the referee that there was little opportunity for Len to do any clean hitting. But he rasped his rival with short uppercuts and evaded Dundee's swings to win the second round by a clear margin. The tough Italian kept barging in, taking some points-scoring punches from Harvey en route, but once at close-quarters entangling the Britisher with his holding and mauling tactics until Len could manage to push him off. This persistent, rough-house aggression kept Dundee in the fight, but all the clean work was coming from Harvey and would have been duly noted by an English referee.

Most of the rounds followed a similar pattern, simply because Dundee was solely intent on getting in close for safety and then indulging in mauling and wrestling, even 'palming' his opponent on occasions, all without rebuke. Len stuck to his task, winning his rounds by clear margins and sharing those when the clinches were more prolonged. At the finish he walked back to his corner with a smile of confidence and Archie remarked that he had made sure of that one. Then Joe Humphries, the celebrated announcer, climbed in to gather the cards from referee Jack Denning, a former boxer, and the two judges, George Kelly and George Patrick: 'By a unanimous decision of all three officials – Dundee is the winner.' 'I don't believe it,' said Len's trainer, but Harvey took it very philosophically. 'That's America,' he said as the Garden rang with intense booing and programmes, ice-cream cartons and peanut bags were thrown into the ring.

The majority of the ringside reporters thought Harvey was the winner. Those who agreed with the verdict pointed out that whereas Len had done all the clean points scoring, fights in the States were judged on the number of rounds won and this entitled Dundee to the verdict. It was a shameful way of covering up for the ineptitude of the referee and the two judges. Writing in his monthly magazine *The Ring*, Nat Fleischer stated:

Although Harvey lost the verdict, there were many among the large gathering who felt that he had won, or at least, was entitled to an even break. The bout was exceptionally close and could have gone to Harvey by a shade, because of the two knockdowns he scored in the opening round. I gave Harvey six rounds and Dundee six, but even with the score even, it is my opinion that when a man scores two knockdowns for counts of 'nine', he is entitled to the decision. Regardless of that, however, Len made many American friends.

When they got back to their hotel, Mrs Harvey was anxious to telephone her parents in London and tell them what had happened. Transatlantic calls in those days cost £5 per three minutes, and when she got through Florence was delighted to hear her young son speak for the first time: 'Hello Mummy, hello Daddy.' Of course, the whole thing had been carefully rehearsed and prepared as a surprise for them and there were a few tears of joy and emotion as she listened. 'Hey, it's too costly to cry into a phone,' said Len, taking away the receiver. Then he spent the next twenty minutes chatting with her brother, Larry, about the Cup-Tie results and how the Arsenal had fared. He had forgotten all about the disappointment of the evening.

There was no doubt in the minds of Harvey's companions that they had been well and truly taken for a ride by the gangster element that seemed to have New York boxing in its grip at that time. By making Len a strong favourite the bookmakers had cleaned up nicely with the adverse verdict. All that Harvey had got out of it was the privilege of paying two managers instead of one. He was under contract for three fights in New York and when Tom McArdle, the Garden matchmaker, and William Carey, its President, suggested a return with Dundee, Harvey was more than willing. Understandably, Dundee was not enthusiastic. He had taken a lot of punishment in that first fight with the Briton and was not anxious for an encore, even if he had been smiled on by Dame Fortune and been declared the winner. But in view of the controversial verdict the New York State Athletic Commission ordered Vince to toe the line and they duly met five weeks later.

Once again there was a packed assembly in Madison Square Garden, but there were no shouts of 'Go home and pay your war debts' as there had been on the first occasion. They all realised that Len had been robbed in the first fight with Dundee, now they were looking forward to seeing him win without recourse to a referee or judges. Right up until he got into the ring he was a firm favourite, again at eight to five, but just before the starting bell there was a sudden rush of Dundee money in large amounts that certainly looked suspicious.

It was almost a replica of the first fight, except there were no knockdowns, although the Italian was almost battered to a standstill in the first five rounds. Harvey hit him with everything but the ringposts and while the fans applauded Dundee's durability, they were far more impressed by the British champion's brilliance. Only his iron jaw and his ability to absorb tremendous punishment enabled Vince to remain in the fight. Again he took all that was coming to him as he bulled his way in to close-quarters, to tie up his opponent and indulge in all the rough work imaginable in an effort to ruffle the Cornishman out of his cool and upstanding boxing.

Dundee continued to plunge forward, walking into a withering fire from Harvey, then spending much time in holding, pushing and clubbing with his free hand whilst claiming Len with the other. Again, he was allowed to get away with murder by the referee, this time Arthur Donovan, a man of considerable repute, but obviously not an admirer of classical boxing. In the last round Len all but put Dundee down. He had the American staggering like a drunken man and reeling to his corner at the final bell.

When the decision was given against Harvey even Dundee could not believe it. The fans booed and hissed and the police had to get into the ring to prevent its invasion by the irate ringsiders. Both the referee and one of the judges cast their cards in the American's favour, only Charles F. Mathison, quoted by Fleischer as being 'the most capable of all New York officials', gave the verdict to Harvey. Len just shrugged his shoulders and got out of the ring as quickly as possible. Obviously the gamblers had cleaned up again. He had been their lamb led to the slaughter. But what a lamb! That night Dundee was taken to Belle Vue Hospital by ambulance and remained there several days to recover.

Again quoting *The Ring*:

> Although the boos that greeted the verdict were exceedingly prolonged, it seemed to me [Fleischer] that the popular disapproval of the decision was brought about by the desire of the fans to see the Englishman win because of his gentlemanly actions, both in and out of the ring since his arrival, and a general desire, always in evidence in New York, when a foreigner fights a native son, to give the visitor a break.

It is a pity that two of those in charge of the fight did not share this meritorious sentiment. After this second rebuff it was forced on Len to realise that he was a mere pawn in the hands of gangsters, racketeers, bootleggers and the like over whom the State Athletic Commission was practically powerless. So with his usual philosophy he shrugged his shoulders and went about with his wife enjoying the New York sights.

One night they were in Texas Guinan's famous night-club, enjoying the cabaret and a meal when suddenly all the lights went out. There was a queer hush about the place and when the lights came on again Florence was surprised to find herself the only person sitting at a table. Then it transpired that everyone else had taken shelter *under* the tables and that was where she found her husband. When she asked him what he was doing down there, he said, with a smile, that he thought it was the appropriate time to duck: 'I being more used to doing that than you,' he explained. 'Well,' she replied, 'I only thought it was the lights had fused – what else could it have been?' 'I dunno,' said Len, 'but nobody else was taking any chances, were they?'

They asked Harvey to go to Sing Sing, the famous penitentiary, and give an exhibition of boxing to the inmates. Florence was only allowed as far as the Governor's office, but she was over-awed by the flashing searchlights and the machine-guns mounted on the walls. Afterwards Len told her that the convicts had proved to be one of the nicest and most appreciative audiences he had ever had. They got to know Damon Runyon and Paul Gallico and a lot of other boxing writers, and all were most friendly. Also there was Ownie Madden, a speakeasy operator, bootlegger and what have you, who seemed to be regarded as a public enemy. He was a quiet, suave, well-dressed, well-spoken man, with great personal charm and he placed a luxurious limousine at their disposal. Later on they discovered it was armour-plated.

The time was coming up for Len's third contracted fight at the Garden, Jackie Fields, a former world welter champion, being the selected opponent. Then manager Friedman, whom they called 'Good Time Charlie', suddenly disappeared as he had been put under suspension by the Boxing Commission for some misdemeanour, while Jack Kearns, who was managing Fields, decided similarly to depart forthwith for Miami. Ben Jeby, a not too well-known middleweight was brought in as substitute and it was necessary for a new contract to be drawn up. Len had returned to Orangeburg, so was not in a position to attend to such business matters and it was a very unsatisfactory state of affairs. There was Harvey, with one manager sitting in the Captain's Cabin in London's Haymarket spending his commission, while his American prototype was living it up on the beach at Miami. So it was left to Florence to take charge of affairs.

Len suggested that she should go and see James A. Farley, who for many years had been a highly respected Chairman of the New York State Athletic Commission, but had recently resigned to take up duties as head of the State Democratic Party. While he was head of the Boxing Commission the crooks, the gamblers, and the manipulators among the managers, fighters and promoters, had always found in him a deadly enemy. Mrs Harvey went to his offices, where he was head of a timber corporation, and told him of their difficulties. He sympathised with her over the two bad verdicts that Len had suffered because of the incompetence of New York officials, but was afraid he could do nothing about these as he was no longer a member of the governing body. He was very friendly and asked her how it was that a young fighter like Len and his equally young wife, should be in a city such as New York completely on their own. When she explained what had happened regarding the self-styled American manager, and that so much pressure was being put upon Len that he could not train properly, he suggested that she should elicit the aid of Jimmy Johnston, a well-known manager, and one who had looked after the affairs of British boxers in the past, notably, Ted (Kid) Lewis.

So along to Tammany Hall she went and got her interview with Johnston, known to all and sundry as the Boy Bandit. To her surprise she found he was totally in agreement with the decisions that had gone against Len and wanted to know what she expected him to do. 'You are British, aren't you?' she asked. 'You were born in Liverpool and I should think it is up to you to support a British boxer. We are not asking you to do something for nothing. Len must have a licensed manager in New York and that is all that is expected of you.' Jimmy softened up after that and said he would see to everything and the match was arranged for 20th March.

All seemed well until she received a telephone call from her husband in which he told her he was leaving Orangeburg as he could not stand the constant besieging by newspaper men and photographers, plus the medley of people who were surrounding him day and night and interfering with his work. 'I would like to finish off my training at Lou Stillman's gymnasium,' he added. 'Will you try and get me fixed up there?' Stillman's gymnasium was world famous. It was between shops on Sixth Avenue and was reached by a narrow and very dirty flight of stairs. Lou, with a perpetual cigar in his mouth, was standing at the top, hitting on the head with a cane those who were trying to get in without paying the required dollar. It was no place for an English girl, or any woman for that matter. But the crowd on the stairs parted to make way for her and finally she told Stillman that she had come to book a ring for her husband. He informed her he was fully booked for the rest of the week, but asked Tommy Loughran, former world's light-heavyweight champion, if he would give up his last day of training to Harvey. A gentlemanly character, Tommy obliged and Len was able to get in a final work-out.

As soon as she saw Len at their hotel, his wife realised that he was far from well. 'We'll see a doctor,' she said and one was called in. He confirmed that the boxer had a temperature and was suffering from influenza, but added, 'It is not for me to say if he is fit to fight. In my view he would be better off in bed, but Len will have to see the Boxing Commission's doctor as well.' 'Well, he'll say the same as you, won't he?' asked Florence. 'Not a chance,' he said. 'Providing Len can stand up, they'll pass him fit to box.' 'Then we may as well go through with it,' replied Harvey, 'and the sooner it is over the better.'

Once again there was a large crowd in the Garden to see the British

Champion's third American contest and again he was established a firm favourite to win at eight to five. Len had spent the last three days before the match in bed recovering from the 'flu. His wife, his trainer and the two brothers Johnston, Jimmy and Charley, tried to get him to appeal for a postponement, but Harvey would not hear of it. Obviously he was fed up with New York and was anxious to fulfil his obligations and get them over and done with.

On her way to the arena, Florence passed a jeweller's shop kept by a man named Lipskey. She had got to know him during her stay in New York and he was locking up his door as she went by. 'Hullo, Mrs Harvey,' he greeted her. 'Come in and let me show you a lovely bracelet I've just brought,' and when she admired it, he asked if she would like to wear it that evening. 'Why, that's very kind of you, but do you think I ought to wear it?' she replied, rather bewildered. 'Sure, I'd love to have you wear it. Maybe it will bring Len luck tonight. Here you are, put it on. See these safety catches? You wear it and give it back to me tomorrow.' So at the ringside that night she wore this rather magnificent bracelet, but forgot all about it in her anxiety to see how her husband would fare.

Jeby was the same age as Harvey, came from New York, but had been boxing only three years, mainly in bouts of short duration, although he had dropped a ten-rounds decision to Dundee the previous year. Managed by Hymie Caplin, Ben stood 5 ft. 8 ins. and was another thick-set tear-away fighter who came in regardless of what punishment he took in the process. He swarmed in with a persistent double-handed attack and although Len tried his hardest to put him away in the early rounds and punished him severely, he was far from being at his best and was often bundled into the ropes, where he was buffeted about until he could push Jeby away and get clear.

Len won four clear rounds, shared three and was considered to have lost the others. Yet he came out of the ring unmarked, whereas his opponent's face bore full testimony to Harvey's brand of punching. As soon as the verdict was announced in Jeby's favour, Harvey went across the ring and congratulated him. Len had no fault to find with the verdict this time, but Ben had been fighting a man very much under par physically, and knew it. He had the greatest admiration for Harvey's boxing skill and wrote regularly to Len in the warmest tones right up until his death.

On the way back to their hotel, Len noticed the glittering bracelet on his wife's wrist and wanted to know how she had come by it. Explanations followed and he asked her if she knew how much it was worth. 'Oh, about £200, I suppose,' she replied. 'More likely £5,000,' he retorted. 'And the sooner we get that back to its owner tomorrow morning, the better.' When it was returned they asked the old jeweller how much it was worth. 'Six thousands pounds in English money,' he replied. 'If it is so valuable, why did you let me wear it at the Garden?,' Florence wanted to know. 'Well, you see, it wouldn't be safe to let a valuable like that remain in a safe all night in a town such as this. And I wouldn't dare take it home in my pocket for fear of being robbed on the way. So I thought the best place to safeguard it would be on your wrist; the safest place on Broadway as it turned out. Thanks very much for your help and I hope you enjoyed wearing it!'

There were a lot of things far more important to be considered. Len was determined not to remain a day longer on American soil than he could help. But how to get away? The Garden had an option on his services for three more fights, so Harvey and his wife went to see Messrs. McArdle and Carey, told them how they felt, and asked for their release. 'We are sorry you are going home,' they said, 'because Len has been a tremendous draw in the Garden. But if you've made up your mind to depart we will provide you with first-class tickets at our expense.' It was a most friendly gesture, but they were warned to make their departure discreetly, because if Friedman had gone from New York, he would certainly have left a few henchmen to look after his interests.

Harvey had paid Friedman and Sullivan their cuts from his Dundee purses, but was under an obligation to pay Johnston for the match with Jeby. This cut out the other two, for he did not feel disposed to pay three managers for one fight. When the Harveys received their tickets, they found that passages had been booked on the *Leviathan*, and Len went aboard the night before, leaving Florence in the hotel. He had gone by way of the goods lift, taking their luggage with him, all with the connivance of the manager who had proved very friendly towards them. Mrs Harvey let herself be seen in the lobby, the dining room and the lounge, because of one or two hoodlums who were walking about with writs. All the time they could see her they thought Len was around and were waiting to pounce on him.

Also, offers for contests had come in from places like Boston, Philadelphia and the Pacific Coast, in spite of Len not having officially won a fight on American soil, with each purse getting higher, and those who were battening on his earnings were anxious that he should take these fights so that they could share the spoils. When it came time to leave,

Florence slipped out quietly and took a taxi to the dock. And as soon as she was missed the others came tearing after her. They went aboard the *Mauretania*, a British boat, and searched it for Len; they tried the *Isle de France* nearby, but not the *Leviathan*, which was American. Even if they had it would have been no use, for Len was on the bridge at the Captain's invitation and the boat was on the move before his presence was discovered, by which time it was too late. His pursuers had secured a writ of habeas corpus to take him off, but even if they had got a boat to come after the *Leviathan* which left the dock very slowly, it would not have been possible for them to go up to the bridge as the Captain was in the scheme to get Len away. And in this bizarre, motion-picture-thriller manner, they ended their unhappy American adventure. When they passed the Statue of Liberty, Len turned to his wife and remarked: 'For me this is the best part of the trip – going home.'

Right: Polhilsa Farm Cottage at Stoke Climsland, near Golberdon, Cornwall, where Len Harvey was born on 11th July 1907.

Below: School at Stoke Climsland. This post card was addressed 'Len Harvey, c/o The Offices, The Albert Hall, London' and dated 29th November 1933, the day before he won the British heavyweight title from Jack Petersen. It reads: 'Your old school. The older boys are wishing you luck this evening, so think of Stoke.'

Right: South Hill School, near Golberdon, where Len attended when staying for long periods with his grandmother from the age of seven until he was fourteen.

Above left: Ted and Ada Harvey, Len's father and mother.

Above right: Williams' Nipper (Nobby Short) aged thirteen and a half (left) and Len Harvey, aged thirteen, when they were the mascots of the Devonport and Devonia Boxing Club.

Left: Len Harvey at the time he made his debut at the Cosmopolitan Gymnasium at Plymouth in 1920 at the age of twelve and a half and weighing 4 st. 12 lbs. With him is his father, who was his trainer and manager at the start of his career.

Above left: Nipper Harvey, showing his well-balanced stance even for a youngster.

Above right: Perfect example of the straight left which Len expertly exploited from boyhood.

Below: Members of the Devonport and Devonia Boxing Club in 1921. Len Harvey is seated in front on the right. His father is the second figure on the left in the third row from the top.

Above: The famous 'Ring' at Blackfriars in South London where Len Harvey became known as Britain's Wonder Boxer. It was built as a chapel in 1812, opened for Boxing in 1910 and destroyed by bombing in 1940.

Below left: Mrs Bella Burge, who became proprietress of 'The Ring' when her husband, Dick Burge, former lightweight champion, died in 1918. *Below right*: Arriving in London, seventeen-year-old Harvey is greeted by Matt Wells, ex-lightweight champion. On Wells's left is Dan Sullivan, manager of 'The Ring', who became Harvey's manager. Next to Len is his father, and the man pointing a finger is Archie Watson, Harvey's trainer.

Above left: Harvey (facing camera) has Joe Rolfe in difficulties during their 1927 contest at Holland Park Rink. *Above right*: Len (back to camera) sends Jack Hood to the canvas during their alleged 'drawn' title bout at Olympia in 1929.

Below: Harvey stopping Leo Frick, of Belgium, in two rounds at 'The Ring' in 1928.

Above: Unique picture shows two fathers and their sons. *Left to right*: Ted Harvey, Len, Len Johnson and Bill Johnson, taken before the twenty-rounds contest at 'The Ring' in 1927 which Johnson won on points.

Left: Fighting pose by Len Harvey when at his prime. Note the similarity between this picture and the one showing him as a mere child.

Below: In his 'teens, a happy Harvey with his ukelele, on which he was an expert player.

Above: Len and Florence on their wedding day, 1st January 1928.

Right: Celebrating their thirtieth anniversary in 1958.

Below: With Terry, at the age of six, who died in tragic circumstances in 1947.

Above: Weighing-in with Frank Moody for their famous battle at the Crystal Palace in 1929.

Left: Len Harvey as he was between welter and middleweight.

Below: Knocking out Alex Ireland at Olympia the same year to win the British middleweight title and Lonsdale Belt.

CHAPTER 13

Beating the Men of Iron

Len's first meeting with his manager on returning to London could not be termed cordial. Dan demanded his cut from the Jeby fight and when told that his had been claimed by Jimmy Johnston and there was no more to come, Mr Sullivan waxed very wrathful, especially when he learned that income tax had been deducted by the American authorities before Len had been allowed to leave the United States. He argued that Harvey had been placed in the care of Walter Friedman; Len explained that the 'Good Time' gentleman had disappeared at the crucial moment and that, as it was imperative that a boxer should have managerial representation in New York, one had to be found – and quickly. 'As my manager, you should have been there to look after things,' said the boxer.

There was no answer to that, but in Harvey's mind was the thought that he might be better off by looking after his own affairs. The Frank Moody business could not be overlooked; Mr Sullivan's removal from his management of 'The Ring' by Mrs Burge, who was very fond of Len, was another factor in the coming breach. If in the future an opportunity came for a very lucrative purse in America, he would want to go far better equipped with advisers than on the last occasion.

For the moment, however, he was still under contract to Sullivan, and after a month's rest Len was eager to get back to work. The battle of attrition between the National Sporting Club and Jeff Dickson was continuing unabated, the Club using Olympia for its major promotions, while the young American occupied the Albert Hall. Harvey would have given the NSC the first option on his services had they had a ready-made opponent to offer. But Al Brown, the world's bantamweight champion, was occupying Mr Bettinson's mind at the moment, so Dickson offered to match Harvey with René Devos, also recently returned from the United States where he had kept himself busy among the middle-weights for the past three years.

The Belgian had been European Champion before going to America. Renowned for toughness, but not a destructive puncher, at one time he had been touted as a possible challenger for the world title, but one or two setbacks had deprived him of that high status and he had come home to re-establish himself in Europe. He seemed just the man to give the British Champion a vigorous test and showed that he took his job seriously by completing his training at George Smead's gymnasium at the *Load of Hay* on Haverstock Hill. Harvey installed himself once again at Windsor, and at the weigh-in looked in perfect health at 11 st. 3 lbs., his Belgian opponent being heavier by five pounds.

They were scheduled to box fifteen rounds, but the fans had barely settled down to enjoy this middleweight duel, when it came to an end. As soon as they left their corners, Harvey, showing something like ferocity, rushed his opponent towards a neutral corner, stabbed a left into the face and then, as Devos started a counter, Len crashed over a right to the jaw. As the Britisher came forward, the Belgian clutched his right shoulder to prevent himself from falling, whereupon Harvey whipped in two fast left hooks to the body, each driven with full force to the 'mark'. Devos went down on his knees, squatting on his heels, and with his body bent forward. Len walked away to watch referee Moss Deyong toll out the full count and it was all over, seemingly in a flash, although the official time was given at 107 seconds.

Devos gestured an intimation that he had been fouled, but he recovered his feet and physical self-control far too quickly for anything like that to have happened. He had been fairly and squarely beaten, in fact, taken completely by surprise, while Harvey's work had been a revelation. His dynamic victory was enthusiastically received by his many followers, removing the disappointment they had felt over his abortive trip to America. They could not wait to see him in action again.

Dickson did not keep them long in suspense. A matter of exactly three weeks and Len was climbing into the Albert Hall ring again, this time to try conclusions once more with Jack Hood, the man who had thwarted his ambitions to win a Lonsdale Belt in almost unbeatable time. It being near the end of June and therefore somewhat late in the season for a major show, the promoter asked the two principal boxers to accept a modest fee as he wished to reduce considerably his prices of admission for this occasion. Both men agreed and it was reported that to make the event more worthwhile, a side-bet of a thousand pounds would operate, thus giving the winner a more profitable evening.

The critics were hopeful that the businesslike manner in which Harvey had demolished Devos would be seen again with the Midlander as the sacrifice. They were not disappointed. Held to a 'draw' at their last meeting, Len went all out from the start to win this one as conclusively as possible and that it went the full distance of fifteen rounds was due solely to his opponent's safety-first tactics and remarkable stamina. Harvey came to scale at the full middleweight limit, whereas Hood was not compelled to strip right down to make the poundage. He was probably the lighter man by four or five pounds. No Lonsdale Belt was at stake as the Board of Control refused to give official recognition to the contest as one involving the British title.

At the start it was left lead for left lead until Len tried his favourite trick of turning an opponent into a left drive to the body. Then he was grabbed and there was a good deal of hitting in holds, with Hood the chief offender. Jack was not showing his former brilliance and left it to his opponent to take the initiative. Len wanted no encouragement, but attacked confidently in each round, subjecting his rival to a lot of body punishment. The man from Birmingham got in the occasional jab or hook, but would then go straight into holds, where he came off worse as Harvey was always endeavouring to score with one hand, even if the other was made temporarily immobile.

The further it went the more Hood dropped behind and at the halfway stage Harvey had built up an imposing lead. Jack's supporters knew this and he made a big effort to close the gap, but in the tenth round came very near to being stopped. Twice Hood was forced into the ropes and had to wriggle clear. He looked tired and Harvey pounced upon him, hitting out strongly in a fierce assault that he terminated with a hard drive to the solar plexus and a whipping right to the jaw. The last punch sent the welter champion spinning into the ropes and almost through them. He managed to get back and on to his feet by 'nine' and then underwent some rough treatment as he fought defensively to last out the round.

They had to work hard over Hood during the interval and Harvey gave him no rest when they resumed. He was out to prove beyond doubt who was the master and although Jack's superb defence prevented him from being floored again, he was forced to take punishment from all angles and a variety of punches in the succeeding rounds. Jack made a heroic burst in the last two sessions, striving hard to retrieve the situation with one big punch, but without success. Len kept up the pressure to the very end and did not have to be told he had won on points. He could scarcely have lost a round and seemed as fresh at the finish as when he started.

Promoter Dickson was elated. His conclusive victory over Hood had made Harvey his ace boxer and with his usual flair for showmanship he announced that he had booked the White City Stadium for a full-scale tournament on 27th July and had been able to coax Vince Dundee to come to London for a third meeting with the British Champion. Here was a great chance for Harvey to prove that the American judging of their two New York bouts had been totally inaccurate, but there was more to the meeting than that. On 4th June in New York, Dundee had outpointed Ben Jeby over ten rounds. On 19th June, Mickey Walker had relinquished the world middleweight title. Dundee, therefore, stood out as the leading contender, in fact, laid claim to the vacant throne. So Dickson matched him with Harvey, programmed as challenger, over fifteen rounds and billed the contest as an 'Eliminating Middleweight Championship of the World'.

Why it was not given full title bearing was due, rightly or wrongly, to the businesslike machinations of Mr Dickson himself. He had managed to bring Dundee to Europe because he had guaranteed the American a three-fight contract. Vince would fight Marcel Thil, the European Champion, over twelve rounds in Paris, then Harvey at the White City, then have a match with Hood, providing nothing of more importance matured in the meantime. Somehow or other, Dundee lost in France, which gave Dickson the opportunity to announce with great trumpeting, that the winner of the White City bout (cleverly denoted as an 'eliminator' beforehand) would now meet Thil for the world title. This meant, therefore, that if successful in beating Dundee, Harvey would have one more obstacle to overcome before he could claim full recognition as world champion.

All very neatly worked out, but the best laid plans often fail. Earlier in the month Len had answered the request of Promoter Captain Prince-Cox to come and show his wares in Bristol. The Rovers' Ground had been booked for a Wednesday evening and the Welsh middleweight Champion, Jerry Daley, engaged to supply the opposition over the fifteen rounds course. With prices ranging from 1s 2d to 5s 9d, Len did not expect to be able to retire on the proceeds. But it was a sporting gesture and typical of the man that he would willingly travel a long distance and fight for a small purse in order to help a friend who was doing his best to keep the Fight Game going in the West Country.

Apart from showing willing to have a go, the Welshman had nothing else to offer. He was shorter and of stockier build and Harvey let him make all the running in the opening round, being content to parry his attempts to land a big punch and putting in the odd blow now and then just to let his opponent know that he was in the ring with someone of class. Daley was put down in the second from a crisp right to the chin and took a count of 'six'. He tried to fight back, but before the round had ended he had been compelled to take another count, this time of 'seven', and was then forced to hold on desperately to avoid being floored again. The third was soon over. A left hook to the jaw dropped Daley for eight more seconds then, as he came forward to clinch, another finely-timed right struck his jaw and he fell flat on his face to be counted out.

Harvey gave himself three weeks to prepare for what appeared to be the most important contest of his career. By defeating Dundee, whom he had twice had the better of in New York, and then defeating Thil, whom he had already beaten, the way seemed wide open for the fulfilment of his greatest ambition – to become a world champion. Quickly he got himself into peak fitness at the *Star and Garter*, boxing beautifully against his spar-mates, and being cared for by Mr and Mrs Godfrey as if he were their own son. Also training there was Al Foreman, the British lightweight champion, and one evening they both went to give a charity exhibition at the Fisheries Club at Bray, once the home of Ruby Miller of Gaiety Girls fame, but now a palatial club. It was July and very hot and they drove back to Windsor in an open car, satisfied that their efforts had been appreciated.

A day or so later, on Len's twenty-fourth birthday, Mrs Harvey visited her husband and found him looking in magnificent condition, sun-tanned and, as he told her, fit to fight for a kingdom. However, at lunch with his trainer and sparring-partners, with keen wifely observance, she noticed a slight puffiness under his eyes and also, of more importance, that he was toying with his food and not making his usual hearty meal. Afterwards she drew Archie Watson aside and spoke to him, but he allayed her fears by saying that it was the heat-wave as Len was in fine shape and there was nothing to worry about.

Knowing that manager Sullivan was expected later in the afternoon, Florence waited for him to arrive and then persuaded him to walk with her to the stables as she wanted to talk to him out of Len's hearing. In the cobbled yard she told him her fears and, as was to be expected, there was an immediate explosion. Dan was furious and asked her what she thought she knew about conditioning fighting men; told her she could not possibly understand anything about men physically and that Len looked all right to him and he was a far better judge than she was. 'He's got a good trainer, hasn't he? You know nothing about boxers,' he snapped. 'I know all about my husband,' she answered quietly. On reaching home she asked her father-in-law to go to Windsor and take a look at his son. Ted Harvey had finished with Sullivan, but he always went into Len's corner and did as requested. On his return he said he thought she was worrying for nothing; that Len looked one-hundred-per-cent fit to him. But she was still unconvinced.

Three days later she went again to the *Star and Garter*. Len was finishing his day's training in the gymnasium upstairs and she was talking to the proprietor in the lounge. Suddenly there was a great deal of noise from above and a clattering of many feet down the stairs. 'Len has collapsed,' they shouted. 'I knew it,' she thought to herself and when the onlookers had been cleared out, she went into the gymnasium. One look at her husband told her the worst and immediately she instructed the trainer to telephone Doctor Malden, a local physician who had often watched Harvey in his work-outs and knew him very well. He came immediately and examined the stricken boxer, afterwards telling Florence that Len's throat was in a dreadfully inflamed state and that he would have to be taken at once to hospital.

He also called in Mr Tregreham, a kidney specialist from King's College Hospital, who diagnosed that Harvey was also gravely ill with kidney trouble. He wanted to have Len moved straight away to his hospital, but the boxer was insistent that he be taken home, so his sparring-partners carried him down to a waiting car. The specialist told Florence that her husband was so ill it was doubtful if he would ever be able to box again. He had known several rugby players whose careers had been finished because of kidney trouble. 'How they could have encouraged this man to go on working in the gymnasium day after day when he was in this state is beyond me,' he said. 'Don't they care how ill a man might be? It is criminal to treat an athlete in this way.'

Knowing the repercussions that were sure to follow, Mrs Harvey asked the specialist to issue a press statement setting out the nature of Len's illness, but before this could be done, Sullivan and Dickson appeared on the scene, not, as one would imagine, anxious to know the extent of the boxer's illness, but to try and persuade him to go on with the fight. 'There is no possibility of that,' they were told most emphatically, 'He is not able to stand and will be confined to his bed for a long time, so give up all hope of getting him into the White City ring.' They went off very disgruntled and regretfully it must be placed on record that not once during the thirteen weeks that Len was ill did they come to see him or enquire as to his welfare. Jack Hood substituted and held Dundee to a drawn verdict and the American returned home, subsequently to become middleweight champion of his own country.

An unfortunate illness had robbed Harvey of his big chance. He went to Madeira for a month and when he again saw Mr Tregreham, he was assured that he had made a full recovery, but could consider himself lucky. The specialist also advised Len to have his tonsils removed, as they were large and septic, advice that was not taken unfortunately, with adverse results some years later. At the time Harvey meant merely to put off the operation as he did not want to delay his return to the ring any longer. Then he forgot all about it.

It was four months before Len was ready to fight again and to try himself out, he accepted an offer to box Fred Shaw, from Shipley, in the principal contest at Manchester's Belle Vue on 30th November 1931. Whilst his selected opponent did not present any serious problem, there was a second reason for Len to make his first appearance at this particular venue. Suddenly he had acquired two persistent challengers from Northern areas, one being Jack Casey, from Newcastle, and the other, Jock McAvoy, from Rochdale. Both seemed likely to loom up as official contenders in the near future and Harvey welcomed them as he was anxious to start collecting notches on a second Lonsdale Belt.

Shaw was disposed of in less than three rounds. Whilst content to box himself into a fighting rhythm in the first two, Len backed into the ropes, luring his opponent after him, then suddenly swung a right from nowhere. It was beautifully timed, accurately aimed, and carried the full weight of his body behind it. Shaw went down as if he had been pole-axed. He struggled hard to rise, but it was impossible and the 'out' was called before he could get off the canvas.

At the beginning of 1932, Dan Sullivan had found himself a place where he could again indulge his matchmaking talents, these having been curtailed since his removal from 'The Ring'. On 17th January he opened at the South London Palace, within walking distance of his old haunt, and typically it was Len Harvey who agreed to start him off by appearing in the main event against George Slack, the Yorkshire heavyweight he had outpointed at Leeds over a year earlier. That the boxer did his manager a good turn was evidenced by the fact that a crowd of over two thousand were present on this particular Sunday afternoon.

The disparity in weight was enormous, but a bigger handicap, as far as Len was concerned, was the fact that the rounds were of only two-minutes duration. This no doubt suited Slack, who was there to stay, but irritating to Harvey as, more than once, and just as he was warming to his work, the bell would intervene and he would have to start afresh in seeking an opening. There was an exciting start in round one when Len backed his rival into a neutral corner and put him down with a thudding left hook to the jaw for 'eight', but he had to wait until the thirteenth round before he could repeat the feat, another left hook sinking the Yorkshireman for another 'eight' count. Harvey did everything but knock out his heavier opponent and Slack must have been as strong as an ox to stand up under the severe punishment he received. Len won every round and rightly got the award, but George, too, was given a great ovation for his gameness.

For some time a Newcastle promoter had been hopeful of staging a title fight between Harvey and the local favourite, Jack Casey, who had started by fighting in the streets as a newsboy and then developed into one of the toughest and hardest hitting middleweights of the day. Because of his durability they called him 'Cast-Iron' Casey and John Paget, who owned the New St James's Hall, which he had built himself, wanted to give Jack a crack at the championship. Len was willing enough to travel and put his title on the line, but the Board of Control saw fit to regard the proposed contest as not being of championship calibre. Perhaps the Stewards did not regard Casey as a worthy contender, but they did not say so. What they did do very effectively was to prevent their middleweight champion from making a voluntary defence of his title and also deny him the opportunity of having his name engraved on a new Lonsdale Belt.

So promoter Paget, still keen to stage what he knew would be a sell-out, suggested a fifteen rounds bout at a pound over the middleweight limit and, although naturally disappointed, Len shrugged his shoulders in customary fashion and made the trip. Casey was a big-hearted, enthusiastic scrapper, who put everything into his fighting; out from the start to knock his opponent into the middle of next week; ignoring what might come his way in the process. His sheer force of attack had Len going back and boxing on the retreat in the early stages, a sight that had the miners, who made up the bulk of the audience, noisily exhorting their Cast-Iron idol to make short work of the champion.

On one occasion, Jack swung a mighty right that Harvey took on his left arm. Yet there was sufficient power behind the swing to send the champion sprawling into the ropes. But he was unhurt and came off the hemp to pound away with both hands to the body, Casey joining in to the delight of the onlookers. At long range Len jabbed and clipped his rival about the chin, but he might have been punching at the side of a battleship for all the effect his blows had on the local hero. Several times the excitement was so intense as they exchanged fierce punches that they did not hear the bell and had to be parted and sent to their corners by the referee.

Midway through the fourth round, the champion suddenly cut loose and landed a heavy left hook on the cast-iron chin, followed by a magnificent right to the jaw that knocked Casey off his feet, the first time in his life that he had ever been put down. These two blows had been delivered with amazing speed and made it seem that the man from Sunderland had been struck by lightning. But no sooner had he touched down than Jack was up again, and now the din was so terrific that the referee had to appeal for order. That one attempt to win with a spectacular burst of punching having failed, Harvey went back to his boxing, waiting for his tough rival to give him another opening. The fans were urging Casey on and were hostile to Len when he boxed defensively on the retreat. But the champion knew what he was doing.

Apart from taking toll of Casey's features with a rapier-like left, Harvey was showing extreme cleverness in the way he broke up his opponent's fierce attacks. By smart swaying he dodged many vicious right-handers and then, going to close-quarters, he got the inside position to pick up more points with both hands. It was this hitting with a free hand whilst being claimed by the other that the crowd did not like. They wanted the big-swinging stuff and voiced their disapproval. But through all the disturbance, Len remained unperturbed. He scored freely when he could and smothered up when it suited him. In the final two rounds he tried his hardest to put Casey down again, but although showing distinct signs of wear, Cast-Iron Jack stayed on his feet and the champion had to be content with a well-deserved and undisputable points verdict.

There was slight disagreement with the decision, but it was wholly partisan. Casey ran across the ring to meet Harvey half way and they patted each other's shoulders. When he had changed, Len followed his usual practice of going to his opponent's dressing-room to see that all was well. 'You are a great boxer,' said Jack in admiration. 'I have to be against iron men like you,' replied the champion. 'What do they feed you on – filings?' 'Will you give me another fight?' asked Casey and Len replied, 'Of course, any time you like.'

It was McAvoy, however, who was Harvey's next challenger. A tempting offer came from the Belle Vue promoters, one that made the British middleweight champion a four-figure man. His opponent had been reared as a fighter among the small arenas in Lancashire and then 'adopted' by the Belle Vue syndicate who installed Harry Fleming as his manager. At the same time they were grooming two other Manchester boys into championship material, Jackie Brown and Johnny King. With McAvoy they were to form a great fistic triumvirate. A tremendous right-hand puncher, Jock claimed a long string of seventy-five knockout wins to his credit. He was the Northern Area middleweight king and was known as the Rochdale Thunderbolt.

This time the Board of Control agreed that the fight should be officially regarded as involving the British title and a new Lonsdale Belt was at last provided. Since winning the first outright by defeating McCall, Harvey had won two further fights, against Hood and Casey, that could have been classed as championship bouts. By all that was justice, this defence against McAvoy should have given Len the chance to make a second trophy his own property. But the Stewards, it must be supposed, had taken their time in forgiving Harvey for having stood out against them when they had wanted him to take out a licence and this was the way they showed their displeasure.

The King's Hall at Belle Vue was jam-packed with ten thousand fans for this vital championship match. They were all there to cheer their KO idol on to a devastating victory, although all recognised that McAvoy was up against a superlative boxer. At the bell, the champion's upstanding stance and classic defence was in striking contrast to the challenger's crouching attitude as they moved round the ring sizing one another up. Harvey had had plenty of experience with fighters who came in with hunched shoulders and gloves at waist level, but Len's compact guard must have seemed almost impregnable to McAvoy. Only a persistent aggressor could hope to break through that muscular armoury, but the man from Rochdale was naturally aggressive and after that brief summing-up he plunged in to deliver his thunderbolts from either hand.

McAvoy made the body his target as he swept forward, switching to the head at closer range. At least, that was the objective, but he had straight lefts, hooks and crosses to contend with, while he was rendered almost harmless in the clinches. The referee was Jim Kenrick, a former flyweight champion, and he was kept busy in separating the men. No sooner had they been parted than McAvoy was dashing in again with the champion catching his big swings on his elbows or shoulders, while boxing on the retreat. The fact that their man was always coming forward en-couraged the Manchester fans to think that Jock was getting on top and might at any moment bowl the champion over. But Len's face bore a slight smile as he feinted, parried or got in a steadying punch, a left jab or a neat hook. His blows carried sting, but went unheeded by his tough, hard-as-iron, opponent.

The rounds had a similarity, but the atmosphere was highly tensed, with the crowd urging their man on, hoping that Harvey would join issue and battle it out punch for punch. They could have waited all night for that to happen. Len had patience of inexhaustible quality. His mind was completely shut off from extraneous matters, his sole intent being to contain this dangerous rival and take the first opportunity to weaken and then, if possible, destroy him. Jock's strength and stamina was equally unending. He was another Casey when it came to non-stop attacking, yet he was a far better boxer than the Tynesider, his lefts being lunged in with great power. Only a near-faultless defence could cope with his tenacity and determination.

There was great excitement in the fifth round when Harvey took his opponent by surprise and drove him back into the ropes. It was a typical move by the champion and as Jock reeled against the hemp, Len drove in a terrific right. It missed McAvoy's chin, but the force behind it lifted the challenger off his feet and over the top rope on to the floor. Fortunately his fall was broken by the large lap of a spectator, but for a moment he stood on his head, then slid down, got to his feet and managed to scramble back into the ring and beat the count by a second.

By the halfway stage, the betting which had started at five to two on Harvey was now even money as McAvoy continued to attack, striving his utmost to batter the champion into the canvas. Surely his persistence must be rewarded before long, but the champion was still there, moving gracefully about the ring, getting in his long range shots and refusing to indulge in infighting. After being parted by the referee or pushed off by Harvey, McAvoy would stop for a moment, pull his gloves more firmly on to his fists with his teeth and then tear in again, ramming in his left, swinging his right, switching from the body to the head, but always aiming at a departing target.

In the thirteenth round, Len suddenly dropped his arms as if he had been overcome by weariness. That was enough for McAvoy. In he dashed and out streaked the champion's right. The timing was perfect and the challenger's head was turned to an angle of forty-five degrees under the impact of that mighty blow. McAvoy's knees sagged and he staggered backwards. For a second or two he wavered and Len stood watching, fully expecting him to collapse in a heap and that it would be all over.

He knew that the power he had put behind that right was sufficient to knock a horse down, but there was the challenger still there and coming forward again, his big fists threatening.

That fine delivery had not scored the intended knockout, but it had considerably reduced the challenger as a fighting force and Harvey kept him at the end of his gloves for the remaining two rounds, at times driving the challenger before him, the fans yelling themselves hoarse as the possibility of a sensational finish seemed imminent, even though it might be their local hero who was in danger of being stopped. But Jock, who must have been in something of a daze, had enough fighting instinct left to keep going to the final bell when the referee did not hesitate to raise Len's arm as the winner. It was not a wide margin, but wide enough to leave the championship in the Cornishman's keeping and give him the first notch on the new Belt.

CHAPTER 14

Middleweight Farewell

Now came the time for Harvey to sever his connection with Dan Sullivan. The seven-year contract had been drawn up in April 1924, when Len had his first contest at 'The Ring' and was still three months short of his seventeenth birthday. His father had shared the management of his son at the outset, but gradually his influence had been whittled away until he was ousted completely and had to confine himself to going into Len's corner on fight nights. Until he began to move among the top men in the middleweight division, Harvey was reasonably satisfied that his interests were being well cared for, but later on various happenings, some of which have already been outlined, made him feel that he was not getting the protection or the recompense that was his due. When he reached the age of twenty-one he could have sought the making void of a contract that had been drawn up and signed while he was a minor, but Len valued his father's bond as he did his own and so, for the best part of four years, he had served out his time, although far from happy that he was getting the best results from his efforts.

It was, in fact, a very crucial period in his boxing life. He wanted to fight for the world's middleweight title, he would like to win a second Lonsdale Belt outright at the same poundage, but this would have to be done with the minimum of delay. He was approaching his twenty-fifth birthday and it was becoming increasingly harder to tip the beam at 11 st. 6 lbs. Marcel Thil had won the world title by defeating the American claimant, Gorilla Jones, in Paris, while Len Johnson did not miss an opportunity to remind Len that he was the only middleweight with an unrevenged decision over the Cornishman.

The Board of Control had seen fit to half-lift its bar against coloured boxers by allowing Larry Gains, long resident in Great Britain, to fight for the Empire heavyweight title, so when Jeff Dickson approached Harvey to fight a return contest with Johnson at the Albert Hall, Len offered to put his British title at stake. As he expected, the Stewards of the controlling body gave an emphatic denial to this request, probably because it made clear that if they had a prejudice against coloured boxers, from whom nevertheless they took a licence fee, one of their own champions held no such racial beliefs. When the promoter suggested that he should bill the contest as being for the British title, even though it was not recognised as such by the BBB of C, Len was more than willing. He liked Johnson, as he did all boxers, and felt that he could not regard himself as Champion of Great Britain if he did not give the coloured man a chance to win the title.

Len had gone back to Whetstone for his last three contests, but this time the faithful Archie Watson was absent, having decided to be neutral in the split between Harvey and his manager. This was a pity because Len had formed an attachment to the man who had trained him from the time of his arrival in London and this was no doubt reciprocated. When Len had gone to America, Archie had accompanied him, moreover Len had provided for Mrs Watson in their absence. The Cornishman was always on the friendliest terms with those in his training-camps, especially his sparring-partners, even if that might not seem apparent when they were swapping punches with the big gloves. So Fred Duffett, at whose gymnasium in Camberwell Len had trained during his early days, accompanied the champion to the *Black Bull*, where he got him into the acme of physical perfection, so much so, that Johnson barely got a look in.

In fact, most of the critics were unanimous in writing that Harvey had given the most convincing display of his career. In Johnson he was meeting a man who, because of his long experience with a travelling boxing booth, had acquired practically all there was to know about scientific fighting and ringcraft. Len from Manchester was the more experienced of the two, moreover he had a victory over Harvey to his credit. Yet Len beat him at every phase of the game and even on the few occasions when he was beaten to the punch with some wicked right-hand digs to the body, he showed that he possessed the ability to assimilate punishment when he had to, to remain calm, and quickly get back into his rhythmic stride.

It was not a sensational battle, but to those who understood the finer points of Boxing it was a contest of wits between two accomplished artists of the ring. It was a far different Harvey from the man who had faced those two tough tearaways, Casey and McAvoy. It was a scientific duel that brought out the finest boxing on each side, with the champion displaying just that much more initiative and versatility to keep his aquiline nose in front. He was the speedier of the pair and this was the dominating factor. He beat Johnson to the punch with his leading time and time again, causing the coloured man to lash out with counter-punches to the body in the hope of keeping on terms. Johnson's best effort was a savage right under the heart and he had Harvey gasping from one of these in the fourth round. A mighty blow, it was a tribute to the champion's fine condition that he was able to throw off its effects.

After that the only question in the minds of the onlookers was whether Harvey would be able to stay the full distance, but although he took several other nasty punches, he rode them well and was always scoring, so that when they came up for the fifteenth and final round, he could not lose providing he stayed on his feet. Johnson was well aware of this and disregarding all defence for the first time, he stormed into his opponent in an effort to make one punch pay for all. Concentrating on his right to the body, Johnson slammed in his punches as an immediate counter to a Harvey lead, banging them in before the champion had time to cover up or get out of the way. Three great rights buried themselves in the Cornishman's body and with each one it seemed that he must go down. But courage and sheer fighting craft saw Harvey through. He stalled, held and covered up. But more than that, he fought back in such dynamic style to be there at the finish, deservedly triumphant, to receive the full verdict.

Len had now beaten four leading contenders for his title in less than twelve months, yet, thanks to the BBB of C, had but a single grip on the new Lonsdale Belt. The Stewards, who had prevented Harvey from defending his championship against Jack Casey, now did an about-face and nominated the so-called Sunderland Assassin to meet Archie Sexton, of Bethnal Green, in a final eliminator to decide who should next be the official challenger for the middleweight crown. That did not leave the titleholder empty-handed as Jeff Dickson was making plans to match Len with Marcel Thil for the world championship, the fight to be staged at the White City, London, on 4th July, white gloves to be worn by both men to enable the fans at the back to follow the punches.

The Cornishman did his own negotiating for this match, the break with Sullivan now being complete. Dan had taken action against Harvey in an attempt to draw the commission he claimed was due to him from the Ben Jeby fight in New York, but he lost the case and was ordered to pay his own and Len's costs, the judge telling him quite plainly that he could not countenance a man living off another's earnings with 3,000 miles between them. Presumably Sullivan paid his own lawyers, but he neglected to pay those Harvey had been forced to hire in his own defence. So Len paid them himself because he did not want to cause his one-time manager further financial embarrassment, although he was destined to recover his money before long. This is how it came about.

While at the *Star and Garter* there were among the spectators at his training sessions a number of soldiers from Windsor Barracks, one of whom was Jack Doyle, a young Irish Guardsman, who came every day and pestered Len to allow him to spar with him. It was not in Len's nature to discourage anyone and Doyle showed such enthusiasm that eventually he agreed. Finding that the youngster had a fair idea of what it was all about, and impressed by his size and punching power, Harvey passed a message to Sullivan, inviting him to come and have a look at a promising boy who had all the potential for grooming into a heavyweight champion. Dan had one look at Doyle in the ring with Len, bought him out of the Guards and proceeded to launch him on what was to be a sensational, but also lamentable career. In a short while Irish Jack was earning big money, whereupon Harvey had a writ served on Sullivan and duly recovered the costs he had been awarded.

When he had agreed terms with Len, Dickson suggested that he should take over the management of the British Champion. Len did not see the purpose of such a move, but Jeff pointed out the great influence he had as a major promoter, especially in continental rings, and promised that if Harvey did as he was told and followed the programme outlined for him in advance, he would make far more money, as Dickson was in a position to bring almost any American he liked to box in Europe and had just built a vast new Palais des Sports in Paris which, with his London enterprises, would give him virtually a boxing monopoly on this side of the Atlantic.

'I'm ready to be advised, but I don't like being told what to do,' answered Len. 'Just what have you got in mind?' 'Well,' answered Jeff, 'if you win in London, I expect you to give Thil a return title fight in Paris.' 'And if I lose in London?' 'Then you will get another chance in France.' 'But I intend to beat Thil at the White City. I've beaten him before and think I can do it again. And if I beat him, I don't see why I should have to fight him once more. It seems far too cut and dried to me. If you don't mind, I'll do this my own way, without any strings attached. I want my services to be available to any promoter who is prepared to pay me what I think I'm worth. I refuse to be bound to one man. I've had enough of that already.' Len did not say so, but he had a feeling that the American promoter was not all that honest in his fistic dealings and did not want to be involved with him.

Dickson had not been prepared for a rebuff to his schemes and became angry. 'If you don't sign with me, I am in a position to ruin you as a boxer. What's more, I can promise that you'll never win the world's title.' 'That doesn't happen to be in your hands,' answered Len quietly. 'That's for Thil and me to decide.' Not quite! When Harvey climbed into the open-air ring he discovered that the referee appointed by the International Boxing Union was a Swiss who did not know a word of English, but was fluent in French, which put the British champion at a distinct disadvantage before a punch had been exchanged. Furthermore, they were boxing under IBU rules and if these varied in any way from what Len was accustomed to, the referee was powerless to explain any differences.

It was up to Harvey to be his own referee and beat the Frenchman so decisively that there could be no possible argument. This he tried to do from the very start, coming across the ring to stab the champion in the face with a lovely left that put Thil back on his heels. Immediately a 'mouse' swelled up under Marcel's right eye, half closing it, while a keen right cracked on his craggy jaw, causing him to cover up as his challenger went all out to bring off a quick victory. It was a tremendous start that had the fans in an uproar, but Thil covered up under the bombardment, then managed to get in close, put his bald head on Harvey's chest and busy himself with both fists to the body.

They went into holds, and the referee had something to say. Thil probably understood, but paid no attention. Harvey did not know what the official had on his mind and did nothing, whereupon the action was stopped and M. Devernaz wagged his finger at Len, then signalled them to box on. In plunged Marcel, there was hitting in holds on both sides, in the challenger's case it was self-defence. Again the referee gave an order in French, again it was ignored, and once more it was Len who was warned. Whenever he could, Harvey would try to stand up and box, but having once sampled his long-range punching, Thil did not want any more. He was determined to make a close-quarter fight of it and as soon as there was a clinch, they were ordered apart and if the Britisher was slow to respond he was made the culprit.

Back in his corner Len was also at a handicap. Thil's seconds, who understood what the referee was saying, could advise Marcel accordingly. Len's handlers were just as much at a loss as he was, consequently they could only advise him to box the Frenchman off as best as he could.

Harvey knew as much about infighting as anyone, but as soon as he employed his skills in this department, he found himself restricted by the referee. Thil could hold and hit, but when Len did likewise he was in trouble from the Third Man. The only real boxing seen was by the British champion and this clean work came in flashes, usually at the start of a round, the rest of the time being taken up with Thil intent on battering the body, using his bull-like strength to push his opponent before him.

The referee continued to confine his admonishments to the Cornishman and harrassed him to such an extent that when he returned to his corner at the end of the seventh round, his right eye gashed from a butt from the Frenchman's hard head, Len muttered, 'If this goes on for another round, I shall turn it in. I'm not being allowed to box and it is hopeless.' The boxing writer, Norman Hurst, who had a monetary interest in McAvoy and none whatever in Harvey, was so perturbed at the injustice of the whole thing that he called out: 'Don't lose control, Len. Stick it out. We are all behind you.' Unfortunately, Len was in the ring on his own with two foreigners against him and gradually it became obvious that the will to win was ebbing away from him.

On went Thil to chop, carve, cut and bore his way to victory and Len showed the utmost courage in striving to cope with these bulldozer methods. Jabs and uppercuts failed to halt this Frenchman who was built like a tank and behaved as one. He had no time for upstanding boxing and the constant interference of the referee prevented the challenger from meeting Thil at his own game. M. Devernaz seemed content to permit infighting by one man but not when the two of them were at it. Then he broke the clinches by pulling the men apart, had a few words to say which Harvey could not understand and then let the Frenchman bound back into holds once more, when the whole mauling business would be repeated.

It was a disappointing contest from every point of view. The rounds were too much of a likeness to sustain the interest of the fans, especially those at any distance from the ring, and although there were moments of brilliance from the British champion, these faded away as the bout continued. At the final bell Len knew he had lost, but that did not prevent him from going over to his opponent after the decision had been made public and shaking Thil's gloved hand. Well, Dickson had been right, but Harvey had the satisfaction of knowing that he was a free man and had kept his self-respect.

So, for the time being the dream of becoming a world champion had faded away. Len took his defeat philosophically, enjoyed a well-earned rest for about three months during which he enrolled the services of two people to help him in the furtherance of his fistic ambitions. The first was Wally May, a rotund little man, an expert masseur and physical culturist, cheerful and full of good humour. Harvey had first encountered him at Camden Town when coming to London as a boy and they had remained good friends ever since. The other addition to his establishment was Charlie Rose, another man of small stature, who wrote a boxing column under the name of The Old Guard in the *Daily Express*, was an excellent publicist, and had been the respected manager of such heavy-weights as Frank Goddard and Phil Scott. Just now he had the veteran Australian, George Cook, under his wing, also another Australian, Leo Bandias, and Eddie Steele, a young Norwood heavy. Len was very happy to let himself be incorporated in this lively stable.

Jack Casey had stopped Archie Sexton in seven rounds to qualify for a championship fight with Harvey. The match went to purse offers and John Paget secured it for his New St James's Hall at Newcastle. It cost him £800. But Len needed a warming-up fight or two so manager Rose arranged for him to try himself out against a Belgian light-heavyweight named Theo Sass. The bout was to take place at the 'Olympia' in Bradford. 'It's fifteen rounds,' said Charlie. 'There's not a lot in it, so you can give yourself a nice work-out.' But the boxer could not have been listening.

He sailed into Sass, who put up a guard for the left hook, thus exposing himself to a left to the body, followed by another that made him lower his arms, whereupon Len let him have a left hook to the chin. The last punch was a beauty and the Belgian sank to the canvas for a count of 'eight'. He got up to grab hold of his assailant, but was shaken off and put down by another left drive to the body. Although he reached his feet at 'seven' his condition was such that the referee immediately stopped the contest.

In the dressing-room manager Rose said it wasn't worth the train fare and chided his boxer for not giving himself a longer time to loosen up. The next day one of the critics said that the Belgian had 'little idea of attack and was poor in defence', whereupon Len wrote to his editor in the following terms:

Actually my opponent's idea of defence was to cover and mask up from the start when he realised that my object was to land a decisive punch. It was therefore my task to 'open up' my rival, which I did by simply 'showing' my right hand and then whipping in my left. I never once used my right hand for punching, but did all the damage, including the blow that caused the referee's intervention, with my left. If you can win a fight with one hand, why use two. There is no sense in taking the risk of damaging a hand on a man who is covering up as Sass did. I had to beat him by strategic means and did so.

They had hardly reached home before Charlie was on the telephone: 'Len Johnson has had to pull out of a fight with Seaman Harvey at Leicester. It's only a ten-round supporting bout at the Granby Halls and Jim Panter, the promoter, is asking if you will help him out. The pay is £300 – what shall I tell him?' 'Do you want to do him a good turn?' asked Len. 'Because, if so, tell him I'll be there.' He took the fight at only forty-eight hours notice – what other champion of today would do so? To have a champion of Harvey's quality on view was an extra tit-bit for the local fans and Len beat his namesake very comfortably, the sailor showing great courage against a man who boxed in his best style. The titleholder could have won decisively in the fifth round when he had the man from Chatham in a bad way, but he let him recover and travel the full distance. The points award was a foregone conclusion and when the Seaman left the ring his face bore testimony to his opponent's punching, whereas Len was unmarked.

The championship fight with Casey was scheduled for 12th December but ten days beforehand, Harvey returned to Plymouth for a fight, his first there in over seven years. He was given a vociferous welcome when he ducked through the ropes in the Promenade Pier Pavilion, his opponent over fifteen rounds being Glen Moody, the Welsh middleweight champion and a brother to Frank. If Glen had any hope of avenging the family honour, this was soon dissipated as he was forced to play second fiddle to the Cornishman from the start.

Harvey's most destructive blows that night were right hooks to the body and he knew how to put plenty of steam behind them. The Welshman took several short counts in the fourth and fifth rounds, going down each time Len planted a heavy blow under his heart. He was dropped from the first punch he received in the sixth; he may have slipped because Len helped him to his feet, gave him time to get going again and then drove a right into his ribs with such force that he went down in a writhing heap, whereupon the referee called a halt and Harvey was declared the winner.

Arriving in Newcastle, Harvey and Co. found the city seething with excitement and the hall was filled to overflowing for the championship match, which wasn't surprising seeing that the prices of admission ranged from a modest one guinea down to five shillings. They were all there to see if Cast-Iron Jack could go one better this time and win the championship and promoter Paget had spared no pains to have everything just right for the occasion, even going to the extent of installing special basins in each corner, complete with a tap and running-water, something of the style to be found in a dentist's surgery.

Len was very impressed with this innovation. Although he had fought in innumerable rings it was the first time he had encountered anything like this. He considered it an ingenious novelty, although he thought differently after the first round. In this the challenger showed greatly improved boxing skill. He was far less crude in his moves and at the same time his punching power had not diminished in the slightest. Before they had been fighting for a minute Harvey found that he was up against an even more formidable opponent than had been the case at their first meeting ten months earlier.

He had no difficulty in reaching Casey's face with a left lead, but Jack countered with very hard blows from his own left. The local man forced the pace to the delight of the spectators and when the bell sent them to their corners honours were about even. To Len's disgust, however, his watering appliance absolutely refused to function. Try as they might, his seconds only wasted time in trying to make it work and the champion had to go through the interval without as much as a damp sponge to refresh him.

Coming up for the second, Len enticed his challenger into a clinch and said: 'Hi, Jack. Is that water gadget working in your corner?' 'Yes,' replied the Sunderland Assassin, 'isn't yours?' 'The hell it isn't,' said Harvey, as he allowed himself to be pushed off and then snapped a left into Casey's face. Back came a left hook, then another, the champion responded and they swapped punches until they went into a clinch and were parted by the referee. The challenger was successful with his long left drives, but although he tried many vicious rights, Harvey was too clever to be caught by any of them. He was always peppering Jack with a straight left, planting them into his rival's face with plenty of power behind them. But he might have been hitting a brick wall for all the effect they had.

At the bell Len found his corner still as dry as the Sahara Desert, but one of his seconds had managed to secure a bottle of water for which he was grateful. 'Don't worry, Len,' they told him. 'The promoter's sent for a plumber,' and there was a big grin on the champion's face when he came out for the third round. 'Got any water yet?' kindly enquired Casey, as he whipped in a left hook, followed by a right which was blocked. 'Not yet,' answered the champion, uppercutting his challenger with relish. 'But it'll be there any time now, they've sent for a plumber.' Almost as he spoke there sounded the tinkering noise of hammer on pipes, which made the crowd laugh and the fighters smile. But soon they were back to business again with Casey crowding the champion, coming in behind his long left, then whirling away with big punches from both hands, while Harvey pecked at him with his leads, crossed and uppercut his head and body. But nothing he did seemed to hurt Cast-Iron Jack.

During the next interval, Len sent the plumber about his business and the water gadget in his corner remained a dead loss for the rest of the evening. Now he was very much on his mettle and would have to fight his hardest to keep his crown. By giving ground and so forcing the challenger to walk into his punches, it made it seem as though he was weakening under pressure and when he was a little late in avoiding a right swing that brought a trickle of blood from his mouth, the fans went frantic as they urged their hero to sweep the champion out of the ring.

In the sixth round Harvey tried his hardest to finish the fight with one good right hand punch to the chin. The opening came and he put everything he had into a right hook, perfectly timed and full-powered. The punch struck home and Casey faltered. Len hit him with another, equally as potent, but the challenger merely rocked. One more must do it and for the third time the champion's right thudded against the Assassin's chin. He merely bent at the knees and to the surprise of everyone it was Harvey who drew back. Casey came on and Len was kept busy containing his aggressive rival until the bell sounded. Back in his corner, Len muttered to his chief second: 'I'm in agony, Wally. I've knocked up my right trying to put him out, I can feel the pain right up to my shoulder.' 'You'll have to use your right in defence only,' advised his trainer. 'Threaten him with it and ward off his left leads. Concentrate on keeping him out with your left.'

No matter how cleverly Len defended himself, he could not avoid all the punches that the Assassin tossed in his direction. More than once he appeared shaken and Casey probably won the middle rounds on sheer aggression as he marched forward throwing a stream of punches from both hands. Suddenly Len stood his ground and battered Jack's rock-like jaw with thudding left hooks, but Casey did not take a backward step and they stood there, toe-to-toe, exchanging shots, although to the close observer it was plain that the champion's were more accurately delivered and better placed.

Casey was outboxed completely in the next two rounds, being kept at a distance by some excellent lefts and then being tied-up when he managed to break through and get to close-quarters. Then, midway through the twelfth, Jack pounded through a shattering right-hand punch that caught the champion on the point of the chin. It was the vital punch of the fight. Harvey was hurt and everyone knew it. He staggered backwards and sagged into the ropes. Now the fans were frantic with excitement and the noise was deafening. It seemed that Len was out on his feet; that it needed only one more big punch and the championship must change hands.

Then, as Casey moved in for the 'kill', Harvey smiled at him. It was not a wide grin, but to the challenger it looked very suspicious and he hesitated. Even while his supporters were screaming at him to finish off the titleholder, he held back the one punch that might have made him champion. That was when the real fighting skill of Len Harvey became so evident. He feinted a left and slid along the ropes out of danger. Only a master craftsman could have 'foxed' his way out of a drastic situation the way Len did that night.

Casey had missed his big chance – had been made to miss it, and Harvey made sure he never got another opportunity. Jack never ceased trying to land another telling blow, but the champion encouraged him to use up his strength by making him miss, sometimes by only the merest shade and each time Casey was countered with jabs to the nose or clips to the chin and soon it was noticeable that the challenger had slowed down considerably and Harvey was hitting him far more freely. The challenger tried hard to bring off a sensational last round victory and the fans thrilled as they watched the champion keep his foe at bay until the final bell. There was no dissension when the referee declared Harvey the winner, but how they cheered Casey when he left the ring. And for ever afterwards when referring to this contest, Len would always remark: 'Don't talk to me about that fellow Casey. I should have known better than to fight him the first time; I should have had my brains tested for taking him on again.' But he had a twinkle in his eye when he said it. As champion he felt it was beholden on him to take on any contender and it is a fact that all the while he was a champion at one weight or another, he never refused a legitimate challenge from anyone.

He had a full six months' grace before he need defend his title again, but now he was a free agent he could look around and make plans –

plans that took the boxing fraternity and the sportswriters by surprise at the temerity of his ideas. Having beaten Reggie Meen for the heavyweight championship, Jack Petersen decided to relinquish his light-heavyweight crown and at once Harvey submitted himself as a logical contender for the vacant title. But he was not to get a straight crack at it. The Board of Control decided that he and Eddie Phillips, the Bow coachdriver, should fight a twelve-rounds eliminator, the winner to meet Harry Crossley, the former champion, to decide the championship proper.

Hardly had this been announced than Charlie Rose issued a challenge to Jack Petersen for the heavyweight title, offering to put up £500 to bind such a match, the same sum to be regarded as a side-stake. 'I am authorised by Len Harvey to state that he is so confident of being able to outbox Petersen that £250 of the sidestake will be his own money.' It was a bombshell and, of course, hit the headlines. How could a mere middleweight take on a hard, speedy puncher like Petersen, to whom he would have to concede all the physical advantages? Then they started measuring the pair up and found there wasn't all the difference between them that might be imagined. Certainly the Welshman was $1\frac{1}{2}$ ins. taller and weighed nearly a stone more. But Len was the same size round the chest, while his arms were considerably bigger, the circumference of his biceps being half an inch more, while his forearm was $1\frac{1}{2}$ ins. bigger than Petersen's. But there was a difference of $4\frac{1}{2}$ ins. in their reach.

Jack of Cardiff had a lot of admiration for Harvey's boxing ability, but for the moment he could not take Len's challenge seriously. He had several bouts lined up and promised that when he was free of work he would willingly put his title at stake against the Cornishman. He was ready to raise the sidestakes to £1,000, but insisted that they must fight on a winner-take-all basis. But Harvey had made his point and implanted in the public mind that a match between himself and Petersen was by no means out of the question.

So Len and Wally May went off to the *Black Bull* to prepare for Eddie Phillips. Four years younger than Harvey, Eddie had been brought into prominence by the Stadium Club and in twenty-three contests covering three years had been beaten only once, while seventeen of his wins had been accomplished inside the scheduled distance. He was a tall, upstanding boxer, lacking only in experience. The Harvey *v.* Phillips match was put up for bidding and secured by Jeff Dickson who had it sharing top-billing at the Albert Hall with a heavyweight clash between Don McCorkindale, the South African, and the young German, Walter Neusel, who was making quite a name for himself in British rings.

The referee was C. H. (Pickles) Douglas, who was a renowned martinet when it came to controlling a contest. Len was made favourite to win at the long odds of three to one, no doubt because of his far greater experience, and these seemed justified when he took the first two rounds with some snappy left-hand leading interposed with some neat rights to the side of the head. By the third, however, Phillips had got over his nervousness and finding he could match Len in reach, began working his left to the face and the fans were treated to a fine display of skilled boxing at long range. Clinches were few and were promptly broken up by the referee and there was a comic moment when he snapped: 'Don't hold, either of you!' and Len stepped back with a look of innocence on his face. 'Stop the acting, Martin Harvey,'* called a wag from the ringside and this caused a laugh, Len enjoying it as much as any of them.

They kept the pace fast and Phillips showed excellent footwork. He seemed to be gaining confidence with every round and in the seventh got through with a powerful right to the jaw that shook up the middleweight champion. But Len was back with a fast counter-attack and showed his superior class when he tempted Eddie to drop his guard and then sent a splendidly-judged left hook to the mark, followed by a right clip to the chin that tumbled his opponent to the canvas. Phillips was more surprised than hurt and bounced up to come back into the fight, keeping the exchanges at long range as much as he could and so preventing Harvey from using his superior skill at close work. Again in the tenth Eddie got through with a right to the jaw, a high-powered punch, but Len displayed his strength and craft by shaking off the effects and joining in a brisk rally that had the crowd roaring with delight.

Each time Phillips managed to get in a good blow his coach-driving pals raised the roof, urging him to 'get into top gear'. But Len matched him in speed and enterprise and they fought on very even terms in bright and attractive fashion to the final bell when the referee's decision of a 'draw' was enthusiastically received by a well-satisfied assembly. It was a disappointing verdict so far as Harry Crossley was concerned, while the Stewards of the Board of Control were back to square one in settling the light-heavyweight championship.

Len had agreed to defend his middleweight title against Jock McAvoy at Manchester a fortnight later, but was forced to ask for a postponement as the right hand he had injured in the fight with Casey had been knocked up again in the match with Phillips. The Belle Vue people put back the

---

* Martin Harvey, a popular tragedian of the day.

championship fight by a fortnight, but this was not nearly enough and Len begged to be granted more time. When this was refused he went to a specialist who told him that he had displaced a knuckle and although it could be put back, the inflammation would take some time to heal. 'If you take my advice you won't box for six months,' he told the boxer. When Len asked for a longer respite before meeting McAvoy, the Board of Control doctor thought the hand was sound enough for it to be used and that was an end of it.

Charlie Rose was all for demanding the full six-months period to which Harvey was entitled. He had fought Casey in December and the Manchester fight was dated for 10th April. Wally May told Len he was mad to go handicapped into a contest with a fighter of McAvoy's calibre and risk losing his title. But Len was all for getting the fight over and done with. Further delay would only mean putting back what he considered would be a lucrative step into the heavyweight ranks. 'After all, I'm champion, and it is up to me to defend my title at any time. It's bad luck, but I'll have to go through with the fight.' So his trainer did his utmost to restore his right hand as a fighting weapon, and Harvey presented himself at Belle Vue on time.

Naturally, it was in Len's interests to withhold the information that he would be a one-armed fighter for his title defence, therefore it was not surprising to find the fans wondering why he made very little use of his right hand, especially when he lured the attacking challenger into position for its delivery. Len looked confidence itself at the start, as if he thought that having beaten McAvoy once, he could do it any time he liked. That fact he was to prove on later occasions when he had two sound fists to fight with. But at Belle Vue, it needed a superman to hold off the continual and determined assaults to which his challenger subjected him in each of the fifteen rounds.

Harvey had to fight a rearguard action for most of the way and although he scored valuable points with his left lead as McAvoy marched in, and caught the majority of his rival's heavy punches on his gloves, elbows, arms and shoulders, he was fighting far too defensively for local referee Harry Myers who stopped the bout in round six and asked the champion for more action. Len spoke to the official, a smile on his face, perhaps he was inviting him to swap places; they were ordered to 'box on' and the challenger continued his advance.

Only once did the Rochdale Thunderbolt look dangerous and that was just before the bell ended the ninth round. He swept through the champion's guard with a mighty right uppercut, but Harvey drew back sufficiently to lessen the impact and warded off Jock's attempts to follow up his advantage. His damaged hand forced Len to fight an almost entirely defensive bout and he must have lost rounds on the referee's score card purely because he left most of the attacking to his challenger. He had to work his immaculate left while on a steady retreat and as a result it seemed that he was being chased out of his championship.

Knowing he had nothing to fear from the champion's right, that deadly weapon he had felt the weight of in their first encounter, McAvoy took more chances as the fight went on, striving hard to break through Harvey's defences and get home a decisive punch. But in this he failed and he had to go on to the final bell to win the verdict, the championship and the coveted Belt. Len had lost the trophy in what was virtually his sixth title fight against the best middles in the country, and he must have felt sadly disappointed as he saw it wrapped around Jock's waist while the ten thousand fans filled the rafters with their triumphant cheering. When he had been rubbed down, taken a shower and dressed, Len went along to McAvoy's dressing-room and pushing his way through the crowd of well-wishers, took Jock's hand and congratulated him. 'You're the champion now,' he said, adding with a grin: 'And this is where your troubles begin.'

CHAPTER 15

The Great Year – 1933–4

The British light-heavyweight title still without a holder, the Board of Control re-matched Harvey with Phillips, this time over fifteen rounds and ignoring Crossley altogether. The fight went to bids and was secured by the National Sporting Club, who once again booked Olympia for a mammoth production, this time excelling all previous efforts by staging three championship matches; one between Jackie Brown and Valentin Angelmann, of France, for the Manchester lad's world flyweight crown; one between Johnny King, the British bantamweight champion, against Bobby Leitham, the Canadian titleholder, for the vacant Empire championship, and the light-heavyweight title duel. In addition, Al Brown, the world bantam king, had Dave Crowley, from Clerkenwell, as an opponent over ten rounds, while in a battle over a similar distance, the newly-crowned British middleweight champion, Jock McAvoy, took on Oddone Piazza, the Italian titleholder.

With sixty-five rounds of boxing to be decided and not starting until 8 p.m., it was not surprising that it was well past the midnight hour before Len and Eddie took the ring. They actually fought one day later than was stipulated in their contracts, and must have been glad to get out of their respective dressing-rooms. In fact Harvey became so bored with the long and tedious wait that he suggested they play cards. Fortunately a pack was available and they began to play 'Solo'. After a while Len turned to his trainer and said: 'What about inviting Eddie to join us? Pop next door, Wally, and ask him.' Trainer May was aghast at the suggestion. 'Are you serious?' he asked. 'You'll be in the ring with him at any minute.' 'Of course I'm serious,' replied Len. 'What's the harm? He's probably as fed up as I am with waiting. We can stop the game as soon as we're called, can't we?' It was all so casual, a typically Harvey relaxed gesture; thinking of anything else but the impending fight; giving a thought to another person's comfort as much as his own. 'I don't think it would be a good idea,' said Wally. 'He's got his own boys to keep him company, besides they might think you're trying to take the mickey out of them.' 'As if I would,' answered Harvey. 'Come on – I'm going "abundance".' The big crowd, a number of whom had to leave before the show was over because of public transport problems, had their money's worth, especially as prices started at five shillings and only rose to three pounds for ringside seats.

In the same ring a few weeks earlier both Harvey and Phillips had been introduced as forthcoming opponents. They shook hands and appeared to be the best of pals, which was nothing unusual for out-of-the-ring Len was 'hail fellow, well met' with everyone, while Eddie was equally fraternal with all fighting men. Harvey was looking extremely smart in a dinner jacket, while Phillips was wearing a man-about-town lounge suit in a heather mixture pattern. Their appearance as championship contenders gave the lie to all those critics of Boxing who liked to consider it a low-down sport, fit only for uncouth ruffians.

Len trained at the *Black Bull*, having the help of Ted Mason, a Maidstone light-heavy, and Eddie Steele, from Norwood. Harvey's right hand was given plenty of testing, both on his sparring-partners and the heavy bag, and it was pronounced as strong as ever. Phillips got into shape at Southend. He told the pressmen who came to watch his workouts that he had learnt a lot from his previous bout with Harvey: 'I hope to let him see I am a good pupil,' he told them, to which Len replied: 'Well, I'm still learning and it remains to be seen which of us has improved most since we last met.' All very modest and sincere.

Again they supplied a model contest of high-class boxing and if some of the fans were feeling impelled to yawn because of the late hour, they were soon brought to a state of acute wakefulness by the brisk and keen exchanges. Harvey was full of confidence and at once assumed the initiative, leading with long lefts to the face and bringing over a neat right every now and then. Phillips was not intimidated, but stood his ground and gave back in like measure. But usually he was just beaten to the punch and although Len could be credited with the first three rounds, the margin in his favour was not wide. In the fourth, however, he found an opening for a particularly good right-hander to the head and when Phillips returned to his corner at the end of the round he was wearing a nasty cut over his left eye.

The wound yielded to treatment and did nothing to lower Eddie's morale, in fact it had the reverse effect for he swapped punches with eagerness and brought off a first-class sensation by clipping the Cornishman on the chin with a snappy right, causing him to drop to the canvas. A great roar resulted, but Harvey had not been hurt and was up, dusting his gloves on his trunks by the time the count had reached 'four'. Then he demonstrated his complete recovery from the knockdown by taking the fight to his opponent and scoring well enough to earn a division of the round.

Harvey took the sixth with his superior boxing and wider repertoire of punches, but Phillips was fighting back with great verve and, forcing the pace, had a shade the better of the next few rounds, giving as much as he got, so that Len had to give ground now and again and bring out all his vast experience in order to cope with the younger man's aggressive spirit. Perhaps Harvey was letting his rival expend his energy whilst keeping out of possible danger, for by the thirteenth round a big change came over the proceedings. Now it was the Cornishman who was on the attack and the Londoner began to wilt under punishment.

As game as a pebble, the tiring Phillips fought back as best he could and the crowd rose to both men as they struggled for survival. Here the former middleweight king took complete command and gave an exhibition of real championship stuff, almost putting Phillips down with a mighty left to the jaw that sent him staggering. There was only one man in it now, but Eddie continued to offer courageous resistance, resolved to be on his feet at the final bell. He was, but he had lost, and the fans were fully satisfied that the right man had won when the referee indicated Harvey as the winner.

So Len Harvey was a champion of Great Britain for the second time and once again he cast his eyes towards even greater fame and a further challenge was issued to Jack Petersen, offering to increase the side-stakes to £1,500 and taking up the champion's former edict that they should fight on a winner-take-all basis. But the Welshman had other irons in the fire. Meanwhile Jeff Dickson offered Harvey a fight in Paris, suggesting as an opponent Carmelo Candel, from Oran, who had been boxing professionally for five years, had never been knocked out, and had stood up to Jock McAvoy's thunderbolts for ten rounds to lose on points. Recently, however, he had achieved the distinction of stopping Jack Casey in five rounds, which made the Frenchman appear a formidable proposition. Perhaps the ingenious Mr Dickson fancied him to lower Len's colours!

Harvey did not like boxing for Jeff, there was something about the American promoter that made him uneasy. But he had to earn a living and with no pressing challengers in sight, he decided to accept the match.

Besides neither he nor Florence had ever been to Paris. 'We are taking no chances,' she said. 'I've heard all about that rich French food. So we'll take our own joint and vegetables for the meal you will want before the contest and have them cooked our way.' They flew to the Gay City by Air France from Croydon Airport, a hazardous business in those days: the slightest hint of mist or fog and there could be untold delays. The French customs officers thought it extremely funny that anyone should want to bring eatables into their country, renowned throughout the world for its cuisine. The chef at the Hotel Madeleine was also astonished to be told by Mrs Harvey that the food had to be cooked *à l'anglaise*, otherwise she would invade his kitchen and do it herself. 'After the fight I will eat anything you like – even snails,' Len told him with a very straight face. 'But for now, the roast beef of Old England and the bacon and eggs.'

Florence had a surprise when she went into her room. It was full of flowers and on the table was a large cake with 'Welcome' inscribed on it. There were glasses and a bottle of wine and for a moment she thought she had been shown into the bridal suite by mistake. It transpired, however, that the head waiter was none other than Henri, who had owned the restaurant in London where they had held their wedding party. Having heard they were coming to Paris and staying where he worked, he set out to give them the best possible reception. They felt quite at home and not at all as if they were in a foreign country.

The Palais des Sports in the outskirts of the city had ten thousand seats and none were vacant when Len came from his dressing-room. He received the greeting due to a visiting champion, but nothing like the roar given to Candel when he climbed into his corner. The fans knew that Thil had beaten Harvey in his own country and fully expected him to suffer defeat now that he was on foreign soil. This seemed likely when the British champion backed away from the advancing Frenchman, using a light left and displaying no anxiety to use his right. Candel adopted the typical Continental cover as he came forward. But although it appeared that Len was being put on the retreat by the Frenchman, those close enough could see that he was unable to lay a glove on the Englishman, while every now and then his head was jolted back with what seemed a mere flick from Harvey's left.

For four rounds Candel boxed very cannily. At first he was suspicious, then he got more confident and by the start of the fifth round he decided he had nothing to beat and went in with a fierce attack, no doubt thinking he could make a name for himself by scoring a knockout over the celebrated Britisher. When he left his corner the Frenchman stepped up the pace, then rushed at his rival and tossed over a big right. Len drew back sufficiently to make him miss and then sent a sizzling right uppercut to Candel's exposed jaw. It connected with a click and the recipient fell forward on to his face, knocked completely cold. The count was a mere formality and the fans went wild with excitement. They had seen the perfect knockout. A one punch win achieved by a master boxer. They raised the roof as Len was announced as the winner and cheered him as he made his long way back to the dressing-room. 'Harvey Snuffs the Candel' was the headline the next morning in the English papers.

Dickson's feelings must have been decidedly mixed. One of his best French aces had been reduced to nothing. Harvey was a Parisian hero. If he had hoped to get Len beaten, his plans had exploded in his face. When Florence got to her husband's dressing-room he was showing grim satisfaction over his victory. 'That's scuttled another of Jeff's schemes,' he said. 'You can take it for granted that I'll never be asked to box here again.' Nor was he! Later on Florence met Dickson, who gave her a ready smile. He knew she had come from the dressing-room and asked: 'What does Len plan to do next?' 'Why not ask him?' she said, but he told her that Len had refused to speak to him.

The next morning Jeff travelled with them to Le Bourget airport. Throughout the journey from Paris he and Harvey had not exchanged a word and the atmosphere was far from comfortable. Len got on the plane and Florence was about to follow when something made her hold back: 'If you want Len to fight for you again, match him with Petersen,' she said quietly. 'He's too small,' whispered Jeff. 'What makes you think it would be a worthwhile contest?' 'Len has watched Jack more than once,' she replied. 'He is sure he knows how to beat him.' 'How sure?' asked the promoter.

'So sure that he will do it for nothing,' she answered, and ran up the gangway. Here she was met by her husband, who had left his seat and come to the door because the plane was being delayed. 'Don't waste time talking to him,' he said. 'Come aboard and let's be off.' Looking out of the window she could see Dickson standing there, a quizzical look on his face. At five o'clock the next morning the telephone rang. Len was still sleeping, so she did not wake him and crept downstairs to answer, wondering who could be calling at that early hour. 'It's a call from Paris,' the operator told her and then she heard Dickson's voice on the line. 'Did you mean what you told me at the airport yesterday?' he asked.

'Because if you do, I'll get to work immediately to make the match. Petersen will want the earth, but if Len will fight for nothing, I can afford to put it on at the Albert Hall next month.'

Florence was petrified at what she had done – committed her husband, a professional boxer, to fight for the heavyweight championship – for nothing! 'Could you pay Len's training expenses?' she enquired. 'If so, you can go ahead.' He agreed, she hung up the phone and crept back upstairs. What had she done? She knew that Len would desire nothing more than to fight Petersen. But Boxing was his sole source of income, he could not afford to go into a contest as important as this and not receive payment. What would happen if he flatly refused? She lay sleepless until Len awoke. He got out of bed and stood at the window looking out on the day. Quietly she told him what had transpired. 'You are to meet Dickson at the Savoy Hotel at one o'clock,' she said timidly.

Len looked round and stared at her. 'You did the right thing,' he said quietly. 'Now I've got to make doubly sure of winning. But please don't make a habit of getting me jobs for nothing.' The next day the papers were full of the fight. It aroused more interest than any other for years. They called Petersen 'The Welsh Tiger'. He was four years younger than Harvey, had been an outstanding ABA champion, and won both the British light-heavy and heavyweight titles in less than a year's professional battling. He was unbeaten in twenty-four contests, more than half of which had ended inside the distance.

Could Petersen knock out or stop a man a stone lighter than himself, or would Harvey's greater experience enable him to prevent the Welshman from landing his dynamic punches? The prospect caught the imagination of every fight fan throughout the country and the demand for tickets was so great that every one had been sold ten days before the contest was due to take place. On the night hundreds of would-be spectators milled around the Albert Hall and the touts reaped a rich harvest, commanding three and four times the advertised prices. That morning the newspapers had warned their readers that it would be useless to go to West Kensington without a ticket, but the lure was too great and a huge multitude remained outside merely to hear the result. But those who stayed at home were able to listen to a running commentary over the radio by Lionel Seccombe, which the British Broadcasting Company put out on the London, Western, Scottish and Midlands regions, also on the Empire transmitter, commencing at 9.35 p.m.

Probably the only two people in England who had total faith in a Harvey victory were Len himself and his wife. Even Wally May and

Charlie Rose must have had doubts, however loyal they were. If anyone in the big hall backed the Cornishman to win it was because the odds were long enough to take a sporting risk. The appointed referee was C. H. Douglas; a hush descended as the starting bell rang out and the men emerged from their corners. Those packed-in fans were destined to see one of the greatest duels in British boxing history. Yet there wasn't a knockdown, although Harvey did slip to one knee in an early round. Nothing very dramatic occurred, no one was badly hurt, in fact, there were no sensations. But it held the audience spellbound.

It was a contest for the connoisseur, a keen battle between brain and brawn that kept the big crowd tensed up from start to finish, because there was always the promise of the unexpected, an atmosphere of suspensed hope that one or the other would strike home a conclusive blow. Harvey took things very quietly, almost sedately, for the first five rounds, allowing the fiery Welshman to expand his energy in trying to land his vaunted pay-off punch. Time after time, Petersen would send his famous right swishing over in the direction of his challenger's chin, but Harvey either rode these intended finishing blows by a swift movement of the head, or got out of their path by a matter of inches.

Each time Jack missed, so Len would pop him one on the nose with a straight left. Petersen would plunge in and take these jabs as he came forward striving desperately to nail his rival with just one solid blow. In her ringside seat, Florence chain-smoked as she anxiously watched her husband skilfully avoiding trouble as he sneaked the points. This was a fight she had made. If Len was beaten he would be on a hiding to nothing. But the rounds sped by to the cheering of the crowd and he was still there, coming up cool and confident each time, giving her the occasional wink as he went back to his corner.

There is nothing so tiring as being continually made to miss, and before long the heavyweight champion began to slow down. Then Harvey came even more into the picture, beating the Welshman to the punch, landing telling counter-shots, making Jack bleed from the nose and mouth. At close range Petersen was all at sea. He was so used to scoring at long range that he was pretty helpless 'inside', whereas Len hooked and uppercut practically at will. The Cardiff heavy got annoyed at this treatment. He wrenched himself away, was clipped on the break, made a desperate lunge at his opponent from long range, missed badly and was trapped again.

Several times referee Douglas saw fit to caution the challenger for holding with one hand and hitting his opponent with the other. He would pop round to one side and knock down an offending arm, only to find the boxer transgressing with the other. From Harvey's point of view it was all legitimate warfare. He was coping with a man bigger and heavier than himself and could not afford to be barged about the ring. Furthermore, he had to restrict Petersen's wild attempts to score at close range and the referee gave Jack a stern warning during the ninth round when he butted the Cornishman severely under the chin.

The further the fight went, the more it became obvious that the Welshman's unbeaten record was in grave danger of being broken. None were more conscious of this than his cornermen, especially his father, who bemused his already bewildered son by pouring forth a never-ending stream of advice. This was changed during each interval with the result that eventually Jack had no plan of campaign save the sole idea of landing the one punch that would pay for all. Harvey never gave him a chance to do that and long before the end Petersen had lost control of his boxing ability and was being tricked out of the decision. He became clay in Len's masterly hands, yet was always dangerous and never for a moment did the challenger dare relax his watchfulness and defence.

When the last round was signalled, Mrs Harvey slipped out of her seat and made her way back to the dressing-room. She wanted to be the first to greet her husband – win or lose – on his return. She felt she could not wait another three minutes to know if their great gamble had come off successfully. He had won all right, but it was a hard-won victory and the points margin in Len's favour could not have been wide. But it was enough for the referee, who raised Harvey's hand while the fans raised the roof. They weren't all in agreement, but the few who disagreed were out-shouted by the vast majority that acclaimed Len as the new heavyweight champion and gave him a standing ovation. He and Jack met half-way across the ring to shake hands and exchange good-will pats on the shoulders. Harvey's friends swarmed into the ring, but Len did not stay long. He hastened away to tell Florence the news, but her eyes were shining with joy for she already knew. The great roar that had gone up to echo in the dome of the big hall had told her, without any possible doubt, that her husband had won another famous victory.

Just as happy was Jeff Dickson. He hurried round to Len's dressing-room to congratulate him and his wife. 'You were quite right and I admire your wonderful faith in your husband,' he told her, then turning to Harvey said: 'I'm paying you five hundred pounds over and above your expenses. You have put new life into boxing in this country. Now what about a return fight? The fans will be clamouring to see you and

Petersen in action again and I'll pay you as much as I have had to pay him for tonight.'

'Oh no, you won't,' answered Len. 'This heavyweight title owes me a lot of money and it has got to earn it. If you want another box-office winner, put me in with Larry Gains for the Empire championship which he holds. That will be a sell-out and if I beat him, and I believe I can, there won't be a hall in London big enough to hold the crowd that will want to see Petersen try to win back his championship.' Dickson thought it a brilliant idea. 'I'll be in touch with Gains right away, and contact you immediately I have his agreement,' he said.

It was not until the next day that the press and public realised that Harvey had created a record by being the lightest man ever to hold the British heavyweight title, also that in the space of six months he had been champion at three separate weights. A fortnight later Harvey gave a champagne party at the Stadium Club in Holborn to which the leading lights in the Fight Game, plus the press, were invited. Here he met Petersen for the first time since their great battle and each was full of praise for the other. 'A great boxer and gentleman,' said Jack about the man who had recently taken away his title. 'A good sportsman,' answered Len. 'And as soon as I have fought Gains, he can have a try to regain the championship. We might be fighting for two by then,' he added. Jack bestowed a gallant kiss on Mrs Harvey and asked her to keep her husband up to that promise. 'You have no need to worry about that,' she told him. 'When my husband says a thing, he means it.'

Dickson arranged for the fight with Gains to be staged at the Albert Hall on 8th February and the Board of Control sanctioned the match as carrying with it the Empire championship. Few of the critics thought Harvey could win this one. True he had astonished them by defeating Petersen, but Gains was a different proposition altogether. Larry was in the 14-stone class. He had been boxing professionally almost as long as Len, but not as a mere child, so that he was even more experienced. He had taken the Empire title from Phil Scott with a two-rounds victory and successfully defended it against Don McCorkindale and George Cook. He had also achieved the 'impossible' by defeating Primo Carnera, when the giant Italian was at the peak of his power.

Len and Florence went on a Mediterranean cruise before it was time for him to go to Whetstone to prepare for Gains. One of his admirers was connected with the Blue Star Line and the boxer was able to enjoy a special rate. Of course, it was excellent publicity for the Company to have such a prominent sporting personality aboard, and the photographers were always busy, both at the time of departure and whenever the liner put into a foreign port for a day or so.

At the *Black Bull* he had as sparring-partners Ted Mason and a Canadian light-heavy, Ted Phillips. Others came and went, a number of boxers who knew and liked Harvey popping in to see him and have a round or two, all of them eager to lend a hand. There was great camaraderie among professional boxers in those days. For the majority of them it was their sole means of livelihood. They were hard times for most, but a happy spirit pervaded and they were all assured of a jovial atmosphere in Len's company. Gains trained at Market Bosworth where he specially engaged the services of George Slack who had twice fought Harvey. He also had the assistance of Eddie Peirce, the South African, and George Brown, the Stepney ex-policeman.

Once again it was 'house full' at the Albert Hall, the big question being whether Harvey could upset the old ring adage that 'a good big 'un will always beat a good little 'un'. Most thought it would be a question of reach: the coloured fighter had several inches in his favour. Harvey's only advantage lay in the fact that although he was in his twenty-seventh year, Larry was just past his thirty-third birthday. Little Jim Kenrick was the appointed referee and he operated from inside the ring from the start.

Again it was more a battle of brains than brawn, one that would live long in the memory of those that saw it. The close observer could almost see the two men thinking, as move followed move with the precision of two masters of chess. The gloves flashed out, but every time with thought behind them. Gains was well aware that he carried the heavier punch, but he did not throw his right hand aimlessly. He made all the openings for it first and if it did not land on the spot or with the power intended, it was because of his opponent's superb defensive skill and mental alertness. Harvey refused to be fooled into any false move. He knew too much to walk in and have a fight with a man who could hit with the heavy power that Larry had at his command. Anyone who had not seen Gains use his full destructive punching on anyone else would have imagined that he could not hit with any hardness after seeing him against the Cornishman, for that was the way Len's evasiveness made it seem.

The reason that Gains did not win by a knockout or ever show any likelihood of doing so was not that Len was too tough. It was because not once in those forty-five minutes of tense boxing did Harvey's fine science falter. Moreover he had planned his strategy well in advance and stuck to it throughout the entire fight. He did not try to beat Gains to the punch with a straight left to the face, he concentrated on driving a long left into the coloured boxer's body. Hammering away at his ribs, causing Larry to drop his right elbow as a shield, a point from which he could not launch his powerful right arm with fullest effect.

Len put up a beautiful display of boxing until the twelfth round. He scorned to mix matters, being content to sneak his points by means of his superior speed. In point of fact, he turned his disadvantage in weight into an advantage, at times making the bigger man appear slow and lumbering. With four rounds left and knowing that his lead could only be slender, Harvey let himself go at a man who was showing the first signs of tiring. He drove Larry before him, breaking through his defences and battering him against the ropes. The crowd had not expected to see action of this sort from the smaller man and now they went delirious with delight. Gains could sense that his title was slipping away whilst his opponent was applying so much pressure and he endeavoured to put in a counter rally, but Len would not give him a chance.

The Cornishman was scoring with two blows to one and gradually punching the coloured man out of his championship. A powerful right hook to the chin staggered Gains in the fourteenth round. For a moment his legs wavered and it seemed that he must go down. But he pulled himself together and managed to keep out of further trouble to the bell. He was up for the final round, resolved on saving his crown at all costs, but Harvey was even more determined to win yet another title. He surged into Larry, going all out to score a knockdown and it was a tribute to Gains' courage and resistance that he managed to stay on his feet. Like the great champion he was, Larry flogged his remaining resources in an attempt to stave off disaster. But Len was there to give a grandstand finish that would settle his superiority beyond doubt. With confident zeal he punched so fast and furiously that Larry had been fought to a standstill by the time the last bell sounded.

Gains lurched to his corner, a large lump over his left eye, looking drawn and exhausted, while Len marched back to his smiling seconds, breathing evenly and entirely unruffled. After an hour's strenuous battle of nerve and muscle he looked as if he had just come in after a walk in the park. Referee Kenrick took a moment to add up his score card and was moving towards Harvey's corner as he did so. At once a great roar resounded throughout the big hall. Harvey had not won by a wide margin, but he had won and his win was popular. But those who had listened in to Lionel Seccombe's description of the contest could hardly believe their ears when he had to admit that despite his commentary, which for the most part had run in Gains' favour, it was to Harvey that the referee had given his verdict. In fact the broadcast version was so out of tune with the newspaper reports the following morning that letters of protest poured into the BBC's offices and the sporting columns contained many complaints at the misleading radio account of the contest.

Writing to the *Evening Standard*, Mr P. J. Moss said:

> I cannot allow Mr Lionel Seccombe's statement on his broadcast commentary of the Harvey-Gains contest to pass unchallenged. As chairman of the Referees' Association, chairman of the Southern Branch of the BBB of C, and an administrative steward of that body, also as an amateur 'starred' referee who has controlled the last two British Empire championships and the last world title bout in this country, I say most emphatically that from start to finish Harvey's superiority was never in doubt. I scored the actual points and here is the result: Harvey won seven rounds; Gains won three rounds; five rounds were even. My score sheet at the finish read: Harvey 74 points, Gains $72\frac{1}{2}$ points. Harvey has attained his position by brainwork, clean-living, careful training, added to perfect physical attributes. But it has ever been our custom to belittle our champions in the eyes of the world. As for Mr Kenrick, his work as referee was admirable.

The great controversy caused by the misleading broadcast was a gift to the cinematograph people who had obtained the rights to film the Empire heavyweight contest. Thousands flocked to the Movietone News Theatre in Shaftesbury Avenue, London, to witness a full-length silent version with a commentary by that other great British heavyweight personality, Bombardier Billy Wells. The film was shown for some time in London, while a shortened version was included in every picture theatre programme throughout the country.

It had been a great and wonderful year for Leonard Austin Harvey. In March 1933 he had been middleweight champion. In June he had become light-heavyweight title-holder. In November he had gained the heavyweight championship and by the following February he was the acclaimed Empire heavyweight king. It was a fantastic record, never likely to be beaten. But for a damaged hand he might even have won a second Lonsdale Belt outright and become the holder of four titles at one and the same time. But for a non-English-speaking referee he might have gained the first leg of his boyhood ambition to follow his great Cornish hero and win the first of the three world titles he sought. But time was still on his side and even after thirteen years of busy ring life he was just as full of ambition and determination to add further to his already illustrious career.

CHAPTER 16

That One Unlucky Punch

At this point in his boxing career Harvey was the most popular fighter in Great Britain. Manager Charlie Rose received on average between fifty to a hundred letters a day congratulating Len on his great wins over Petersen and Gains, asking for his photograph, seeking his help; while there were many from aspiring young boxers asking for advice. He responded to charitable calls for financial help; he opened fêtes, gave free exhibitions, judged various competitions and sent autographed pictures of himself for auctioning in aid of worthy funds. No one was refused. He even found himself installed at Madame Tussaud's famous waxworks exhibition in Baker Street.

It can be taken for granted that promoter Dickson was a very happy man. Harvey had upset the heavyweight apple-cart with a vengeance and Jeff had a ready-made winner on his hands in a return between Len and Jack for which the whole of the fight fraternity was clamouring. But this was far too big a prospect for an indoor event. The place to stage it was the White City, which had already been established as a successful fight venue. It was capable of holding up to a hundred thousand fans and a capacity crowd, such as a return Harvey *v.* Petersen bout promised, would yield a handsome profit.

Harvey wanted a contest to keep himself in fighting trim and Dickson was keen to keep his ace boxer in the public eye. He suggested a match with Jimmy Tarante at the Albert Hall, and once again the Cornishman left the *Black Bull* and returned to the *Star and Garter*. With him was Wally May, as trainer. It was his immense popularity as much as anything that caused Len to transfer from Whetstone to Windsor. When training at the *Black Bull* he attracted enormous attention and consequently a great deal of noise with car doors slamming, the crowded bars and the sound of young boys and girls running around excitedly. It had been a quiet and secluded residential country place before Len began coming there, now the local inhabitants complained about their peace being disturbed, especially at week-ends. Harvey charged a penny a head to watch him go through his afternoon training stint and would collect up as much as £50 by this means, all of which was given to the London Children's Holiday Fund. But once he realised that his presence at Whetstone was creating a nuisance to the neighbourhood he gave up going there, although with reluctance because he had always enjoyed being there.

Tarante (real name James Rogers) was coloured, with a Cherokee Indian strain in his blood. He was twenty-four, a light-heavy, and had been boxing for more than five years, starting in America where he had thirty bouts. As he was unbeaten in the United States and had won thirteen of his contests by the knockout route, it was surprising that Dickson had been able to induce him to come to Europe. Here he was equally successful, boxing mainly in Paris, but also in other continental cities, plus five appearances in London, each time winning inside the distance. He had suffered eight defeats in European rings. Sad to say, three of these set-backs had been due to disqualification, for Tarante was a great thumper to the body and in his anxiety to land his pet punches was inclined to strike off the target.

This is precisely what happened against Harvey. They were scheduled to travel twelve rounds, but after being cleverly outpointed by an immaculate Harvey for three rounds, Jimmy got irritated and wild in the fourth round and struck dangerously low, so low in fact that referee Kenrick was on the point of ordering the American to his corner, when Len stopped him: 'I'm all right, Jim,' he said. 'Don't rule him out, it was accidental, but tell him to be more careful.' So Tarante got his warning, but it fell on deaf ears. In the fifth round he brought the Cornishman down with a palpably low delivery and with Len in obvious pain as he tried to get up, the Third Man had no other option but to disqualify the offender.

The double title fight with Petersen was not due for fifty-three days and three weeks of that period would be needed for training. So Len had time to recover from the Tarante mishap and was delighted when he arrived at the *Star and Garter* to find Eddie Phillips offering to be his chief sparring-partner. It was a fine gesture on the part of the Bow boxer, but he did have an axe to grind: Harvey had announced that in the event of his successfully keeping his heavyweight titles against Petersen, he would relinquish his British light-heavyweight crown and, as he had already defeated Tommy Farr in an official eliminator, Phillips was the recognised contender. He and Len had already boxed twenty-seven rounds together. Was there anything else for them to discover of each other, especially when wearing the big gloves? 'If I boxed with him for the rest of my life, I would still be learning,' declared Eddie. 'He has an answer for every move I make.'

The forthcoming White City battle was the talk of the country and Dickson's box-office had a busy time. There were day-by-day stories from the training camps; feature interviews with both men; forecasts as to how it would end, plus the usual flow of rumours that abound when a big sporting event is about to take place. The weekly paper *Boxing* disclosed the physical differences between champion and challenger, as follows:

	Harvey	Petersen
Height	6 ft. 0 ins.	6 ft. $1\frac{1}{2}$ ins.
Weight	12 st. 7 lbs.*	13 st. 0 lbs.
Neck	$16\frac{1}{2}$ ins.	17 ins.
Chest (normal)	41 ins.	41 ins.
(expanded)	45 ins.	45 ins.
Waist	33 ins.	34 ins.
Thigh	23 ins.	22 ins.
Calf	$15\frac{1}{2}$ ins.	15 ins.
Ankle	$9\frac{1}{2}$ ins.	$9\frac{1}{2}$ ins.
Biceps	15 ins.	$14\frac{1}{2}$ ins.
Forearm	$13\frac{3}{4}$ ins.	$12\frac{1}{2}$ ins.
Reach	76 ins.	$80\frac{1}{2}$ ins.

The crowd did not quite come up to the promoter's estimate of a hundred thousand, but it was not far short and the tournament must have been a huge financial success. Not surprising, since the two principals were the most popular boxers the country had seen for years. The ticket-holders were handled without a hitch and the smooth progress of the spectators to their seats spoke much for the good organisation. The weather held good, for although dark clouds had threatened all day, only a few spots fell and passed unnoticed by the fans. One of the keenest of the ringsiders was Harry Jenkins, the man who had given Len his start at the 'Old Cosmo' fourteen years earlier.

Once again C. H. Douglas was referee and the start of the contest was fought on very similar lines to the first meeting between the pair, with Petersen launching a heavy attack, bounding in to try and destroy

*This was three or four pounds above Harvey's weight at that time.

his opponent as quickly as possible and Harvey boxing coolly and defensively, drawing his man into counter-punches and using all his defensive skills to prevent himself from being swept out of the ring. Naturally when the Welshman was made to miss he came forward again with extra fury and frequently Len had to come in close where he was an expert at inside work and where Petersen's extra reach was of no value to him.

This made it a tricky contest to handle, but the referee knew his business and broke up the clinches when they threatened to become prolonged. Jack's plan was to leap in with a long left and bang over a big right. Harvey had either to go back out of range, which would have meant being continually on the retreat, or come in and either take the punches on his gloves and arms, or move his head to make them go hurtling into space. At close-quarters, he brought all his infighting technique into play, tactics that annoyed the Welshman, who had either to push the champion off, or pull back out of range, in the process of which he usually had to take a snappy left to the face.

It was not an artistic duel and at times was inclined to be rough. Harvey was more than holding his own against his heavier and taller opponent and it was on the cards that before long Petersen would have been put out of his stride and made to make the kind of errors that had caused his downfall at the Albert Hall. Even after four rounds he was beginning to show signs of raggedness and then came the event that changed the whole situation; one single punch that was to have a catastrophic effect upon the eventual result.

It happened soon after the start of the fifth round. Petersen came out fighting, even more determinedly than before. He flung a tremendous right at his rival's body followed by another aimed at the head. For a moment Harvey was taken by surprise and before he could get out of the way, another smashing right went into his ribs. The impetus behind this last mighty punch threw him and his rival together as Len came forward to go into a clinch. They were immediately ordered to break and as they did so it was seen that the champion's left eye was completely closed. It could have been caused by an accidental butt, the inside of a glove or a punch at close range. Whatever the reason, it spelt disaster for Harvey who in a moment had been half-blinded, robbed of vision as surely as if his eyelids had been stitched together.

The big crowd did not need telling that now Harvey was fighting under an almost insurmountable handicap. To face a fiery fighter like the impetuous Welshman you needed vision in two good eyes; to be forced to hold him at bay with one was asking the impossible. As soon as he realised what damage he had done, Jack piled on the pace and Len was hustled all over the square as he attempted to box on the retreat, having to turn half-southpaw in an effort to keep Petersen's big punches in focus. In the interval they could do nothing to bring down the swelling, but Harvey came forth to do what he could with a situation that had got beyond his control.

Petersen could see victory in his sights: the big opportunity to become a champion once again. He became one all-out fighting force and to deal with him Len had to close the gap between them and bring the battle to a close-range affair. This produced holds, there was tugging and wrestling as Jack tried his utmost to pound his opponent into the canvas. Finally referee Douglas stopped the proceedings and gave them both a lecture. 'Let us have a boxing match, not a brawl,' he said. 'If you go on like this, I'll be forced to send you both out of the ring and you are both such good fellows that I don't want to do that.'

During the scrimmage an old wound had re-opened on Petersen's left eyebrow. It was bleeding profusely and when they resumed he had to protect his injury. So Harvey came into his own again and, half-blinded as he was, he could still put in his punches where they scored points and beat the Welshman with sheer ringcraft, thus putting up a remarkable recovery from what had seemed near defeat. They patched Jack up during the minute's rest and he came out as eager as ever to win with a battery of big punches. He fairly threw himself at the champion and Len was caught by a heavy left hook that struck him full in the right eye, causing the flesh beneath it to swell up alarmingly.

How Harvey lasted out the round no one knew and as soon as he got back to his corner his father and Wally May urged him to retire. But Harvey muttered that he was not beaten yet and was off his stool at the sound of the bell to walk, as it were, into the jaws of death. Petersen met him with a long left into the face, then another, followed by a tremendous left swing that sent Len reeling. But he recovered his balance and hit out as Jack advanced, standing square to keep him in his fading vision, moving out of the way of punches by sheer instinct. His face looked a terrible mess but he kept on his feet and again his seconds implored him to give in, if only to save himself from suffering a real injury.

Up for the eighth and as the Welshman set off again on his path of destruction, he was met by a fine right to the face that pulled him up in his tracks. Another right followed and either of these two blows would have ended the fight had they been delivered by an unimpaired Harvey. For a moment Jack was nonplussed, then he went in behind a jolting left, realising that he could throw away the fight if he let his impetuosity get the better of him. Len was pawing the air now, he was practically blind and although he ducked and dodged, grabbed and held on, it was only by a miracle that he was able to last out the round.

'This is plain ridiculous,' said Ted Harvey. 'Let me call over the referee and tell him you can't go on any more. You can't possibly see him.' To which this remarkable man with the unbeatable spirit replied: 'Of course I can't see him. But I know where he is. I can hear his feet shuffling and his breathing when he gets close. How many more rounds are there to go?' 'You are only past the half-way stage,' said trainer May as he tried to do something for Len's right eye which was bloodshot and running with water. 'I'll go up for one more,' declared this brave man. And he kept going up for one more round, almost sightless, yet defying his determined opponent to knock him off his feet.

If Harvey had not had enough by the end of the twelfth round, referee Douglas had. He had been walking over to the champion's corner during the interval for the last three rounds and now he would not let it go on any longer. 'I strongly advise you to give in, otherwise I shall stop you from going out for another round,' he said kindly, and Len nodded his head. The referee walked over to Petersen's corner and raised his arm to signal the fact that Harvey had retired. The vast crowd applauded loud and long, just as much for the gamest of losers as for the new titleholder. Len was helped out of the ring and stumbled back to the dressing-room. Here he received sufficient first-aid to enable him to peer out of one eye. He stood up and walked over to a mirror: 'Look at Nelson without his telescope,' he said with a grin. No complaints, no excuses, no recriminations. Because of one unlucky punch he had lost his two hard-won titles.

The Board of Control doctor strongly advised Harvey to go at once to a hospital for treatment, but Len had other ideas. They had an eye specialist friend, Dr D. Gayer Morgan, who lived at Highgate, and they telephoned him from the White City. He told them to go home and said he would meet them there, but asked them to try and get some ice, plenty of it, on the way. They stopped at the Dorchester Hotel in Park Lane, where a bucket of ice was readily supplied once its urgency was known, for everyone from the manager down to the kitchen boy had been agog about the big fight for the past few weeks. When the specialist examined Len's eyes he found no serious damage had been done. He advised two or three days indoors to allow the swellings to go down and the watering to cease. 'I can't do that,' said Harvey. 'I'm determined to see the Derby on Wednesday.' 'In that case,' he was told, 'you'll have to sit up all night with an ice bag to your left eye, otherwise it will never be opened in time. And keep applying ice to it all day tomorrow.'

He then made out the following statement to be issued to the press: 'I have examined Harvey's eyes. There is a scratch on the front of the right eye,* which means that with the left eye closed, he was quite incapable of seeing anything clearly. The vision of this eye must have been blurred by the scratch and the consequent watering.' From which it can be taken for granted that Len's chances of winning with three more rounds to go were just about a thousand to one. Yet he would have gone on with his task if his seconds and the referee had not prevailed upon him to give up. He spent the next day in bed, but on Derby Day there he was on Epsom Downs, sporting a wonderful black eye, yet full of good cheer and intent on enjoying himself. Quite by chance he ran into Jack Petersen and they chatted away quite happily, the recent fight forgotten, each intent on finding the winner. Then he went off on another Mediterranean cruise, following which he and Wally spent a month on a Cornish farm at Newquay, a quiet, clear-aired spot in his home county where he could fully recuperate from his ordeal at the White City.

Back in the boxing world Harvey received a notification from the Board of Control that he must defend his light-heavyweight title against Eddie Phillips and that the highest bid for the contest was £750, offered by the Belle Vue syndicate at Manchester. Now Len had no objection to putting his remaining championship at stake and considered the man from Bow as his legitimate challenger. But he thought the purse accepted by the Stewards was totally inadequate and told them so. Even the boxing writers were of this opinion. They pointed out that Harvey and Petersen had shared equally a £10,000† gate at the White City, and

---

* There was a suggestion that a loose lace from Petersen's glove had caused the damage.

† Although newspaper stories quoted Harvey as receiving £5,000 for defending his British and Empire heavyweight titles against Petersen, Len always maintained that he received far less than this amount. Unknown to the promoter he had a check made at two of the entrances to the White City and as a result found there were discrepancies in the final accounts. What annoyed him was to discover that many so-called 'celebrities' were being admitted free of charge; people who could well afford to pay, whereas every ticket Len had taken to distribute to his friends had been paid for in hard cash. Harvey in fact estimated that the money he received from this particular fight, after all his expenses had been met, was in the region of only £1,000.

although it was not expected that a match between Len and Eddie, even with a title at stake, was worth as much, they thought the Manchester offer miserably low.

Len appeared before the Stewards and was told that unless he agreed to accept the purse offer which they had accepted, he was in danger of being called upon to forfeit his title. 'If you value a British championship at only sixty per cent of £750, then it isn't worth keeping,' he replied. 'But even if you take it away from me,' he added, 'the general public will still consider that I am the true British light-heavyweight champion.' He was asked to return the Lonsdale Belt but insisted that it was his to hold until they had appointed his successor, or had found a promoter willing to pay a more reasonable price for a contest between his challenger and himself.

In the autumn the fistic fraternity became aware that an entirely new promoter was entering the field. The National Sporting Club had regrettably gone into liquidation, thus depriving all the outright winners of its Lonsdale Belts of the pound a week pension they had been promised on reaching the age of fifty. Dickson remained supreme in London, but not for long. The Empire Pool and Sports Arena had been used most successfully for the British Empire Games of 1934 and managing director Arthur J. Elvin now had ideas of using this spacious indoor arena for the staging of professional boxing tournaments. He engaged the services of Sydney Hulls as matchmaker and decided to make his opening night an auspicious occasion with a highly publicised £1,000 Heavyweight Novices Competition, the winner and any other promising boxer who might emerge being guaranteed every assistance in the furthering of a fighting career.

To top this popular attraction he needed a contest of outstanding appeal and it can be taken as a tribute to Len Harvey's high standing among British boxers that he was chosen to open the new arena as the star performer of the evening. It was a great honour that Len fully appreciated and demonstrated the esteem in which he was regarded by Mr Elvin, which was to grow into a closer and even more trusting relationship in due course.

Harvey's opponent over twelve rounds was to be Walter Neusel, the German heavyweight who had established himself as a great favourite in British rings during the past two years and had just returned from a successful trip to America where he had won five of his six matches with one drawn. In England he had beaten Larry Gains, George Cook and Reggie Meen, also had two blistering bouts with Don McCorkindale, one of which had been drawn, the other ending in Walter's disqualification for alleged low hitting. His last appearance had proved disastrous, having been stopped in eight rounds by Max Schmeling in Hamburg because of a badly lacerated eye. It was estimated that he would outweigh Harvey by at least two stones.

There were 11,500 fans in Wembley Arena on the night of 26th November, 1934, the day after Neusel's thirty-first birthday, when Walter, followed by his renowned manager, Paul Damski, got into the ring. Harvey had his father and Wally May with him and Charlie Rose hovering around. Len had been brought to a peak of ultra fitness at Windsor and although he appeared somewhat dwarfed by the big German when referee Douglas called them together for a few preliminary words, he had his usual confident look, as if no physical difference existed.

Obviously it was Harvey's plan to make full use of the ring, to skip round his slower and more cumbersome opponent while spearing him at long range with points-scoring punches. All the time he could do this and fend off the weighty blows that Neusel swung at him from both hands, it was an attractive and tense contest. But as soon as the German bore in by sheer weight and strength in an attempt to trap his rival on the ropes or pin him in a corner under heavy fire, Harvey had no option but to close in and bring all his art to bear in order to prevent himself being punched full of holes at short range. Neusel liked infighting, Harvey preferred to do without it, while the referee wanted none at all. Between them they had a good time, but it was not what the fans had paid to see.

Each time they came from their corners, Neusel would slug away with both hands at Harvey's body, and Len would tag him with lefts to the face and then uppercut him when he got closer into range. Then would come the seemingly inevitable clinch and this brought the referee into the picture. 'Don't wrestle,' he would admonish. 'Neusel, you are holding.' 'Pull your left glove out, Harvey,' and so on. In the third round he stopped the action and said: 'You can both box, so let us have some boxing.' 'I'm trying,' Len answered him, and for a while he boxed on the retreat until Neusel caught up with him again.

That he was indeed trying was seen at the start of the fourth when he got in the first punch of the round, a beautiful straight left to the face that halted the German's advance, then a volley of good clean punches from both hands, showing all too plainly how easy it was to hit Neusel at long range. The fans cheered, but Harvey could not keep it up as Walter forced his way in, brushing aside Len's left or merely ignoring it as he marched forward with his short punches to the body.

Most of the clean work came from the Englishman, one particularly good straight left in the ninth round opening a cut over the German's right eye. It bled considerably and Neusel had to hold up his right elbow to protect his injury from being worsened. This gave Len the opportunity to bang in some left hooks to the body, but Walter had plenty of flesh-covering there and took the hard blows unflinchingly. The tenth was spent mostly in infighting with not many clean punches exchanged and at this stage there could not have been a lot between them, for what Harvey had gained at long range, he lost at close-quarters where Neusel's advantage in weight was more noticeable.

In an attempt to finalise matters, Len sprang from his corner at the start of the eleventh and crashed home a powerful left, then a right to the German's head. Neusel was rocked and had to take several more well-placed punches before he could get inside Len's straight punches. Walter's right eyebrow was bleeding again and Harvey made another attack, hitting out with enterprise and was so anxious to get out of a clinch that he caught the referee with a punch as Mr Douglas came in to separate them. 'Pickles' laughed, as did Len, but Neusel could not see anything humorous in the incident. He was not looking either happy or confident at this moment, for his face was covered in blood and appeared puffed and swollen. Len did not improve matters by getting in several more shots to the German's damaged face and when the bell ended the round the fans showed full appreciation for Harvey's effort to make an open fight of it.

The last round was as bad as the previous one had been good, for Neusel was determined to prevent Harvey from picking him off at long range and at once got in to thump away, his head on Len's shoulder, while he held him in a bear-like grip whenever the Britisher tried to get away. Sometimes Len had to hold in order to do some scoring on his own account, and when the final bell sounded they were in a close-quarter scrimmage. To the keen observer it seemed that Harvey had done just enough to win, but mindful of the way he had been forced to censure both men, referee Douglas called them together and held their arms up simultaneously to declare a 'draw'. But if appearances had anything to go by, Len must have been the winner, for whereas Neusel looked like a Red Indian, Harvey left the ring unmarked.

Early in 1935 another attempt was made to create a union of boxers. There had been several efforts in this direction, but all had failed, principally because of the inertia of the fighting men themselves. Now a National Union of Boxers had been formed with the backing of the

Trade Union Movement and Jimmy Wilde assumed the role of President, ably assisted by an enthusiastic Len Harvey, who had been right through the fistic mill, from the novice to the top-of-the-bill class, and knew only too well how all boxers had been and still were being exploited and robbed of their inadequate earnings by promoters, managers, agents and all those deriving a living from the sport. The self-instituted Board of Control, which should have made the protection of boxers its prime concern, was still in its infancy and being run on the same principles as had been the case with its parent body, the committee of the National Sporting Club, and infamous acts were being blatantly committed against the fighting men simply because the Stewards had not the machinery or organisation for a proper governing of Boxing.

Len, as Vice-President of the NUB, made an impassioned speech at the first general meeting of the Union held at the St Bride's Institute, just off Fleet Street. It was printed in full in *Boxing* under the heading: 'Len Harvey hits out: fighting speech by one who has been through the mill', and passages from it were quoted in the majority of the daily papers. He called upon every boxer to join in his own interests, and said that only by becoming united could they overcome the evils that beset their profession. 'Let us lay the foundations of this Union well, so that we can look back and be proud of what we have done.'

There was less need for Harvey to take up the case of the under-privileged fighter than for almost anyone in the country. He had had his father and his boys' club to aid him in Plymouth; he had been advanced in his career by his association with Dan Sullivan as manager of 'The Ring', and when his own talent had developed, he had been among the leading boxers in the country for the past ten years. But if he had been one of the fortunate ones in this respect, he was not blind to what was going on around him; not unconscious of the 'hungry fighters' who made up the rank and file, the unemployed, the poorly paid labourer who often travelled miles on an empty stomach to fight for a mere pittance, some of which was whittled away by the parasites that infested the sport. He had never had to suffer in this way, but he knew of hundreds up and down the country who did, and it was for them he was fighting*.

Although Len had asked his wife not to do any more matchmaking

---

* The National Union of Boxers progressed until the outbreak of the Second World War in September 1939. It did not flourish as its founders had hoped, but did much to enhance the standing and conditions for boxers generally and gave rise basically to the rules and regulations of the BBB of C that exist today for the welfare of its licence holders.

for him at the time of the first contest with Petersen, he did not mind when she returned home one day to say she had met Mrs Bella Burge and promised that her husband would give his services for a Silver Jubilee tournament which the owner of 'The Ring', was proposing to stage there on 29th April. He got in touch at once with that kind friend of his youth and offered to top the bill for her against any light-heavyweight she cared to name. 'What about the champion of France?' 'He'll do,' answered Harvey and it was arranged for them to box ten rounds as the main attraction. Apart from a number of minor bouts, exhibitions were given by many great champions of the past, together with some of the stars of the day, while three members of the famous Lloyd Family, with whom Mrs Burge had been associated in her theatrical days, Rosie, Alice and Daisie – sang some of their famous sister Marie's old songs, in which the packed assembly took a loud and vigorous part.

Marcel Lauriot came out to face Harvey under the usual continental crouch which provided no puzzle to his experienced opponent, who took a step forward and hooked him hard with his left to the jaw. The blow shook the Frenchman, three straight lefts to the face straightened him up, then another powerful left hook to the chin caused him to crumple up at Harvey's feet. It took him nine seconds to get himself off the floor and during the count Len happened to see a look of horror on Mrs Burge's face, who could visualise her main item of the evening's entertainment ending in the first minute.

That would never do. So when Lauriot was upright once again, Len allowed him to recover and then gave the crowd an exhibition of perfect boxing, at the same time encouraging his opponent to fight back. Len was always scoring with left leads and the occasional hook that checked the Frenchman's rushes, but he never really opened out again. Harvey's defence was dazzlingly clever. He would let himself be taken to the ropes and there he would duck and sway or hold Lauriot off with his arms. He was making it an exhibition and the crowd thoroughly enjoyed it.

The visitor was tough. He stood up well to the precision punches that caught him in every round, and he was always trying to retaliate with swings to the body. But Harvey had an adequate defence for these crude shots and even seemed to encourage his opponent to hit out as it gave him every opportunity to display his skill at avoiding trouble. The further it went the more one-sided it became until some of the fans were urging Len to finish it. But there was nothing to be gained by knocking out a game, if outclassed rival, and it went the distance with Harvey the winner by the proverbial mile.

CHAPTER 17

So Near to Ambition's Dream

The rest of 1935 was almost barren of fights for Len Harvey, mainly due to the fact that Jack Petersen was in the heavyweight limelight with his two great battles with Walter Neusel, both of which ended with the gallant Welshman's retirement due mainly to eye injuries. The second of these clashes occurred at the end of June, whereupon Len pointed out to all concerned that having held the German to a 'draw' he was entitled to (a) another fight with Neusel or (b) a rubber meeting with Petersen, with whom the score was one-all. The only other heavy of high standing was Larry Gains, over whom Harvey had already shown his superiority. As usual, however, the Board of Control did not feel inclined to agree with Len's views and he was ordered to meet Eddie Phillips in an eliminating contest, the winner to be regarded as the leading contender for Petersen's British and Empire titles.

Earlier in the year Phillips had taken over the vacant light-heavyweight crown by defeating Tommy Farr on a fifteen rounds points decision at Mountain Ash in Wales. Although Harvey had beaten the new champion once and boxed a draw with him previously, he was thus called upon to assert his superiority yet again and when a Plymouth syndicate offered a purse of £1,000 for a Harvey v. Phillips match, it was accepted by the Stewards. So, on 26th October, the pair met for the third time. It took a great deal of aggravation to upset the Cornishman, but much as he welcomed the opportunity to box before the Devon seaport fans again, he felt at heart that his journey was not all that necessary and poor Phillips had to bear the brunt of his annoyance.

There were between six and seven thousand spectators in the Millbay Rinkeries and they saw one of the finest boxing matches that a student of the Noble Art could wish for. Those who had forecast that the men knew too much about each other to make it worthwhile were wholly confounded, and those who came to admire Harvey's renowned handiwork saw him at his very best, while Jack Smith, from Manchester, who refereed the contest, had one of the easiest jobs imaginable.

Harvey fought with a dash and determination which marked him as not only a clever tactician, but also a fierce and punishing fighter. On more than one occasion he had his opponent sagging at the knees under the weight of his hard and well-placed punches, and Phillips showed great gameness and proved he was in the very best condition by being able to absorb the weighty stuff that Len handed out and yet avoid being put off his feet.

Len's left was the chief factor in his success. The manner in which he shot it straight from the shoulder into Phillips' face was truly classical, while the clever manner in which he timed his rival's counters and either slipped, drew back, or ducked them, sometimes seemingly by a hair's breadth, was an object lesson in sound boxing judgment and mastermanship. The light-heavyweight champion tried hard to get through with punches to the body, but the majority of these failed to land with any real force and some appeared to go slightly low, although this may have been due to Harvey's trick of beating down these deliveries. He knew he was taking this risk, but never once complained of being hit low or even indicating to his opponent that he was going below the line. In the main, however, he negatived much of Eddie's midsection work by taking the punches on his gloves, forearms or elbows.

Fierce and determined as were the exchanges, it was always a battle of skill with Harvey the strategist and Phillips following the trend set by his rival. It was intriguing to see Harvey edging backwards, drawing Phillips towards him until a corner of the ring was almost reached, when suddenly out would shoot Len's left full in the face, then a rapid head swing under Eddie's countering right, and then a swift and telling right to Phillips' head. These tactics were a feature of almost every round. Wearing a champion's mantle brought the best out of the Londoner and he was ever striving to beat his clever rival to the punch. He did in fact draw blood from a stinging shot to the mouth, but it did not inconvenience Len in any way. Eddie also got the occasional left through to the body, while, smart as he was, Harvey could not avoid all the rights that came his way, although he reduced the power behind most of them by his clever headwork.

With his cheek bones badly bruised and eyes swollen, Phillips fought gamely, always coming forward under a controlled attack, but usually taking more than he could hand out. He had his worst time in the eleventh round when a perfect right to the jaw shook him to his toes and another that followed immediately had him really groggy. It looked as if he might be put down and out, but Eddie stalled and defended desperately to rob Len of a decisive victory and to earn Phillips applause from the fans in recognition of his great courage. Harvey made another big effort in the final round to score a knockout, but although battered and weary, Phillips fought back with all his remaining strength and stamina to be there on his feet at the finish. Harvey did not have a walk-over by any means, but it could be claimed that he had not lost a round.

Afterwards in the hotel he sent Wally May to the one next door, where Phillips was staying, to see how Eddie was faring. 'He looked pretty used up to me when I spoke to him in the dressing-room afterwards and I'd like to know if he is all right.' When the trainer came back he astonished Len by saying Eddie and his manager, Sam Russell, were on the point of catching a train home. 'Sam is going racing tomorrow, so can't stay overnight,' explained Wally. 'Why didn't you advise Eddie to remain here and travel up with us tomorrow? I know I'll be glad to turn in tonight and I'm sure it would be better for him to get into a proper bed, rather than try to sleep in a railway carriage.' It was another outstanding example of Harvey's interest in the well-being of his opponents, and also how he felt about the way some boxers were neglected by those who were supposed to be looking after them. Unfortunately, far too many managers considered their job done after securing a man a fight and then going into his corner to watch it.

With Harvey fully established as a heavyweight title contender, interest among the big men was stirred up again and Jeff Dickson was in with the first offer – £6,000 to Petersen; £4,000 to Harvey. But perhaps Jack was no more keen to box for the American promoter than was Len, in fact the latter never again fought under contract to Dickson. It was left to Arthur Elvin to make an offer for the fight which was acceptable by both men, although the purse was not as large as that quoted by the man who had staged their two previous contests. Petersen was reported as receiving £4,500, but as challenger it is to be supposed that Harvey got less. The Welshman trained at his own gymnasium in Cardiff, while Len went off to new quarters at the Barn Club, a road-house on the Barnet by-pass. With him as spar-mates were Eddie Steele, Jack Fox and Len Rowlands, with Wally May to supervise the callisthenics and massage.

Within a few days of the fight date being announced, Wembley Arena was sold out and little wonder. Everyone wanted to see the rubber meeting between these two who represented fire and ice in their respective fighting make-ups. Because many considered Harvey unlucky to lose the second contest due to the mishap to his eyes – the sole occasion in his long career when he had failed to go the full distance – and taking into account his win on the first occasion – Len was made favourite at two to one to win the 'rubber'. Another feature to be taken into account was the fact that since their last meeting Petersen had been subjected to two beatings at the hands of Neusel, the last time having to succumb because of exhaustion as much as anything else.

For the first time since he started out on the professional trail Petersen was without the aid of his father in the corner. He looked buoyant and confident, while Harvey was his usual phlegmatic self, cool and unconcerned until the bell started them off when he came out in brisk fashion, obviously intent on making a fight of it. He attacked with a quick left and right, but missed with another right as Petersen drew back out of its path. Jack seemed slow in getting into his stride, he fenced and shifted his ground as Len shot lefts at him, then worked Harvey into his own (Petersen's) corner and crashed over a right to the jaw.

It was a good punch and came so swiftly that it took Len by surprise. Fortunately it landed a little too high to be really damaging, but carried enough power to put the Cornishman down on his right knee. He took a count of 'five' during which he watched the Welshman very closely, then got up and had to go on the retreat as Petersen went all out to make the most of his advantage. Len had to bring all his evasive skill to bear in order to avoid disaster, and made his opponent miss with three powerful rights in succession, each of which could have ended the contest had they landed.

That first-round knockdown practically determined the course of the contest. It made Len fight on more cautious lines than had been planned. He had made up his mind that as he had weight and height to give away, his best scheme was to carry the fight to his opponent and endeavour to put him out of his stride. But that knockdown made all the difference and for the next three rounds Harvey had to cope with a cock-a-hoop champion who thought he saw an opportunity to score a quick victory. At the same time the Welshman had to make sure that the cuts around the eyes that had cost him dearly against Neusel were not re-opened by Harvey, and this put a restraint on his normal attacking fire.

So when Len had weathered a couple more rounds, he opened out with a renewed attack in round four, in which he got in two of his favourite left hooks to the chin. A heavy right under the heart was meant to lower Jack's guard and expose him to another at his head. But Jack did not fall for this move as he had in the past. He could not afford to risk a hard punch on that suspect eyebrow and preferred to expose his ribs rather than his face. Those who had seen his reckless way of fighting in the past were surprised to see the Welshman so much more subdued, bringing out the boxing ability he possessed rather than flinging punches wildly in the hope of getting one home on a vulnerable point.

Actually he did not have as much to fear from Harvey's right as he imagined. In the past this had been Len's most lethal weapon, one that had delivered many an opponent into his arms. When he had got it home well-timed, true and with full power on an opponent's chin, it took a good man to take it and survive. But ever since that title fight with Casey in Newcastle at the end of 1932, it had not been the same instrument of destruction. In fact since then, apart from the knocking out of Candel in Paris, Harvey had been forced to go the full distance in all his contests. His damaged right had cost him his middleweight title and his striking power had been reduced ever since. Just at the time in his career when he was at earning peak, he found himself less than the hundred-per-cent fighting machine he had been when middleweight champion.

Against Petersen it was all too plain that he dare not let his dexter hand go with the power and pace as of old. He no longer struck straight with it, but used it more in the manner of an overarm loop, which naturally made it a lot less effective. He got through to Petersen's chin with it on a number of occasions without shaking the Welshman. He troubled Jack a lot more with his left hooks when they landed, but with Petersen doing most of the forcing, Len's opportunities for scoring decisively were infrequent. It was a good, keen fight and an interesting one, yet without sensations apart from that first round knockdown. It was clean and referee Charlie Thomas easily broke the clinches and there was no prolonged wrestling.

Harvey made a grand-stand effort in the last two rounds, hoping to snatch the fight out of the fire, but Petersen's determination to keep his titles, plus his new-found way of keeping a brake on his natural exuberant style, enabled him to hold off the older man's final spurt. Len gave everything he had to try to level the points between them or put himself in front sufficiently to catch the Third Man's eye. But it was an abortive effort. At the end he knew, as the majority of the spectators knew, that he had just failed. He had been beaten beyond doubt, but not by much, and none could say that he had not given a thoroughly good account of himself.

Harvey was in his twenty-ninth year. He had been earning his living entirely by his fists for sixteen years. What hopes were there now of his ever being able to compete among the heavyweights again? But he was far from finished as a fighter and once more his thoughts turned to the light-heavyweight class. Phillips was still British champion and holder of the Lonsdale Belt. Having licked Eddie twice, a second notch on the trophy could be achieved. But before such a thought could be carried any further there came an event that put a different complexion entirely on the 12 st.-7 lbs. situation. In August 1936 the Greyhound Racing Association had opened Harringay Arena, an edifice that could fully compete with Wembley, and Sydney Hulls had been enticed away to do the matchmaking. That left Arthur Elvin without anyone in that capacity and while there were many expert and experienced licence-holders in that category who would have jumped at the chance of stepping into Sydney's shoes, Mr Elvin, who knew precious little about the Fight Game, and what he did know he didn't like, fought shy of placing himself at the mercy of the philistines of Boxing.

He wanted a man he could trust implicitly. A man with no other axe to grind beyond the job in hand. Someone whose record in British Boxing was beyond reproach, whose name had never appeared in a newspaper other than connected with Boxing. A person who held the respect and admiration of all, gentlemanly in appearance and bearing; noted for his sportsmanship and fair play, above all, someone who had the Noble Art at his finger-tips. He chose Len Harvey!

Here was a man he felt sure would develop the Boxing side of the Wembley sporting enterprises better than any other, whose record in the ring was nothing short of marvellous, whose name was a household word, whose popularity was unchallenged. Harvey, he was convinced, could help him in keeping Wembley Arena as the leading fight centre in London. He invited Len to come and see him, told him of his plans, obtained the former champion's interest in the project, then waited to hear what ideas Harvey might have for a great opening night under the new regime.

'We have to face the prospect of keen competition from Harringay Arena,' Mr Elvin reminded his new matchmaker. 'We need something out of the ordinary that will stand up to any opposition.' 'The utmost in a Boxing attraction is a contest involving the world's heavyweight championship,' Harvey told him. 'You cannot do that, but it is in your hands to do the next best thing – a fight for the light-heavyweight championship of the world. John Henry Lewis is the present holder and I would like to fight him for his title here at Wembley.'

'But you are my matchmaker,' said the astonished Arthur. 'And I've made you a good match,' replied Len. 'It is one that will appeal to both the press and the public. Jock McAvoy gave Lewis a hard fight for the title in New York to lose a close decision. I believe I can go one better and beat him. The last British holder of this particular world champion- ship was Bob Fitzsimmons and that was as long ago as 1903. He was a Cornishman like myself – it makes a good story for the boxing writers.'

Elvin liked the idea the more he thought about it. They got to work and met with instant success, the coloured champion's services being secured on a flat guarantee of £4,000 free of tax, plus £200 for training expenses and four first-class return tickets to New York. The next thing was to get the approval of the Board of Control, bearing in mind that Phillips and not Harvey was the reigning British titleholder. In view of Len's recent victory over Eddie in an official eliminator, the Stewards gave their sanction for the Wembley project, then the details were sent out to the newspapers.

The news of the impending world title fight in London was received with acclaim in all quarters, and even though not a lot was known about Lewis, the Wembley publicity boys soon discovered that he was only twenty-two years of age, had been boxing professionally for six years and had engaged in seventy-one contests, of which he had won all but ten, four of these being drawn. He was born in Los Angeles, California, stood 5 ft. $11\frac{3}{4}$ ins. and in most other physical aspects was of much the same build as his challenger. That he carried a useful punch was demonstrated by the fact that thirty-six of his contests had ended inside the distance.

The Wembley matchmaker went down to Southampton to meet the American and his coloured manager, Gus Greenlee. He escorted them back to London and installed Lewis in his own new training-quarters at the Barn Club. Then he found a fresh place for himself at the Dumbell Hotel at Taplow, near Maidenhead on the River Thames, and both men settled down to prepare themselves for the battle ahead; John Henry for the second defence of his world crown and Harvey for his second attempt to win one.

There was a crowd of 11,800 to see the fight and they paid £15,200 between them. The fact of a Britisher fighting for a world title was the dominant factor in the drawing of such a big attendance, for every ticket- holder knew that in Len Harvey they had a man determined to achieve a life's ambition. When he entered the ring at 9.40 p.m. they gave him what must have been the greatest reception he had ever received and he knew that they were a hundred per cent behind him. Like true British sportsmen they gave the world champion a heart-warming welcome, so that he too must have felt he was among friends. Jack Smith, from Manchester, was referee. The weights were announced as Lewis 12 st. $5\frac{1}{2}$ lbs. while his challenger was lighter by $1\frac{1}{2}$ lbs. The coloured man had sustained a slight cut over his right eye in training and was permitted to come into the ring wearing a taped dressing over the wound.

At the starting bell Harvey walked straight out and planted a stiff left into the champion's face, then banged over a right to the jaw that Lewis rode cleverly. This brisk opening let the champion know what he was up against and he showed his skill in the exchange of left leads, in the use of which it was soon plain to see they were pretty evenly matched. Both countered well, each was clever in blocking, parrying and avoiding punches. The pace was fast and the footwork on both sides economical and graceful. There was some clinching, but the referee broke them speedily, and at the end of the first round, which had been full of interest, the score must have gone slightly in the challenger's favour.

Harvey continued to be the aggressor, starting with a swift left to the nose followed by a short right to the ribs. Lewis forced his way in close and there was some infighting that ended in a clinch. This was broken and as they came apart Len feinted with the left and shot a crisp right to the chin. Lewis had not settled down as yet and was leaving the initiative to his opponent who made the most of it. But the champion got in several left jabs and was busy when they got to close range. Again Harvey's round.

They circled round and exchanged lefts. Lewis was more aggressive now and drove his challenger into a corner. Harvey came forward to clinch, but the coloured man had anticipated this move and caught the Britisher with a finely-timed right to the jaw. Len boxed on the retreat with Lewis following up, then Harvey stood his ground and they put up an exciting rally in which plenty of punches were exchanged. But they were back to fencing with lefts at the bell. The round went to Lewis.

Again the champion forced the fighting and although the Britisher showed clever evasion, he was not able to keep pace with Lewis in picking up the points. There were several spells of infighting that ended in clinches which were broken up by the referee. Towards the end of the round it was noticed that the dressing over the American's right eyebrow was looking discoloured as if the wound underneath was bleeding. Lewis again took the round, but it was Harvey who captured the fifth, making a bold assault from the start, sending his straight left into the face, one crisp punch removing the piece of tape that covered John Henry's slight eyebrow injury. Lewis concentrated on the body, outscoring Harvey with the rapidity and placing of his punches. Just before the bell, however, Len shook his rival with a sizzling left hook to the head, a trifle too high to be really damaging.

As the fight progressed so it became more of a close-quarter battle, it being the coloured champion's plan to batter away two-handed, his head on Harvey's chest, while he moved steadily forward, forcing the older man back. Harvey hooked and uppercut, but had to do so on the retreat and was forced to clinch as a protection against the American's busy fists. When the referee parted them on one occasion, Lewis stepped back with his guard down and Len whipped over a quick right that missed the champion's chin by a coat of varnish. Lewis looked surprised and Len received a warning from the referee for his opportunism.

By the halfway mark they must have been on even terms, but Lewis kept the pace hot, was always coming forward to attack the body, and Harvey was having to pull out all he knew to do his share of the scoring. Occasionally he got in a good blow that raised the hopes of his supporters, but he appeared to be tiring under the continual body punishment and the speed of action which the younger man was able to maintain. Yet to the close observer it seemed as though the challenger was pacing himself through the middle rounds, concentrating on defence, but losing no opportunity to get in a solid punch whenever the opening presented itself. At the end of the tenth round, Lewis was ahead and Harvey's chances of success looked bleak.

The eleventh was another energy-sapping round for the challenger, but he fought back with great fortitude, even though the coloured man was now concentrating on the head and caught Len with three hard rights in succession. Only Harvey's ability to ride the punches saved him from disaster, in fact, they aroused him into swift retaliation and they swapped punches to enliven the crowd into louder shouts of encouragement to the Cornishman. They guessed Len must be behind, but knew also that he had it in him to still bring off a magnificent victory.

Four rounds to go and Harvey opened the twelfth with some remarkable counter-punching as Lewis came in very determinedly to try and finish off what he imagined was a near-beaten opponent. Len met his attack with blazing fists, abandoning his defence in order to trade punch for punch. Time and again the aggressive champion was caught by solid blows from his challenger and he was a disillusioned man when he returned to his corner for Harvey had shown renewed strength and ability to fight back.

Now came the best part of the battle. Once more Lewis came surging in, but this time he was met with a barrage of punches from all angles. He was taken completely by surprise and the fans roared their appreciation as Len tried hard to put the champion down. One great left swing made Lewis stagger and he just managed to half-parry a magnificent right to the chin. Spurred on by his success, the Britisher went all out and scored three to one at long range, then bustled in to outpunch the champion at short-arm distance. It was a marvellous recovery from a man who shortly before had seemed to have exhausted all his vitality. Now it was Lewis who was going back with Harvey battering away to the body and head, getting through the American's defence again and again. Harvey took the round by the widest margin of all those previous. From the spectators' point of view it was the best round of the whole contest.

There was a grim look on the face of John Henry as he came out for the fourteenth. He tried to force his way in, but once more found fierce opposition that became a whirlwind attack as Harvey strove his hardest to win decisively. Left hooks to the head, right hooks and upper-cuts to the body caused Lewis to wince and give ground. He tried to hang on, but was shaken off and forced back as Len pumped in both fists. There was a greyness in the champion's face, his eyes were the starting eyes of a man in dire distress. The arena thundered as Len gave his rival no rest. Another full-blooded left was pounded into John Henry's face and a smashing right to the jaw shocked his whole system. He hit back in sheer defence and they slammed away, while the feet of the fans beat a resounding drumming to match their non-stop cheering. Again Harvey's round by a wide margin.

It was now or never. Lewis had sunk thankfully on to his stool when he returned to his corner and his seconds were working desperately to refresh him for the final round. In Harvey's corner they were urging him for one last great effort that would put him ahead on the referee's score card. The bell and they clashed in the centre of the ring. In sailed Harvey, carrying the fight to his rival, who was forced to join in and was glad to clinch. They were parted and Len tapped his rival's nose with a measuring left and then banged over a right that carried all the power he could put behind it.

The punch caught the champion on the chin, but he clinched again to recover and then worked both hands to the body. Harvey did not want any close-quarter work, his only hope lay in delivering a knockdown punch. He got himself free, smashed in a left hook to the head, then jabbed and jabbed into the champion's face and flung his right again. It grazed the jaw and John Henry, realising that his title was in danger, blazed forth with both hands to the head and they had another punch-up from which the challenger emerged with a nasty cut over his left eye.

The sight spurred the American into furious action and Harvey joined in. Defence was cast to the winds as they punched it out in a free-hitting spell that was void of clinches and the arena rocked with excitement. They were still at it when the final bell sounded and it was left to the referee to part them and send each to his corner. There was a breathless moment then Jack Smith walked over to Lewis and raised his arm before the coloured champion had reached his corner. To say the decision was badly received is to put it mildly. The booing was loud and sustained and continued while the champion received his World Trophy from the Board of Control and until both men had disappeared to their respective dressing-rooms.

Interviewed there, Len said: 'I am not making any excuses. I did my best, but it was not good enough in the opinion of the referee whose judgment I accept. But my right hand that has troubled me so much in the last two years "went" in the third round and I think that lost me the fight. This fellow Lewis is good, but not invincible. I am not quibbling over the verdict, but judging by the sound afterwards, there were many who thought I was just in front.' Lewis said: 'Harvey is a far better fighter than they led me to believe in America. I had to work hard in those last few rounds to keep my title. I guess it was some fight.'

Some of the opinions expressed by the critics the next morning are worth recording. Fred Dartnell in the *News Chronicle*: 'Although the verdict was heartily booed by the crowd, I think the outburst was caused by the admiration which had been roused by Harvey's gallant attempt to pull a losing game out of the fire in the closing stages. I have seen Harvey in nearly a hundred contests, yet I have never seen him put up a more fearless and spirited fight, all the more meritorious when remembering that his previous bout was ten months ago.' Norman Hurst – *Daily Sketch*: 'As Jack Smith lifted up the arm of the winner thousands of people in the huge arena booed so loud and long as to deafen the applause for the American. Harvey put up one of the most courageous fights I have ever seen.' Jimmy Butler – *Daily Herald*: 'It was worthy of the highest traditions of great championship fights. Harvey has never fought a better battle. He mixed consummate boxing with magnificent aggression and was confident right to the last second.'

Joe Bromley – *Sporting Life*: 'The contest was saved as a spectacle by the amazing rally Harvey staged in the last three rounds. For a man who had become famous for his defensive tactics, he went "fighting mad" and hit the coloured champion more often in the last nine minutes than in the whole of the preceding twelve rounds. Lewis is a great champion. He was able to score often without reply and made practically every punch tell. It was a wonder that Harvey was able to stand up under such punishment and says much for his courage and stamina that he was able to take the American the full distance.' Trevor Wignall – *Daily Express*: 'Harvey has no reason to be sorry for himself. He was unquestionably the loser, but he went down gallantly and well.' Geoffrey Simpson – *Daily Mail*: 'Harvey fought himself to a standstill in a glorious late bid for victory. It was punch for punch in those last two rounds, as even as could be, but the coloured man was with him all the time, taking the best blows that Harvey could give.'

L. V. Manning – *Daily Sketch*: 'A magnificent failure. Harvey climbed higher last night than ever before in his long career. At the finish he was standing proudly on his feet, head unbowed, with the building ringing cheers for a brave loser – the man a world champion could not knock out. That Len won the fourteenth round and certainly shared the honours of the last deserves to rank as the crowning achievement of his ring career. I hope he doesn't fight again. It was a grand curtain and one would like to keep the memory unspoiled.' Ben Bennison – *Evening Standard*: 'Lewis won by a generous margin of points. Though the verdict was greeted by a chorus of disapproval, it was just and proper, in fact, the only verdict.'

So Harvey's second attempt to win a world title had ended in glorious defeat. It would not have surprised anyone had he decided to retire from ring activity, in fact, some of the critics respectfully suggested him taking such a course, pointing out that he would be keeping his connection with the Fight Game in his capacity as matchmaker to Wembley Arena. As usual Len did not commit himself. 'We'll wait and see,' was all he had to say to his questioners.

Right: Len Harvey shakes hands with Jack (Kid) Berg at Waterloo Station as they leave for New York in December 1930. Unfortunately the Cornishman did not experience the 'Good luck' wishes of his friends.

Below left: Harvey with his American manager, Walter Friedman, at Orangeburg, New Jersey, when he was training for his first contest with Vince Dundee. Pushing the barrow is the Egyptian heavy, Salah El Din. Len was well and truly taken for a ride in the USA.

Below right: Harvey in 'safety' with the Captain of the *Leviathan* before sailing out of New York for home.

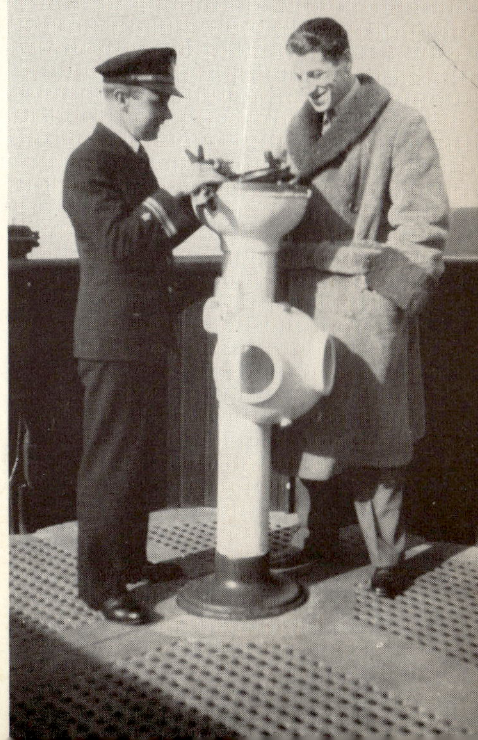

Above: Len Harvey (left) and Jack Petersen fight before a packed assembly at the Albert Hall.

Below left: Petersen lunges and misses as Harvey cleverly draws back.
Below right: Len achieves the 'impossible' and wins a hat-trick of titles by defeating Petersen for the British Heavyweight Championship.

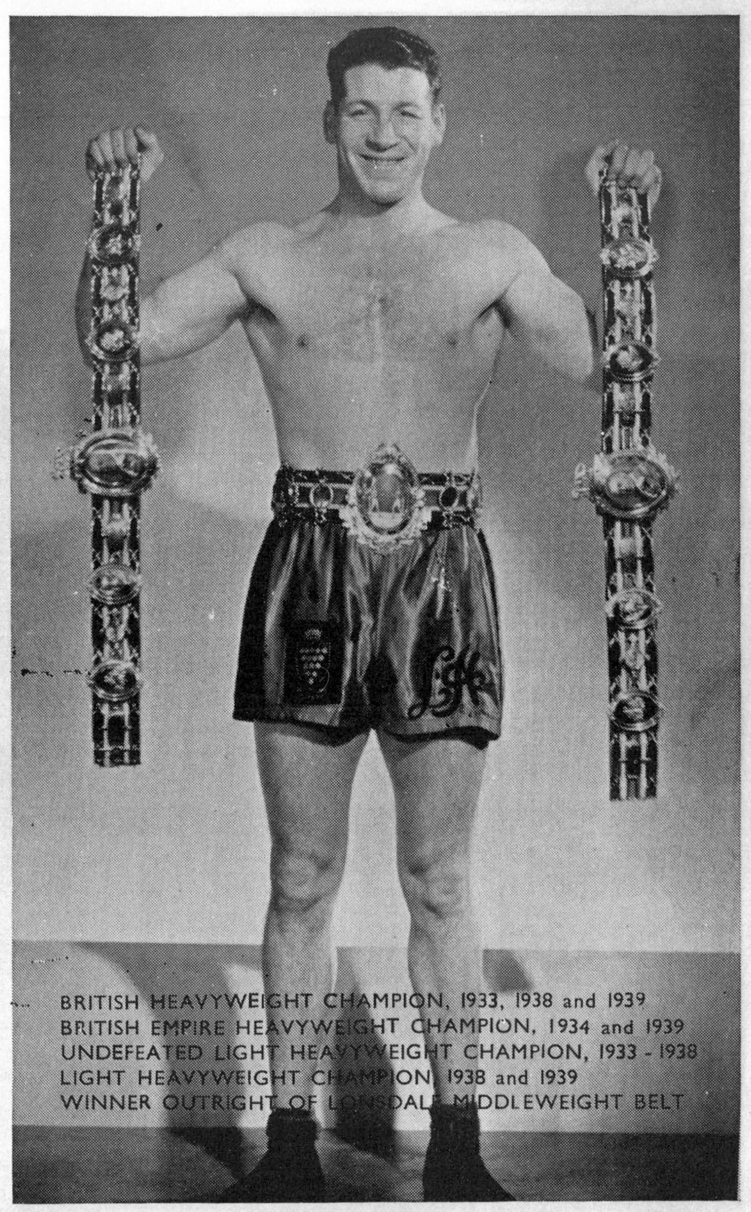

Len Harvey proudly displays his three Lord Lonsdale Belts. The one round his waist is the British middleweight trophy which he won outright; the others are emblematic of the light-heavy and heavyweight championships. Note Duchy of Cornwall badge on right leg of trunks, his initials on left.

Above: World Champion Marcel Thil, of France, on the canvas early in their contest at the White City in 1932. *Below*: Swiss referee reprimanding in French a perplexed Len Harvey who fails to understand him.

Above left: Heavyweight Champion Len Harvey has Jack Petersen on the defensive. *Above right*: Petersen regains title as Harvey is forced to retire with a damaged left eye.

Below: Matchmaker Len Harvey watching Benny Lynch sign to fight Small Montana for the world flyweight title at Wembley Arena. Behind Lynch is his manager George Dingley. On the right is Arthur Elvin, managing-director of Wembley Arena.

Left: Champion John Henry Lewis takes a left lead from Challenger Len Harvey.

Left: Lewis crowding Harvey into a corner. Note the Champion's head.

Right: Exchange of lefts. Harvey scores but makes Lewis miss.

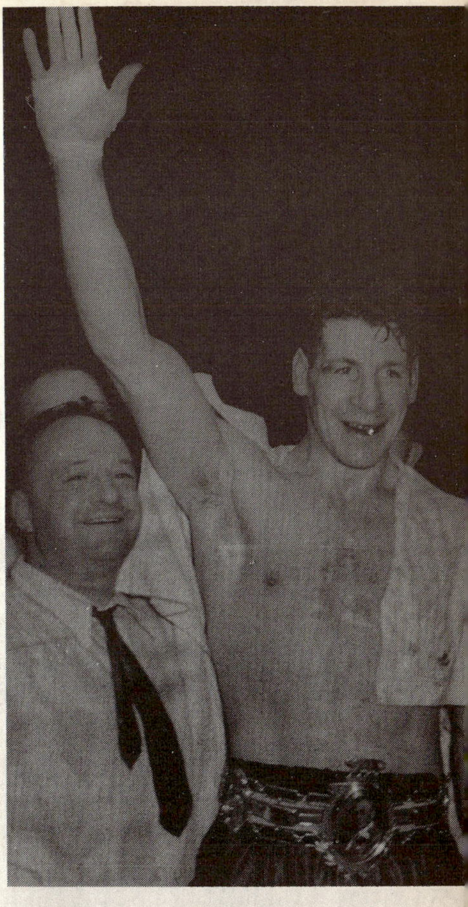

Above: Harvey traps McAvoy in a corner and reaches him with a long left.

Right: Len Harvey's victory smile as he receives the decision and the Lonsdale Belt. On his right is trainer Wally May.

Below: Harvey sets up a vigorous attack against Jock McAvoy from Manchester.

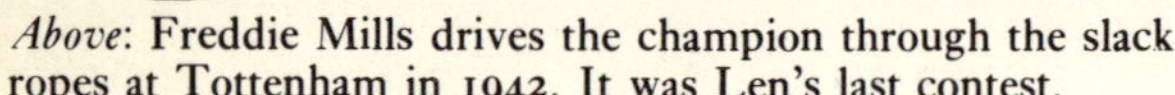

Above: Freddie Mills drives the champion through the slack ropes at Tottenham in 1942. It was Len's last contest.

Right: Pilot Officer Len Harvey, RAF.

Below: One of the last photographs taken of Len Harvey at the launching of Larry Gains' autobiography, which Len is holding (1976). Back row, left to right: Alec Steene, Jack Powell, Eric Boon, Alan Rudkin, Terry Downes. Front row, left to right: Tommy McArdle and Larry Gains.

CHAPTER 18

Champion Once Again

Harvey had proved himself a good matchmaker for Wembley Arena, even if he had personally provided fifty per cent of the enterprise for his first presentation. Arthur Elvin had been delighted with both the Lewis fight and the gate money it had attracted. He was eager for more and when asked if he would go to another world championship fight, wanted only to know more details. 'The best flyweight champion this country has produced since Jimmy Wilde is young Benny Lynch, from Glasgow,' Len told him. 'He is the legitimate holder of the world title, but in America they are recognising Small Montana, from the Philippines, as champion. I suggest you bring him over to fight Lynch in a match that will decide an indisputable flyweight champion of the world.'

Elvin wanted no urging and no time was lost in coming to terms with both men. When Montana – real name Benjamin Gan – arrived with his manager, Johnny Rogers, Harvey was again the perfect host, meeting them off the boat and taking them to the Barn Club where they were comfortably installed and supplied with sparring partners. Lynch, with his manager George Dingley, set up his training camp at Taplow, and both places were visited regularly by the Wembley matchmaker, who attended to all details until they were both safely climbing into the ring. The match had been a winner from the moment of its announcement and Len had arranged an added attraction, Jack Doyle being paired with Alf Robinson in a supporting contest, with another Novices' Heavyweight Competition as make-weight. With Lynch putting up a brilliant fight to outpoint a clever and courageous opponent, it was another big moment for British Boxing, even if Doyle disgraced himself by being ruled out in the first round for striking his rival when he was on the canvas taking a count from one of the Irishman's mighty right hand punches to the chin.

Next came a proposal for a return meeting between Walter Neusel and Harvey as a main event at Wembley. Len offered to put up a side-stake of a thousand pounds, but the German was all for raising this to £2,000, and would not consider a lesser sum. 'I do not want a match of bank balances,' Len told the press. 'I want to fight Neusel, because I think I can lick him.' Some time later, when Walter was training at the *Star and Garter* for a fight, and Len was paying him a visit, someone wanted to know why Neusel did not seem anxious for another fight with Harvey. 'Oh, he wants to wait until he's grown a bit bigger, don't you, Walter?' said Len playfully.

Doyle was still a magnetic attraction in London, so the Wembley matchmaker suggested that he should be provided with an American opponent. 'There's a big husky Chicago fighter, a bit past his best, but quite capable of giving Doyle a good fight, who after all is still only a novice,' he told Mr Elvin. 'He calls himself King Levinsky. He's a wild swinger and with Jack tossing punches the way he does, it should prove exciting.' So the match was made and a well-meaning sportsman, who was anxious that the Irishman should restrain himself this time and not incur disqualification, offered to pay Doyle a pound for every straight left he landed during the contest. This gesture prevented the fans from seeing the punch-up they anticipated, because Doyle showed that he could box when he wanted to and gained a comfortable points victory, earning himself over a hundred pounds in the process.

Again Len took care of the visitor, installing him at Taplow, while Doyle worked out at Windsor where his boxing career had started. At a press luncheon prior to the contest, Harvey was chairman and at the appropriate time asked the assembly to rise and toast the King. Levinsky put on a big grin, remained seated, clasped his huge hands together and shook them over his own head. 'Not you, mate – we'll toast you later,' said Len with a smile. 'This one is for King George the Sixth.' 'Well, I'm King Levinsky the Foist,' retorted the American amidst great laughter.

The main item on this programme was another piece of intelligent matchmaking. Jock McAvoy, still holding the middleweight crown he had taken from Harvey four years earlier, had been challenging Eddie Phillips for his light-heavyweight title and Len brought them together, having in mind that the winner could be a potential challenger to John Henry Lewis. To the general surprise the Rochdale Thunderbolt knocked out the champion in the fourteenth round, an event that gave Harvey the idea that there was nothing to prevent himself from making a return to the 12 st. 7 lbs. division, as he could still make this weight with ease. But not yet!

Jack Petersen had lost the British and Empire heavyweight titles to Ben Foord, the South African, who had in turn been beaten by Tommy Farr, who subsequently knocked out Neusel and was all set to go to New York and meet Joe Louis for the world championship. Defeat caused Petersen to announce his retirement and Len was genuinely sorry at the Welshman's departure from active Boxing. 'He was a splendid sportsman, both in and out of the ring,' Harvey said in an interview. 'He always pleased the public with his plucky fighting and I am sad to think that the eye trouble that has caused his retirement was started in his first fight with me.' Every so often they met at public functions and were the closest of friends. And when, in later years, Petersen was featured in a *This is Your Life*, programme, Len was only too happy to take part. Just as he was setting out from home, Neusel called by chance to see him. 'You're just in time, Walter,' said Len. 'Jump in and I'll take you to Cardiff. They are doing a special television programme on Petersen this evening and they'll be glad to have you in it.' As Petersen and Neusel had met three times in stirring contests, the inclusion of the German greatly enhanced the show and the producers were very appreciative of Harvey's gesture.

The National Sporting Club, having been resuscitated under the management of John Harding, was running regular shows at the Empress Hall, Earls Court. For one of their tournaments Jack Doyle had been engaged at a fee of £2,000 to fight Gunnar Barlund, of Finland, over ten rounds. Suddenly the Irishman announced that he had damaged his right hand and could not box, so Harding approached Len to come in as a substitute. Being a star boxer himself never prevented Harvey from helping out a promoter and we have already seen that he willingly took the place of another boxer in a supporting contest at Leicester in 1932. Nor did he demand a high price for his services when he knew that what was offered was as much as the promoter could afford. He was, however, startled when the NSC offered a thousand pounds for Len to fight Barlund, who was a match for anyone at that time. 'That is just half what you proposed paying Doyle,' he replied curtly. 'Does that mean you regard him as twice as good a draw as myself, for if that is so, you had better find someone else to help you out. I'll take what you offered Doyle, but not a penny less. If you can afford it for him, then you can afford it for me.' There was no answer to that line of argument and Maurice Strickland, the New Zealander, took on the job, but his fee was never disclosed.

Alex Creamer, a Glasgow promoter, now approached Harvey and

suggested a match with Manuel (Kid) Abrew, a coloured heavy from Edinburgh, who had built up a big reputation in Scottish rings. It would be an outdoor promotion at Shawfield Park, and Len, who had not boxed for ten months, gladly accepted the terms offered for a ten rounds bout, even though he disliked boxing in the open-air, feeling that such promotions were robbed of the atmosphere so essential to the sport of Boxing. However, he went off with Wally May and his sparring-partners to the fresh air of Hampstead Heath, training at *Jack Straw's Castle*, which had past associations with the Fight Game, Tommy Burns, the former heavyweight champion of the world, having trained there at one time.

Apparently the heights of London suited Harvey admirably for he was at the peak of fitness when he crossed gloves with Abrew before twenty thousand Scottish fans. Len was conceding fully a stone in weight and six years in age, yet his form was a revelation. He fought with rare judgment, sizing up his opponent and administering a sound, but devastating beating until he had fought him to a complete standstill. It was a triumph of cunning and experience over youth and strength. The coloured man was never over-awed by his opponent's reputation, although he was often perplexed. He tried to set up one strong attack after another, but reckoned without that solid defence, adroit slipping, and the ice-cool brain of the ex-champion.

Harvey picked every punch he plied. At close range he was the master and his short blows, hooks and uppercuts had his opponent bleeding from the mouth and nose at the halfway stage. Abrew was tough and game, but he had no answer to Harvey's close-quarter work. At long range the Scot tried hard to put over a big punch, but could never find the target and as he came in behind his punches, he was an easy target for Len's famous left hook. Once Abrew slipped to the canvas and the crowd applauded Harvey for sportingly stepping back until his rival was on his feet again.

Harvey turned on the heat from the ninth round and Abrew was subjected to a sustained hammering. He had tired under the punishment he had taken and was now easy to hit. Harvey walked round him and picked up the points at will. He expected any moment that Abrew's corner would give in for him, but the game Kid kept coming up. In the fourteenth Len drew him forward, then crossed a peach of a right to his chin that dropped him glassy-eyed and badly dazed. He scrambled up at 'two', too far gone to take a longer count and Len tried hard to finish it off as speedily as possible. But referee Charlie Thomas could see that Abrew's position was hopeless and rightly intervened a few seconds before the bell was due to end the round.

I was writing a weekly feature called 'The Punchbowl' in *Boxing* at that time and making a practice of presenting a Certificate of Merit for the 'Best Performance of the Week', and Len's remarkable victory after such a long lay-off was my choice of the moment. The awards had no material value whatsoever, but they were cherished by those who gained them and once when I visited Len's home many years later he pointed with pride to the framed token of his success that he had won so late in his career.

Harvey's feelings towards the NSC and John Harding in particular were not enhanced when he sat at Earls Court one evening and watched the final of a £1,000 Heavyweight Tournament organised by the *Daily Mail* and saw the ultimate winner, Jack Smith, from Worcester, being presented with a Lonsdale Belt. 'That is my property you are giving away,' he called out in protest, and he was right. It was the original NSC belt, presented in 1919 to Noel (Boy) McCormick and which had been in the hands of eight subsequent champions, including Harvey. In fact, he was the only one of those Belt-holders who had never been defeated for the trophy, so had a legitimate claim to it. But as no one saw fit to right this obvious wrong, Jack Smith took the Belt home and some years later it was sold by auction. The Belt in circulation at that time, and in the possession of Jock McAvoy because of his victory over Phillips, was a Board of Control trophy.

There was a final skirmish between the Cornishman and John Harding. With Farr having a prolonged stay in America, there was no chance of fighting for the British heavyweight title, so Len turned his attention to McAvoy. The score between them was one each, so a third meeting was a 'natural'. Harvey suggested a side-stake up to £2,000 and with McAvoy willing, it was left for a promoter to offer an adequate purse. An enormous Exhibition Hall had recently been opened adjacent to the Empress Hall at Earls Court and Harding, representing the NSC, stated his willingness to stage a Harvey *v.* McAvoy 'rubber' fight there. This was regarded by both Len and Jock as extremely good news until they learned that the Club would go to no more than a £2,000 purse. On a sixty/forty per cent basis, this was not a profitable proposition for the loser to contemplate as, with the side-stake operating, he would be considerably out of pocket. Even the winner could expect no more than £3,600 and, as Harvey pointed out, the new hall was capable of containing twenty thousand spectators, which should produce a 'gate' of which £2,000 would be a fleabite.

He turned down the NSC offer out of hand and when a critic accused him of 'quibbling', and said that he was not serious in his challenge to McAvoy, he replied: 'Those who query my integrity regarding this £2,000 side-stake should know by now that when I make a statement it is not for cheap publicity but a gesture of the confidence I have in my ability to beat McAvoy or any of the other big fellows, including Farr, to whom I have issued challenges. One thing is certain. Boxing is my profession. When going into a fight I am out to get the best I can for my services. Furthermore, I refuse to be jockeyed into accepting terms that I know can be bettered elsewhere. Fifty per cent of the gate would suit me admirably and my money is in my hand ready to be put down on the word "Go".' Len agreed that a promoter was entitled to the 'lion's' share of the gate, but not part of the 'cub's' money as well. Too many, in his view, were very greedy.

When the National Sporting Club's spokesman announced that the Club was prepared to act as the governing body of British Boxing as it had done in the days before the re-constituted BBB of C, Harvey was up in arms with a vengeance. Writing in the *Sunday Express*, he made no bones about his indignation at such a suggestion.

> With this proposal I entirely disagree. As it stands at the moment, the NSC is on the same basis as any other promoting body in the country and there would be a tremendous outcry if we, at Wembley, or any other promoting syndicate, made the same suggestion.
>
> Co-operation between boxer, promoter and controlling body has been a long-felt want, but first we must look after the fighters themselves, without them there would be nothing to control. The promoters can look after themselves, they have done so very nicely up to now as I know full well. What they should do is to give due respect to the men who make their promoting possible. Certainly there is a need for a controlling body of the right sort. Not to act in any dictatorial manner, but in the nature of arbitrators with no axe to grind other than the raising of British Boxing to the peak to which it rightly belongs.

Once again Len was being the voice of Boxing, striving as much for the six-rounder boy as for the champion.

His rebuff of the NSC did not go unnoticed by the Board of Control. A week later the Stewards announced that Harvey had been recognised as McAvoy's outstanding challenger and the pair were given up to 4th February to secure the best terms they could get for a championship fight. Immediately A. J. Elvin offered forty per cent of the gate up to £8,000 and sixty per cent thereafter or he would pay McAvoy £1,250 as a fixed guarantee. This was almost immediately topped by Sydney Hulls at Harringay, who proposed fifty per cent of the gate up to £7,000, any amount over that sum to be shared by the boxers without any deduction. This meant that if the takings reached £10,000, the boxers would receive a total of £6,500 between them. Within a short time the Harringay offer was accepted and contracts signed by McAvoy's manager, Harry Levene, and Harvey himself.

In all Len was managing his own affairs very satisfactorily. The next day he was off to Hampstead with his retinue and settling down to prepare himself for the re-capture of a British championship title. Before leaving home, however, he tendered his resignation to Arthur Elvin as match-maker for Wembley Arena. He felt that he needed a full month to prepare for the match with McAvoy and therefore could not give full concentration to the job at Wembley. His decision was accepted as being the gesture of an honest man and he remained a firm friend of the managing director thereafter.

Up in Manchester the champion was preparing himself with grim intent and did not hide the fact that this time he fully expected to win by a knockout. If he could achieve that feat he knew he would be creating a record, for so far no one had put the Cornishman down for the full count. When Len heard this threatening news at *Jack Straw's Castle*, he grinned and said: 'Well there's no harm in him trying. But I shan't try to knock him out, it will be far easier to win on points.' Then disaster overcame the challenger. A week before the scheduled date of the contest, Harvey damaged his left hand and had to ask for a fortnight's postponement. He did the damage by turning his hand in an effort to avoid hurting one of his spar-mates and had to refrain from using it during the rest of the training period.

Unknown to everyone but his trainer, this injury failed to yield to treatment and remained a passenger throughout the entire fifteen rounds he fought at Harringay on 7th April 1938. He was still unable to really let go with his right hand and, thinking in hindsight, it must have taken the utmost in pluck and confidence to enter the ring against such a dangerous opponent without the full working capacity of his tools of trade. But Len kept his troubles to himself and it was not until afterwards that the true facts of his double handicap was made known. After the contest the glove had to be cut off his hand because it was so swollen and the next day he had an injection at Guy's Hospital to deaden the pain.

The champion was the first to attack, in fact, he opened the exchanges in every round. Jock moved in close and immediately let loose his heavy hooks, both to head and body. Harvey came in, but McAvoy was able to whip in several murderous body smashes before Len could tie him up. They broke mutually and the same thing happened again. McAvoy ducked under his rival's left lead and weaving in let forth another stream of punches, but Harvey turned him away and shot a left to the head. Len's cleverness in breaking up Jock's attacks often caused the champion to stand back and bite the thumbs of his gloves before dashing in with a fresh assault.

A stinging straight left to the face stood the champion back on his heels, but it also cost Len the use of his leading hand, and although he disguised the injury at the time of receiving it, he did not deceive either the fans or his opponent. Now he was under even greater pressure and McAvoy came storming in with his jabs or swings and then got to work with searing punches to the midsection, sometimes swinging them over Harvey's impotent left arm. Len was now forced to rely on his right and hooked and uppercut his aggressive opponent at close range, his left being used as just a prop, no power being put behind it at all.

Coming out of a clinch in the third round, Harvey was seen to have sustained a nasty cut over his right eye and those who fancied his chances had their enthusiasm dampened at the sight of the blood streaming down his cheek. He had to box cleverly throughout the next two rounds, acting almost solely on the defensive, protecting his eye wound, tying the champion up whenever possible and coasting through to keep out of serious trouble. In the fifth, however, he made McAvoy blink when he shot over a perfect right that struck the champion between the eyes. Now a change came over the situation. Before Jock had recovered from that unexpected blow he was freely punished, the challenger propping him off with the left, crossing him with the right and then hooking him under and over at close-quarters.

The bout almost came to an end in the sixth. Finding it easy to penetrate McAvoy's guard with a straight right, Len let this punch go whenever an opening revealed itself. He rarely missed and towards the end of the round he drove in a punch that should have finished the contest. It caught McAvoy flush on the jaw. Jock's knees sagged, his arms dropped and he stumbled forward, his glove tips touching the canvas. By a superhuman effort he managed to right himself just as the gong sounded to end the round. Had there been time for just one more punch, Harvey might have finished it there and then for McAvoy was out on his feet.

The next three rounds went to the challenger while McAvoy was gathering his forces together again. He was tricked into taking more rights to the head, found his own punches blocked and was reduced to inactivity in the clinches. They fought on grimly, with the champion always trying to catch his man with a decisive punch and his chance came in the tenth when he followed a left hook to the jaw with a wicked right that caused Len's knees to buckle and made him grab hold of Jock and hold on like a limpet. McAvoy struggled to get free, but the cool challenger kept him there until his head cleared, then turned him harmlessly into the ropes.

This partial success spurred McAvoy on to even fiercer efforts. He pressed Harvey harder than ever, giving him no rest, and forcing the Cornishman to bring out all his defensive technique in order to survive. Well-placed rights from Harvey merely bounced off his tough opponent who took his punishment and came back with both hands working like a machine. Make no mistake about it, Jock was putting all he had into every punch he threw and when made to miss it was not because he was hitting wildly, but solely as a result of Harvey's cleverness in evasion and blocking ability. If he could not use his left as an attacking weapon, at least Len knew how to bring it into play as an effective barrier to the majority of McAvoy's mighty blows.

During the last few rounds Jock hurt his challenger with some real 'shock' punches to the body. Stoic as he was, Len could not help wincing under these smashes to his ribs, but he gritted his teeth and shook his tormentor time after time with hard rights to the jaw. More often than not, he did not bother to measure his man first, but led with the right to beat the champion to the punch. At close-quarters he offset McAvoy's worrying hooks to the body and head by a direct and deadly uppercut, but the famed Rochdale Thunderbolt remained a man of iron and Harvey had not the power to put him down.

There was a tense moment as they came up for the last time. Immediately they went in for a two-fisted 'bundle' and how the crowd cheered as they gave punch for punch in the centre of the ring, neither yielding a yard, standing toe-to-toe putting in everything they had to try and win conclusively. Harvey was even using his damaged left, heedless of the pain it must have been causing him every time he made contact. With a blood-smeared face and showing distinct signs of weariness, Harvey hit back at his resolute rival and they fought it out bitterly to the end of the round. Almost before the echoes of the final gong had sounded referee Percy Moss raised Harvey's hand and the 'house' burst into a thunder-clap of sound. The prompt decision on the part of the official caught the press and public in two minds. There were many who considered McAvoy unlucky because of the aggression he had shown throughout, but the verdict in Harvey's favour was popular enough. Again a Lonsdale Belt was put round his waist to denote that he was a British champion once more. Afterwards McAvoy said: 'Harvey has an ice-cool brain. He knows every trick of the trade and no one can equal his defence.'

Startling events in the heavyweight ranks caused Harvey to think in terms of winning back another title. Tommy Farr had gone off to America and while there had informed the Board of Control that he no longer regarded himself as British heavyweight champion and they could do as they pleased with the title. The morning after they heard this sensational news, the Stewards received a letter from Len requesting that he should be nominated to meet Eddie Phillips for the vacant championship, point-ing out that as Eddie was their official contender because of his victory over Ben Foord in a final eliminator to challenge Farr, and as he (Harvey) had already beaten the Bow fighter in a heavyweight eliminator three years previously, it was only logical that the two should meet to decide the championship proper. Harvey's argument was so logical that the Board of Control immediately issued an edict to this effect, whereupon Len gathered up Wally May and a set of sparring-partners and again took up temporary habitation at *Jack Straw's Castle*. Here there was an atmosphere of complete confidence, but Phillips, who trained at Windsor, had equal cause to feel happy as to the outcome of his fourth meeting with the Cornishman. He felt that Harvey had lost a lot of his old-time punching power because of hand injuries, while he had produced sheer gloved dynamite in disposing of tough Ben Foord in nine rounds.

Harringay Arena once again enjoyed a capacity attendance for the Heavyweight Championship fight. At the weigh-in Harvey had scaled 12 st. 13$\frac{1}{2}$ lbs. which gave him an advantage of 4$\frac{1}{2}$ lbs. over Phillips, so for once he was not giving weight away. The referee was Jack Smith and as it transpired he had a busy time in the short while the contest lasted. That Len meant to win this one as soon as possible was plainly seen when, with the very first punch, he smote his opponent clean on the chin with a left hook that shook Phillips throughout his whole frame and completely destroyed his morale. To say that Harvey had the fight won with that single blow is no exaggeration.

He tried it again, but Eddie saw this one coming and drew back to avoid it. The Cornishman was intent on an early victory, however, and had his rival on the retreat before a very forceful attack. A right hook jarred Eddie and he was forced to be on the strict defensive, while Len made good play with his straight left and frequently crossed the right over to the jaw, one dazzling shot missing Phillips' chin by the merest fraction. Towards the end of the round it was noticed that Harvey's left glove had been badly split, no doubt as a result of that terrific opening punch, and the referee ordered it to be changed in the interval.

When they came up for the next round, Phillips' seconds made an objection to the new glove that Len was wearing, but Jack Smith was not interested and ordered the men to 'box on'. Harvey went straight in with a speedy and aggressive attack, hitting out freely with either hand and picking his spots whenever Phillips left an opening. Halfway through the round Eddie steadied his old enemy with a stiff right under the heart, his best blow so far, but Len was soon back with a two-fisted assault, a wicked right hook just grazing the point of the Bow boy's jaw. Another to the same point got home and shook Phillips up and he was glad to go into holds. Then, almost on the bell, Harvey connected with another fine left hook to the chin that sent Eddie somewhat shakily to his corner.

Still on the attack, Harvey had his opponent hanging on after taking yet another left hook on the jaw. The Londoner appeared as open as a gate for this shot and Len certainly made the most of it. Then Eddie got tired of being steadily outpunched by Len's long left and cut loose in very fierce style, a desperation attack that might have overwhelmed anyone less cool than Harvey. The crowd roared at what they thought was a turning of the tables and their encouragement was almost Phillips' undoing. He charged into Harvey, both hands at work, but was plainly guilty of butting Len under the chin, for which he received a stern reprimand from the Third Man. Len had not complained and they touched gloves before setting up a fierce punching rally, Eddie whaling away to the cheering of the fans, but Len calmly picking his shots with fine judgment.

Phillips was up smartly, eager for battle, but it was Harvey who got in the first punch, yet one more beautiful left hook that crashed against Phillips' chin and paralysed him. Immediately a right thudded against his jaw and while he was reeling from the impact, another crisp left hook to the point deposited Eddie on the canvas. He took a count of nine seconds before rising and was then freely punished by well-placed punches until Len whipped over a right that was intended to finish the contest. It whizzed past Eddie's jaw and the fact of it missing seemed to make Phillips lose complete control of himself. He fought back with such fury that the sheer force of his attack drove the Cornishman back. Again the crowd sensed a startling upset as Len retreated for the first time in the contest.

Flinging himself forward Eddie swung a mighty left to the body that was dangerously low and which made Harvey flinch. Another, even lower, caused Len to gasp and motion a protest to the referee. But Jack Smith took no action and Eddie responded by swinging first left and right 'downstairs', the last of which put Harvey down on his hands and knees, clutching himself in agony. That was enough for the Third Man, who sent Phillips to his corner, then helped Len to get up and led him to his seconds. 'Phillips is disqualified – Harvey the winner' boomed out the announcer. There was little demonstration against the verdict, the general opinion being that Phillips had been shorn of his mental balance when he committed the fouls that caused his defeat, but which were clearly unintentional.

So Len Harvey was a dual British titleholder once again and a fortnight later in the same Harringay Arena, on the night Eric Boon defeated Dave Crowley for the British lightweight title, Len was presented with another Lonsdale Belt. Interviewed by pressmen afterwards as to his future plans, he said: 'They tell me that Larry Gains is suggesting that we fight once again for the Empire championship and has issued a challenge to that effect. I have never turned down a challenge, and providing a promoter puts up a suitable purse, I am quite prepared to meet him without any delay. At the moment, however, I am awaiting the result of the contest in America between Joe Louis and my old pal, John Henry Lewis, as there is a distinct chance that John Henry and I will be re-matched for his world light-heavyweight title which I thought I came close to winning last time.'

CHAPTER 19

War Disrupts All Plans

Hardly had Harvey shown his willingness to fight Gains for the vacant Empire heavyweight title than promoter Hulls was eager to stage the match at Harringay, offering a purse of £4,000 or fifty per cent of the gate money. Larry accepted immediately and said he was prepared to let Len pick up £2,500 for himself and Harvey only hesitated because a new promoter, Armaud Vincent, had proposed paying him a flat guarantee of £10,000 for three bouts to be staged at Earls Court; the first against James J. Braddock, who had beaten Tommy Farr a year earlier, then Farr himself, and finally Joe Louis, for the heavyweight championship of the world. It was a dazzling programme that epitomised all Len's ambitions, while at the same time promising to yield a small fortune. But when it proved to lack solid foundations, Harvey dismissed the idea from his mind and signed for the fight with Gains.

At *Jack Straw's Castle* where I visited him during his training, he confided to me his plans for 1939. The Prime Minister had promised the country 'Peace in Our Time', so Len, now in his thirty-second year, was at liberty to propose what he thought would be the peak period of his career. 'First I plan to regain the Empire title by defeating Gains; then there is every prospect that I will have a return world title bout with John Henry Lewis round about June, after which I will give Tommy Farr a chance to regain the titles he forfeited. I want this match as much as any because, good as he is, I think he is made for me. And my price for such a contest, which will fill any outdoor arena in the country, will be £6,000 for myself and not a penny less. And if I win those three fights I will be ready for the big one, either here or in America.' 'Against the great Brown Bomber?' I asked. 'Yes, Joe Louis, because if Tommy could take him the distance and lose narrowly on points, I am confident that I can go one better.'

This was said quietly and without any hint of bragging simply because

it was not in Harvey's nature to make any statement he did not feel
he could live up to. He meant what he said and had every justification
for having such confidence in his abilities. Going into the gymnasium
and watching him go so happily through his routine training with all
the enthusiasm that a youngster having his first fight would enjoy, I could
only admire the conscientious and thorough way he set about getting himself into the peak of physical fitness. What a picture of bodily perfection
he presented. Clear-toned skin; rippling, yet proportionate muscularity;
a sculptor's dream model; power, vitality, strength and stamina combined
to make the superb male figure, plus grace, fluency and litheness, with
the maximum of co-ordination between hand and eye.

Gains got himself into fighting shape at Sam Carter's Hotel at Shoeburyness. It was five years since he and Harvey had fought their first
battle, now he was thirty-seven, age being his sole handicap, because
in all other respects he had an advantage over Harvey, being $1\frac{1}{2}$ ins.
taller and at 77 ins., having an extra reach of three inches. At 14 st.
$5\frac{1}{2}$ lbs. he was the heavier by 17 lbs. which was a considerable handicap
for Len to concede. Could Harvey give away inches and pounds to the
coloured Canadian? The question intrigued the fans so much that they
filled Harringay Arena, whilst the BBC put out both radio and television
broadcasts, ringside commentary being given by Howard Marshall. This
was not a history-making event as the first-ever televised contest in Great
Britain had been the McAvoy/Harvey fight at Harringay a year earlier.

It would be folly to suggest that the fight for the vacant Empire title
between Gains and Harvey was sensational. It was not even exciting,
yet it was grippingly interesting, if only because here was a clash between
two clever campaigners, both of whom had little to learn about the Noble
Art, but who were testing themselves in a conflict between brain and
brawn. Harvey had set himself the particular plan to wear down his
older rival and he did not care how long he took about it. He was always
the first to lead, he picked off Larry's counters, moved about and collected
the majority of the points in every round.

To those in the ringside seats it was a methodical yet thorough business
of winning without any display of fireworks. He was far too good for Gains
to be able to alter either his opponent's tactics or the tide of battle. Those
in the outer spaces, who could not appreciate the scientific destruction
of one man by another, resorted to slow handclapping in the middle
rounds, but this display of boredom came only at intervals from those
parts, meanwhile Harvey went on calmly and deliberately taking the
stamina and strength from his coloured opponent.

It wasn't until the eleventh round that Gains took a hand in the forcing. He had obviously been sent out from his corner to do something spectacular and was successful in catching Harvey with a good punch to the chin. His success was short-lived, however, for Len responded with a flashing right that split open Larry's left eyebrow and started a stream of blood flowing down his cheek. This put paid to any more thoughts of aggression on Gains' part, but Len opened out more now he knew his opponent was hurt and Larry was given a hard time to the bell. He was also made to suffer in the twelfth when Harvey scored to the body and head with good punches and the Canadian showed immense courage under the punishment.

He was still fighting back strongly in the next round, making a game effort to beat his rival. But Harvey was well on top now and fully aware of it. He produced some brisk punching to the body and head, opening the eye wound that had been patched up in the interval, and trying his hardest to put his flagging opponent down. But Gains, his left eye closing rapidly, stuck it out until the bell, then walked slowly back to his corner. He was done and one look at him convinced his seconds that he should not be asked to go up for more. The referee was called over and Gains' retirement announced. Harvey was a triple champion again, all three of his title wins being scored in a Harringay hat-trick.

Answering those critics who denounced the fight as lacking thrills, Len replied: 'I suppose if I had put Larry away inside half-a-dozen rounds and had an eye cut open or broken hand, I should have enjoyed a shower of praise. When will those people who do not have to take them on the chin realise that Boxing is my profession? Their idea that I should be expected to take unnecessary risks in the course of my business is something with which I do not see eye to eye. I plan my contests to win them and as long as my hand is held up by the referee at the finish that should be enough.'

Stage One of the 1939 programme had been satisfactorily completed and when John Henry Lewis arrived at the beginning of May, the second phase seemed to be on the point of maturing. Lewis had suffered a dramatic one-round knockout defeat by Joe Louis and there had been rumours that he was not fit to continue boxing because of eye trouble. The Harringay authorities, who had now installed Johnny Best, of Liverpool fame, as their matchmaker, sought confirmation of these rumours from the National Boxing Association of America and were assured that there was nothing to prevent Lewis from defending his world title against Harvey for the second time. But the British Boxing Board of Control was not satisfied and they ordered the coloured American to be examined by their own medical man, also calling in another doctor for a second opinion. Both found that John Henry was not fit to partake of another contest and he had to return home without a fight, leaving Harvey very disappointed but not dismayed.

Straight away he sat down and wrote to the Stewards, commending them on their integrity in ascertaining the truth about Lewis and then making the suggestion that he and Jock McAvoy should fight for the now vacant world crown as it was obvious that Lewis would never fight again – nor did he for that matter. Len pointed out that for far too long we had let the Americans do as they pleased regarding the setting up of world champions and that it was high time this country took a hand in putting up contenders when titles became vacant. The critics showed surprise when the Stewards took up his proposal and told the American controlling bodies that they would recognise a fight between Harvey and McAvoy as being for the vacant world's light-heavyweight championship. The boxing writers concluded that it must have been an exceedingly good letter as the Stewards told them it would be preserved as a document of historic interest. 'So it ought to be,' replied Len, 'it took me two hours to write.'

It must here be emphasised the great influence Len Harvey was having over British Boxing at this particular time. Those in power respected his common sense and integrity; promoters acknowledged his honesty and business-like abilities; the boxers made him an object lesson in fighting skill, the fans idolised him for his astonishing career and the fame he had gained with so many championship fights. His high standing in the Fight Game was never more obvious than at this moment. The Harringay people paid him the flat guarantee he requested and gave McAvoy the terms he asked. They booked the White City Stadium for the fight and to add to public appeal they made a return fight between Eddie Phillips and Jack Doyle as the chief supporting item. Now Arthur Elvin had paid for the Irishman's return from America and when it was suggested that he should join forces with Harringay in the White City project, he was only too willing to release his hold on Doyle. Thus, probably for the first time in history, two rival promoting bodies got together for the benefit of the sport.

A meeting of those concerned was arranged at the White City, to which the four boxers involved were invited. There was a general discussion and Harvey made the suggestion that the price of the cheapest seats should be reduced from five shillings to half-a-crown. 'This fight is a big occasion in Boxing,' he said. 'There are many who would like to see it, but cannot afford even the five shillings asked for a seat a mile off. Right from my early days I have had a soft spot for the fellow at the back of the hall. He is usually a very shrewd critic who really understands the game and I should be very sorry indeed if he and his like were prevented from going to the White City because of prohibitive prices.' There were no arguments against this proposal and so the man in the street was given the opportunity to see a world's championship contest for a modest half-dollar.

Harvey had come specially from Hampstead, McAvoy from the *Green Man* at Blackheath where he had started training. Later on he was to try Shoeburyness, but eventually returned to Belle Vue where he was far happier and more at home. Phillips arrived from Windsor and Doyle, who smoked a pipe during the conference, had not apparently started training as yet. Harvey and McAvoy chatted together and why not. This would be their fourth meeting, with Jock needing to win this one, not only to get back his championship, but also to put the score on level terms. Meanwhile in New York, Mike Jacobs, who liked to think he held a monopoly over world Boxing, announced that he had matched Billy Conn with Melio Bettina, the NBA champion, to fight for the vacant crown. But no one in Britain took any notice.

All fight-minded people in the country were agog with the coming clash, the middleweight champion challenging the light-heavyweight king, who was British and Empire heavyweight titleholder as well. Sydney Hulls had returned to operate the big show to which it was estimated that eighty thousand would attend and Jack Solomons, who was quickly learning how to become a major promoter, was lending a hand in the organisation. At the weigh-in ceremony, held at the Stadium Club in Holborn, the boxers concerned had to fight their way in. McAvoy had merely to remove his coat to be within the stipulated 175 lbs., but Harvey removed his underclothes before stepping on the scales. Immediately a cry of exultation came from Charles Donmall,* the Board of Control secretary; 'Harvey you are overweight by 4 oz. – you will be given just one hour to remove them.'

'That's strange, Charles,' said Len, a puzzled look on his face. 'Do you mind if I try again?' 'I don't see the point,' snapped Donmall. 'If you're overweight, you're overweight. You can't lose a quarter-of-a-pound between getting off and getting on the scales again.' 'Can't I?'

---

*Harvey could never hit it off with Donmall, whom he thought paid more attention to promoters than he did to boxers.

answered Harvey with one of his quiet smiles. 'Well, just hold this for me, will you Charles?', and he handed the Secretary a quarter-pound weight he had been holding in his hand when he first got on the scales and which he had picked up while waiting for McAvoy to be weighed. The joke was enjoyed by everyone except the victim, who reluctantly had to announce that Harvey, too, was inside the stipulated poundage. Len and Jock shook hands. 'See you tomorrow, then,' said the man from Rochdale, 'it's my turn to win.' 'We shall be meeting on the eve of my birthday,' Len remarked. 'I hope you'll provide me with a suitable present.'

All roads led to the White City that night and by 6 p. m. they were completely congested, with traffic jams of great length getting longer every minute. The doors were thrown open earlier than originally planned to try and ease the multitude that was streaming through the turnstiles, but by the time the show was due to start, the vast arena was no more than two-thirds full and the roads were jammed for a mile or more in every direction. McAvoy arrived, but there was no sign of his opponent, nor of Doyle or Phillips. Solomons went outside to try and find the missing fighters and then found he could not get back again. The press telephones were ringing as sports editors tried frantically to contact their reporters, most of whom were stranded round and about Shepherds Bush. Eventually the show was started to placate those who were getting restless as it was long past the advertised time for commencement.

The Harveys were then living just off Holland Park Avenue, only ten minutes away from the White City. Not wanting Len to be waiting around for too long, trainer May held back until he thought they would have plenty of time to get to the Stadium and have his boxer ready for the ring by about nine o'clock. When they turned out of their road into the main thoroughfare, their hearts sank as it took them some time to get into the traffic stream and then they crept along by inches. As it happened Jack Doyle was in a car behind Len and after they had made very little progress and it was getting late, the Irish heavy got very agitated and shouted to Harvey: 'I am going to walk, come on.' Len sat calmly and replied: 'You must be mad, Jack, you will be torn to pieces by this crowd. I am not moving out of this car and I don't care if I sit here all night. So you take off on your own.' How Doyle finally got into the White City, Len never knew, but the experience could not have done him any good as he was knocked cold in the second round.

After waiting an hour in a car that could creep forward only by inches, and being mobbed by hero-worshippers all the way, Len finally arrived but his match with McAvoy went on forty minutes late and an extra bout was put on in the meantime. Right up to the moment that Harvey and McAvoy took the ring, the fans were still flocking in. At one point the weight of the crowd burst through one of the gates, at another spot an attempt was made to rush into the arena and the police had their hands full in restoring order. Fortunately, the fans were full of good humour and there were no ugly scenes, but over eighty thousand spectators were herded in eventually. Most of them saw only the championship contest, but that is what they had come for, although the clash between Doyle and Phillips was an added inducement. But Len and Jock gave them their money's worth, the best and greatest of their four encounters.

The weights were announced as McAvoy 12 st. 3 lbs., Harvey 12 st. 6¾ lbs., Charlie Thomas was introduced as referee and immediately they went into action, Len being first with a long left to the face. McAvoy came back with left jabs and straight rights, and Harvey weaved in to score with two hard rights to the body. They clinched and were broken immediately, whereupon Len got in one of his pet right crosses to the chin which unsteadied the Rochdale man. Harvey feinted a straight left, then shortened his punch to catch his rival with a telling hook, whereupon Jock closed in and was hooking both hands to the ribs at the bell.

Harvey was again first with a series of straight lefts to the face, but McAvoy had warmed up now and whipped in short arm punches to the head from both fists. Backing off, Harvey slipped to the boards, but was up in a flash and came back at McAvoy with a fierce attack and they swapped blows freely to the satisfaction of the fans. No quarter was asked or given as they exchanged heavy punches and they went to their corners to prolonged applause from the crowd. There were shouts from the fans at the back for the lights around the Stadium to be switched off and when this was done the vast assembly disappeared into the darkness and everything was concentrated on the lit-up square with its powerful arcs under which the grim duel was being waged relentlessly.

The third was another brisk round with Harvey hitting out, but his opponent trying to make him miss by weaving as he came in. Sometimes he beat Len to the punch and at once bored in to bang over his heavy artillery. Obviously the Rochdale Thunderbolt was out to tack a hearty one on his opponent's jaw, but Len kept him at bay with some solid point-scoring jabs, although he had to take a jolting drive under the heart. Harvey answered with a wicked right hook that grazed Jock's jaw and again the fans thundered their approval at the bell.

The first three rounds had gone to Harvey, but McAvoy took the fourth by maintaining a storming attack and forcing his rival to mill on the retreat. Len kept cool under this continual fire, especially the two-fisted assaults Jock made on the body; he was pacing himself and letting the Northerner expend his energy while avoiding as many punches as he could, or robbing them of their power with intervening gloves, arms or shoulders. A fine left to the face from Harvey opened the fifth round, then McAvoy worked his way in but was short with his hooks and swings as Len propped him off with a keen left. Several times Jock swung over a lusty right at Harvey's head, but his blows were either deflected or blocked, or Len closed in to nullify his energetic rival's work at close range. But just before the bell he excited the crowd by landing a heavy left swing on McAvoy's jaw that caused Jock to seek a clinch.

McAvoy's continued aggression pleased the fans and they cheered as he kept trying to reach Harvey's chin with a right. The majority of the onlookers, however, were too far away to see that Len was riding most of the punches, otherwise he must have been swept off his feet. Yet to a close observer it was noticed that Harvey's left cheek was showing signs of bruising. There was a good deal of infighting and they were broken frequently by the referee. But they spent the last half-minute of the round in a free hitting spell that was thoroughly appreciated by the vast throng.

McAvoy made another big attempt to put his man down in the seventh round, forcing his way in and pounding away, while Harvey tried to jab him off and then tie him up inside. Jock switched his attacks from the body to head and back again and when baulked by Len's superb defensive work, he tried his hand at using a straight left, sometimes beating his opponent to the punch with these long range leads. This straight punching took Harvey a bit by surprise and the round had to be credited to the Northerner.

There could not have been a lot in it when they came up for the half-way round, but Len started off speedily, scoring well with lefts to the face that brought a halt to McAvoy's attacking. A great 'Ooh' went up as Harvey missed his rival's jaw with a mighty right cross, and another when he cleverly side-stepped out of the path of an equally wicked left hook to the jaw. Whenever he was under pressure, Harvey's supreme coolness kept him out of trouble and he picked up sufficient points as he jabbed off the advancing McAvoy to gain the round.

Although Jock opened the ninth with several good clumping lefts to the side of the head, Harvey, ever watchful, rode the blows or dodged them, then evened the exchanges by driving a smashing right to the mark which checked his opponent and must have hurt. Seeing Jock falter, Len opened out with a splendidly timed two-handed attack to the head that took the honours of the round, although McAvoy walked strongly back to his corner at the bell.

Instead of slowing up in any way, Harvey now put on extra pace and got in his shots before McAvoy could launch an aggressive attack. A right hook to the jaw shook McAvoy, a wicked right full in the solar plexus made Jock grunt, but his condition was so good that he could absorb these destructive punches. Although showing signs of wilting, he fought back magnificently, but Harvey was always the master and won the round by a considerable margin.

The eleventh was just as hard fought with McAvoy coming with renewed strength to try and force the pace. But all the time Harvey was scoring with that accurate left to the head before they closed in when they exchanged heavy smashes to the body. This led to a clinch and when parted, Harvey incurred the displeasure of the crowd by scoring with a neat right to the chin on the breakaway. It was a perfectly delivered punch as the referee had motioned them to box on, and Len's quickness of thought should have been applauded rather than condemned. It was Jock who wanted to clinch after that one and they fought close until the bell.

The crowd was behind McAvoy when he stormed into Harvey at the start of the next round. He was so aggressive that Len was forced to give ground following a stiff left to the head he could not avoid. Another left sent the champion's head back, but soon afterwards he clipped Jock on the chin with a neat right hook. The rest of the round was spent in close-quarter fighting, each punishing the other. In the thirteenth it was obvious that Harvey knew he was in front and meant to hold on to his lead. Twice in succession he connected with rights to the side of the head and followed with some stiff left hooks that shook Jock even if they did not put him down. His toughness was exemplified here and he gained further applause for himself when he launched a two-fisted barrage, but which Harvey met in strong and confident style.

Now came the highlight of this gruelling battle. Coming out with a strong attack, Len was surprised that his rival had the same idea. But before Len could get his points-scoring left to work, Jock had slammed over a right that crashed on Harvey's chin and shook him noticeably. The fans were excitedly sensing a sudden turning of the tide and roared encouragement as Jock got in another right to the chin, followed by yet another and now things looked desperate for the Cornishman. He was forced to try to get into a clinch, but Jock was out for a decisive win and smashed home both hands to the jaw.

Len was shaken and the crowd yelled at the Rochdale Thunderbolt to go in for the 'kill'. Caught by a left hook to the chin when crowded into a neutral corner, Len almost bent in two and appeared to be on the point of collapsing, in fact, he almost touched the canvas with his left hand, but managed to right himself. It was McAvoy's big moment and he tried hard to make the most of it, but Len had sufficient ring sense and pluck to foil his opponent's big efforts and still remain on his feet to the bell.

Thunder rolled from the outer regions of darkness as the pair came up for the fifteenth and last round. There was still time for the Northerner to score a dramatic last round knockout victory, but the Cornishman had made a full recovery from that punishing last round and even though forced back into the ropes, he brought his opponent up to a halt with a neatly-timed clip to the chin. McAvoy rushed in to assail the body, but Harvey shook him with a good right to the head. Len knew that he had only to stay on his feet and the fight was his. No doubt McAvoy too realised this for he went all out to try and knock his rival off his feet. Cool as the proverbial cucumber, Len boxed Jock off, foiled his attempts to land a devastating blow and was there smiling at the finish of a great fight that had the multitude clapping and stamping with satisfaction at having seen a truly magnificent battle.

Referee Thomas stood in a neutral corner for some moments totalling up his score card, then he walked over to Harvey and raised his right arm. This gesture brought tremendous applause from the fans who, realising how close it had been were only too anxious to give full credit to a superb ringmaster who had defied all the efforts of his vigorous and determined rival to bring him down. Science had triumphed over brute force and they were quick to acknowledge it. The Board of Control not only presented the winner with the Lonsdale Belt, but also awarded him a silver trophy emblematic of the world's championship. As the Stewards had also nominated the fight as involving the Empire crown in addition, it meant that Harvey now held three titles in the light-heavyweight class, plus two in the heavyweight division – the first man ever to hold five championships at one and the same time.

At thirty-two he was one of the fittest men in the world, splendidly constructed, as near the perfect being, both mentally and physically as any human male could hope to reach. That evening he had demonstrated that not only could he conquer the formidable Rochdale Thunderbolt in convincing fashion, but also gain a notable victory over the greatest of all bugbears in a boxer's path – Anno Domini. He proved to be what many people had for a long time been calling him – 'Master of the Fistic Art'.

He confounded the majority of the critics who were of the opinion that in the latter stages of a hard-fought fifteen rounds battle, he would have 'bellows' to mend. But by conserving his stamina and energy, moving to long range and into close range as it suited him, he picked up points with precision punches, wasted very few of them and, indeed, comported himself as one of the greatest ring generals of all time. Not only was it a very fine personal achievement on Len's part, it was a clean-cut display worthy of the highest traditions of the Noble Art as practised in Great Britain from which it originated.

Harvey had gained the first two prizes at which he had aimed earlier in the year. He took a holiday at Clacton-on-Sea, after having publicised the fact that Farr was his next objective. The Welshman had suffered five successive defeats in America, but since coming home had gained a revenge decision over Red Burman and stopped Larry Gains in five rounds. Now Harvey offered him a chance to win back his British and Empire crowns, but there was not an immediate acceptance by Tonypandy Tommy. Eddie Phillips rightly pointed out that he had thrice beaten Farr and therefore was in a stronger position to challenge Harvey, while there were other up-and-coming heavies who were keen to go in with the Welshman. Len knew, however, that his most lucrative meeting with Tommy Farr was just a question of time and while the White City organisers were contemplating yet another big outdoor tournament, all thoughts were turned suddenly to the prospect of immediate war.

During the summer of 1939 Len had been employed by Butlin's Holiday Camp at Skegness, his principal job being the staging of small boxing shows and giving exhibitions which were greatly enjoyed by the holiday makers. In that last week of peace, the camp was closed but Harvey remained to see it handed over to the military authorities. Meanwhile Mrs Harvey and her son had gone on a cruise to Scandinavia and had reached the Kiel Canal when the British Admiralty ordered the immediate return of their ship and they got home with just a day to spare.

Harvey's ambitious plans were foiled and in his heart of hearts he realised that it meant the end of his life as a professional fighter. With characteristic philosophy he packed away his boxing kit and the day after war had been declared went off to join the Royal Air Force as a sergeant-instructor.

CHAPTER 20

Forever Champion

Once in uniform, Harvey devoted his attention to his duties as a physical training instructor with all the conscientiousness and zeal that he had given to his boxing career, and what an inspiration he must have been to the men who were entrusted to his care, for he presented the finest example of what true bodily fitness and development can reach. He also gave exhibitions of boxing as and when called upon and entered into his new life very happily with no regrets about his enforced new way of making a living. During 1941 however, news reached him of a young middleweight from Bournemouth named Freddie Mills, who since joining the Air Force had been able to continue his professional career and was making steady progress towards the top. He had grown into a light-heavy and some considered him a threat to the championship.

As soon as he heard this, Len agreed to box Mills if a tournament could be arranged in aid of the Red Cross Fund, volunteering to give up all leave in exchange for the three weeks he considered he needed for getting himself back into fighting shape. Nothing came of this suggestion, but a year later Mills appeared in a contest with Jock McAvoy which was officially regarded as an eliminator for the British 12 st.-7 lbs. title. Freddie won this in the opening round when his opponent was forced to retire suffering from a pinched nerve in his spine. Pressure was then brought on Harvey to accept Mills as a challenger and John Muldoon, himself an aircraftsman, who had been promoting at the Albert Hall, was able to hire the Tottenham Hotspurs' ground at White Hart Lane for the staging of the contest on 20th June, 1942.

Mills was fortunate to get a fortnight's clear training and was installed at the *Airman Hotel* at Feltham, having an apparently sympathetic commanding officer, but Harvey was not so fortunate. Although he had foregone his leave when the fight was first mooted, he now found himself denied any training period, with no help coming from those interested in the promotion of the contest. In the end it was left to Mrs Harvey to telephone to Len's Wing Commander, asking him to relent, even threatening to tell the press of the handicap her husband was undergoing in not getting sufficient time in which to prepare for such an important contest. Eventually Harvey managed to get away for a single week's training at the *Dumbell* at Taplow, where he had the help of Wally May and what sparring-partners could be secured in those difficult days, with every boxer of military age called up for war service.

Lack of training was not the only disadvantage that Len had to face. Mills was the younger man by twelve years, being six days short of his twenty-third birthday. He had been fighting with regularity for the past five years, having had twenty-two contests since the outbreak of war, whereas Harvey had not fought for almost three years. Len was three weeks short of his thirty-fifth birthday, an age at which more than a week is necessary to get prepared for ring combat. He took it all very calmly, but when they came to weigh-in and he was lighter by $2\frac{1}{4}$ lbs., scaling only 12 st. 3 lbs. 2 oz., it was obvious that he was far from being at his best. He looked pale and drawn, tired and languid, in striking contrast to Mills who appeared full of beans, ruddy, robust and boisterous. An estimated forty thousand fans pushed their way in on this lovely sunny Saturday afternoon, but they did not see much for their money.

It was an all-RAF affair, the promoter and the two principals and the referee, then Sergeant Eugene Henderson. He called the men up for their instructions, they touched gloves and returned to their corners. The bell clanged and immediately Mills made a rush, his arms held low and wide, ready to be swung in with all his body power behind them. Harvey had met dozens of this type of fighter and knew just how to deal with them. A stiff left to the face, a backward step, a move to the side and Freddie was sweeping at the empty air. Another stinging left snapped back Mills' head, but he came on full of vigour, swinging a great right that circled his rival's back, then they went into a clinch.

Here Harvey tied up his challenger so effectively that Freddie was unable to do any damage and when the referee had ordered them to break, the remainder of the round was spent with Mills on the chase and Harvey peppering his face with left jabs, supplemented by a right to the head whenever the Bournemouth boy managed to slip inside a lead. Just before the bell, however, Mills got in a vicious right swing to the body that Len could not avoid and it was obvious that he had been badly shaken. Yet he walked calmly back to his corner, seemingly unhurt, whereas there was a trickle of blood coming from Freddie's nose.

That mighty punch to the ribs had been very effective, however, for Len suddenly seemed to have slowed down. In charged the challenger, eager to get in another pile-driver to the ribs. Harvey snapped his head back with a fine left, but was hustled into his own corner. In blazed Ferocious Fred to be met by a brace of hooks to the body. From behind his back Mills crashed a left into Len's midsection, then whipped over a savage left hook to the head. It caught the champion flush on the chin and, lo and behold, he was down flat on his back.

Freddie trotted off to a neutral corner, referee Henderson came over, picked up the count from the timekeeper and pounded the air over the fallen titleholder. Len got to one knee and calmly stayed down until 'nine' had been called, then stood up ready to receive his challenger who came tearing across the ring, both fists cocked for action. Harvey seemed too dazed to move as Mills set up a barrage of two-fisted blows. They rained upon the champion who slowly bent lower and lower, instinctively swerving his head from side to side, but failing to dodge a single punch.

Suddenly a fierce right uppercut caught Len under the chin and hurled him back into the ropes. He was moving fast in his doubled-up state that he went sailing through the middle and top strands to fall among the press and camera men and then roll off them on to the ground. On his way out of the ring Harvey had caught his head a fearful crack on the edge of the apron surround, so that by the time he had struggled to his feet, he was too dizzy to realise that he was being counted out.

Willing hands helped him back into the ring, but by that time the full ten seconds had elapsed and Mills was the new triple champion. Len had been counted out for the first time in his long career and the second round had lasted precisely fifty-three seconds. 'I'm sorry it had to end that way,' said the sociable Freddie when they met in the dressing-rooms. 'That's all right, champ,' replied Harvey. 'That's the way things go.' No excuses, although he did confide to me afterwards that he thought the ropes were too slack, it being remembered that those were the days before it was made imperative for a strip of thick tape to be attached to the three ropes, holding them together, on each side of the ring, which was on the small side, more advantageous to Mills than to Harvey who liked plenty of space in which to move.

Harvey was still British and Empire heavyweight champion, but within a few months had come to the conclusion that his fighting days were over – for good. On 22nd November 1942 he notified the British Boxing Board of Control that he wished to relinquish these two titles, setting them free to be fought for by Freddie Mills and Jack London, the latter winning on a points verdict two years later. If he had any regrets at all over the enforced curtailment of his ring career, it was the fact that he had missed fighting Tommy Farr, not only because he felt confident that he could defeat the famous Welshman, but for the obvious reason that such a match would have provided the biggest pay-day of his boxing life and been a very satisfying way of rounding it off.

Harvey remained in the RAF until the end of the war, in fact, he was not out of uniform until late in 1946, by which time he had been promoted to the rank of Pilot Officer. For some time he had decided that once he was finished with boxing he would go into the licensed victualling trade, about the only independent living open to a man with no experience of any profession other than fighting. Florence had paved the way by taking the *Nordenfelt Arms* at Erith in 1942 when she realised that the war was going to last a number of years, and Watney's Breweries were quite happy for her to do this, although women licensees were rarities in those days. Not that the firm was doing her any favours as, being situated in the Thames Estuary, the area was subjected to almost continual air raids, both by day and by night. Locally the public house was known as 'The Pom Pom', this being the nick-name of one of the earliest of machine guns, which Nordenfelt had invented.

Mrs Harvey kept this place as a tenant until 1947, having Len's help while he learned the business after he had finally left the RAF. With almost all their capital invested in the premises, but with an assured living, thanks to her foresight, things appeared likely to go on happily. But suddenly they were overtaken by tragedy. Their son Terry had volunteered for the Parachute Regiment when he was only seventeen, so had to wait a year before his ambition could be realised. A born soldier, the urge to fight having taken another turning from that of his celebrated father. He left home in November 1946, and was back for Christmas, highly excited at the prospect of joining the Red Berets. But on 6th January 1947, his parents received a telegram telling them that he was dangerously ill in a hospital at Worksop in Nottinghamshire. They hired a car, private vehicles still being off the roads at that time, and Len drove a long, apprehensive and agitated journey to find that Terry had been brought in that day from Retford Camp and that it was feared he was suffering from meningitis.

Florence stayed in the town for the ten weeks during which every effort was made to save her son's life, spending long hours by his bedside. But the boy on whom they had built such hopes died on 19th

March, a bitter blow from which they never recovered. During the long illness, Len had journeyed from and back to Erith as often as possible, travelling in unheated trains, neglecting to eat properly and being unable to sleep well. With the anxiety and strain he had become very low, both mentally and physically, and one week after the funeral he collapsed suddenly and had to be rushed into hospital suffering from pneumonia brought on by debility and shock. He remained in a coma for three weeks and only the skilled attention of a Harley Street specialist saved his life.

The illness left him with deep scarring of the lungs and his recovery was very slow; in fact, he was never the same man again, the tragic loss of Terry having destroyed this magnificent specimen of manhood who had escaped unscathed through all those ring battles he had endured for twenty years. Barely forty, when he should have been at his very prime of life, he had been struck down by misfortune of the hardest kind, yet none who were not intimately connected with him ever had the slightest suspicion of his sorrow or ill-health. As throughout his entire life, he kept his troubles to himself.

They felt they could not remain in Erith after that and took the *Railway Hotel* at Chiswick, but here Len had trouble with his nose that meant an operation and then it was his wife's turn to become seriously ill. When she had recovered they decided that the Chiswick air did not suit them, so went into the *Derby Arms* at East Sheen, near Richmond Park. They remained there for ten years, but it was never a profitable venture, being too large. This time they returned to North London, where they had started their married life, taking the *Star and Garter* at Islington.

Here they stayed until Len became a senior citizen. This place, like all their previous public houses, quickly became a rendezvous for boxers past and present, fans old and young, and, with the walls covered with fight photographs and poses of Len, a veritable fistic museum that attracted all those who loved the Fight Game. Visitors came from far and wide and from all walks of life to see the great Len Harvey. Those whom he had beaten, the few that had won at his expense; the old-timers, the contemporaries of his day in all the various weight divisions, and the up-and-coming youngsters. His bar was the Mecca for the fight fraternity in all its categories; boxers, referees, trainers, seconds, time-keepers, announcers, photographers and press reporters. They came in eager to shake his hand, to chat, to question, to laugh over the humorous incidents of the past – and if by any chance he happened to be out, their faces would drop, unable to conceal the disappointment they felt at not seeing their hero.

Every day his mail brought letters of goodwill, some seeking information, others asking advice. All were answered for, as Harvey would say: 'If they have taken the trouble to write to me, who am I to begrudge them a reply.' Requests for autographed photos, none of which were refused, must have cost him a considerable amount each year, to say nothing of the postal expenses. As during his fighting career, so through the thirty-four years of his retirement from the ring, he was never known to ignore a request to put in an appearance at some function or another, especially if it was for charity, or to oblige an old friend. And he was guest of honour at luncheons, dinners and such-like celebrations. He opened fêtes and sports meetings, ever ready to officiate in any capacity that came within his compass and time.

He enjoyed watching boxing shows, delighting in seeing others perform just as he did when an active fighter himself, and would often go into the dressing-rooms to give quiet advice and encouragement to those youngsters he thought showed promise. But never once did he entertain the idea of managing a boxer or going into the promotion of boxing tournaments. One of his chief delights was to attend the annual dinner of the Boxing Writers' Club, where he would meet old friends in a light-hearted atmosphere, and one year he was surprised to find himself awarded a silver trophy in recognition of what he had done for Boxing, both in his faultless interpretation of the Noble Art as it should be practised, and for the refined manner in which he conducted himself as an exponent of glove fighting.

The life of a publican was not, however, the ideal vocation for a man of Harvey's temperament and upbringing. It was too restrained, too confined, and although he was business-minded in the things that really interested him, he was not a materially-minded man in any way, and the trials and tribulations of the catering trade were foreign to his reserved nature. He enjoyed the close connection it enabled him to keep with his former profession, but the enforced relaxation from his one-time high standard of physical training brought about physical decline and illnesses that came unexpectedly and with lowering effect.

After ten years at the *Star and Garter* and when he had reached the age of sixty-five, Len was happy to go into complete retirement and they went back to a former home at Penn Road in Holloway. Here with Florence he could relax and enjoy life quietly as never before. For the next three and a half years, even though his health was getting progressively worse, he found happiness and peace, talking with his wife of the exciting life they had led, the fun, the pathos, the people, the places, the good times and the bad. He had no regrets about the years of his youth and young manhood that he had spent as a boxer, holding the view that given the chance he would do it all over again – that if you are born to box – you box!

Even in retirement, his fan mail never decreased. Year in, year out, letters came from all those who remembered him fighting and his great performances in the ring. It was remarkable that so quiet an individual, with his mild temperament and dislike of showmanship and publicity, should make such an impact on the boxing public. He gained sensational victories that will long be remembered, but there was nothing theatrical or provocative about anything he achieved. Those who lived through the 1920s and 1930s, his fighting years (that period in British life between the wars when wages were low and unemployment high, and com-mercialised boxing was at its zenith with up to a hundred shows a week throughout the United Kingdom), made up the bulk of his cor-respondents, the boys and men who knew the name of Len Harvey as a household word. When he was no longer fit enough to answer them personally, Florence became his secretary and continued to reply to their letters.

Len's last public appearance was on 10th July 1976 at a social function organised by the London Ex-Boxers' Association, when he was the guest of honour, it being the eve of his sixty-ninth birthday. Extremely ill, he got out of bed to attend, but was too weak to make the speech he had prepared beforehand, this being read on his behalf by his doctor who came specially to look after him. The next day Len was taken into hospital and on Sunday, 28th November, a little more than four months later, he passed away, death being due to a combination of hardening of the arteries, emphysema and a tired heart. He was cremated at Putney Vale in South-west London, his ashes being interred in his son Terry's grave.

His death shocked the boxing world, for so few knew how ill he had become. It was the sudden departure of one who had been a champion in the minds of his admirers for so long, that he seemed likely to be one for ever.

Len Harvey's Fighting Record 1920–42

1920

Jan. 2	Young King	w.pts.	6	Plymouth
Jan. 16	Young Fern	l.pts.	6	Plymouth
Apr. 9	Stanley's Nipper	w.pts.	6	Plymouth
Jul. 30	Kid Roberts	w.pts.	6	Plymouth
Aug. 6	Young Mac	w.ko.	1	Plymouth
Sep. 17	Young Paul	drew	6	Plymouth

1921

Feb. 4	Young Jinks	w.pts.	6	Plymouth
Mar. 18	Young Jinks	w.pts.	6	Plymouth
Apr. 15	Young Jinks	w.pts.	8	Plymouth
May 6	Young Jinks	w.pts.	6	Plymouth
Jun. 17	Young Richards	w.ko.	1	Plymouth
Jun. 24	Young Jinks	w.pts.	6	Plymouth
Sep. 9	Callicott's Nipper	w.pts.	6	Plymouth
Nov. 25	Johnny Cotter	w.pts.	6	Plymouth

1922

Feb. 4	Young O'Neill	w.ret.	2	Plymouth
Mar. 17	Johnny Cotter	w.ret.	3	Plymouth
Mar. 31	Bill Williams	w.ret.	3	Plymouth
Jun. 30	Young Callicott	l.pts.	8	Plymouth
Sep. 29	Young Callicott	w.pts.	8	Plymouth
Nov. 17	Jack Palmer	w.pts.	8	Plymouth

1923

Jan. 2	Bill Lewis	w.pts.	10	NSC London
Apr. 27	Young Callicott	drew	8	Plymouth
Jun. 22	Fred Bicknell	w.pts.	8	Plymouth
Jul. 28	Young Jinks	w.pts.	6	Plymouth Home Park
Sep. 21	George (Kid) Socks	w.pts.	15	Plymouth
Oct. 22	Pop Humphries	w.pts.	15	Kensington, London
Nov. 30	Bill Riley	w.pts.	15	Plymouth

1924.

Feb. 11	Pop Humphries	w.pts.	20	Kensington, London
Mar. 10	Matt George	w.ret.	3	Kensington, London
Apr. 12	Bill Riley	w.pts.	15	The Ring
Apr. 24	Bill Davies	w.pts.	15	The Ring
May. 17	Young Clancy	w.pts.	15	The Ring
Jun. 2	Ernie Jarvis	w.pts.	15	The Ring
Jun. 21	Young Fred Welsh	w.pts.	15	The Ring
Jul. 3	Wal Jordan	w.ko.	1	The Ring
Jul. 17	Albert Hicks	w.pts.	15	The Ring
Aug. 11	Billy Streets	w.pts.	12	The Ring
Sep. 1	Tim Rowley	w.rsf.	2	The Ring
Sep. 20	Bert Saunders	w.pts.	12	The Ring
Oct. 4	Young Dando	drew	15	The Ring
Oct. 20	Young Dando	w.rsf.	4	The Ring
Dec. 8	Sid Cannon	w.pts.	12	The Ring

1925

Jan. 1	Seaman Harrod	w.ret.	5	The Ring
Jan. 26	Harry Kent	w.rsf.	4	The Ring
Feb. 19	Laurie Guard	w.rsf.	5	The Ring
Mar. 30	Walter Maloney	w.ko.	1	NSC London
Apr. 18	Johnny Thomas	w.ko.	1	The Ring
Apr. 30	*Karel Veldt	w.pts.	15	The Ring
May 14	Paul Leukemanns	w.pts.	15	The Ring
Jun. 13	Peter Bianchi	w.ko.	6	The Ring
Jun. 22	Fred Bullions	w.rsf.	10	The Ring
Jul. 2	Terry Donlan	w.rsf.	2	The Ring
Jul. 20	Paul Leukemanns	w.pts.	15	The Ring
Aug. 22	Harry Gent	w.ko.	2	The Ring
Sep. 2	Bill Handley	w.ret.	8	Plymouth, Drill Hall
Sep. 26	Glyn Davies	w.ko.	2	The Ring
Oct. 29	Henri Dupont	w.ret.	2	The Ring
Nov. 19	Edouard Baudry	w.pts.	15	The Ring

1926

Jan. 4	Alf Mancini	drew	20	The Ring
Feb. 2	Billy Bird	w.ko.	7	Shepherds Bush, London
Mar. 1	Johnny Sullivan	l.pts.	20	The Ring
Apr. 29	Harry Mason (*British welterweight title*)	drew	20	Albert Hall, London
Jun. 14	Billy Mattick	w.ko.	7	The Ring
Jul. 4	Nol Steenhorst	w.rsf.	15	The Ring
Sep. 13	Johnny Brown	drew	20	The Ring
Nov. 23	Nol Steenhorst	w.pts.	15	The Ring
Dec. 13	Andrew Newton	w.rsf.	8	The Ring

* First contest over three-minutes rounds.

1927

Jan. 3	Len Johnson	l.pts.	20	The Ring
Mar. 14	Maurice Prunier	w.pts.	15	The Ring
Apr. 4	Joe Bloomfield	w.dis.	12	The Ring
Apr. 25	Joe Rolfe	w.ko.	10	Holland Park, London
Jun. 5	Piet Brand	w.dis.	6	The Ring
Jul. 7	Emile Egrel	w.rsf.	13	The Ring
Aug. 11	Charles Screve	w.ko.	2	The Ring
Sep. 1	Billy Farmer	w.ko.	2	The Ring
Sep. 22	Primo Ubaldo	w.ko.	2	The Ring
Oct. 16	*Piet Brand	w.pts.	14	The Ring
Oct. 31	Jack Etienne	w.ret.	13	The Ring
Dec. 12	Marcel Thil	w.pts.	15	The Ring

1928

Jan. 19	Kid Nitram	w.dis.	14	Albert Hall, London
Mar. 5	Antoine Forr	w.ret.	7	The Ring
Apr. 24	Auguste Lengagne	w.rsf.	10	NSC London
Jul. 30	Emile Egrel	w.pts.	15	The Ring
Sep. 2	George West	w.dis.	4	The Ring
Oct. 1	Auguste Lengagne	w.ret.	9	The Ring
Oct. 29	Johnny Sullivan	w.ret.	6	NSC London
Dec. 3	Leo Frick	w.rsf.	2	The Ring
Dec. 17	Antoine Dubois	w.rsf.	1	Birmingham

1929

| Feb. 21 | Frank Moody | w.rsf. | 6 | Crystal Palace, London |
| May 16 | Alex Ireland | w.ko. | 7 | NSC Olympia, London |

(*British middleweight title and Lonsdale Belt*)

| Oct. 21 | Jack Hood | w.pts. | 15 | NSC Holborn Stadium |

(*British middleweight title and Lonsdale Belt*)

| Dec. 18 | Jack Hood | drew | 15 | NSC Olympia, London |

(*British middleweight title and Lonsdale Belt*)

1930

| Mar. 24 | Francis Stevens | w.ko. | 3 | The Ring |
| May 22 | Steve McCall | w.ret. | 9 | NSC Olympia, London |

(*British middleweight title and Lonsdale Belt*)

Jun. 15	Charlie McDonald	w.ko.	2	Premierland, London
Jul. 6	Henri Vandevever	w.rsf.	1	Premierland, London
Sep. 29	Dave Shade	w.pts.	15	Albert Hall, London
Dec. 14	George Slack	w.pts.	12	Leeds

1931

| Jan. 9 | Vince Dundee | l.pts. | 12 | Madison Square Garden, New York |
| Feb. 13 | Vince Dundee | l.pts. | 12 | Madison Square Garden, New York |

* Contest scheduled for fifteen rounds but cut to fourteen due to timekeeper's error.

Mar. 20	Ben Jeby	l.pts.	12	Madison Square Garden, New York
Jun. 1	Rene Devos	w,ko.	1	Albert Hall, London
Jun. 22	*Jack Hood	w.pts.	15	Albert Hall, London
	(*British middleweight title*)			
Jul. 1	Jerry Daley	w.ko.	3	Bristol
Nov. 30	Fred Shaw	w.ko.	3	Manchester

1932

Jan. 17	George Slack	w.pts.	15	South London Palace
Feb. 8	Jack Casey	w.pts.	15	Newcastle
Mar. 21	Jock McAvoy	w.pts.	15	Manchester
	(*British middleweight title and Lonsdale Belt*)			
May 11	*Len Johnson	w.pts.	15	Albert Hall, London
	(*British middleweight title*)			
Jul. 4	Marcel Thil	l.pts.	15	White City, London
	(*World's middleweight title*)			
Nov. 14	Theo Sas	w.ret.	1	Bradford
Nov. 21	Seaman Harvey	w.pts.	10	Leicester
Dec. 2	Glen Moody	w.rsf.	6	Plymouth Pier Pavilion
Dec. 12	Jack Casey	w.pts.	15	Newcastle
	(*British middleweight title and Lonsdale Belt*)			

1933

Mar. 13	Eddie Phillips	drew	12	Albert Hall, London
Apr. 10	Jock McAvoy	l.pts.	15	Manchester
	(*British middleweight title and Lonsdale Belt*)			
Jun. 12	Eddie Phillips	w.pts.	15	NSC Olympia, London
	(*British light-heavyweight title and Lonsdale Belt*)			
Oct. 16	Carmelo Candel	w.ko.	5	Paris
Nov. 30	Jack Petersen	w.pts.	15	Albert Hall, London
	(*British heavyweight title*)			

1934

Feb. 8	Larry Gains	w.pts.	15	Albert Hall, London
	(*British Empire heavyweight title*)			
Apr. 12	Jimmy Tarante	w.dis.	5	Albert Hall, London
Jun. 4	Jack Petersen	l.ret.	12	White City, London
	(*British and Empire heavyweight titles*)			
Nov. 26	Walter Neusel	drew	12	Wembley Arena, London

1935

Apr. 29	Marcel Lauriot	w.pts.	10	The Ring
Oct. 26	Eddie Phillips	w.pts.	15	Millbay Rink, Plymouth

1936

Jan. 29	Jack Petersen	l.pts.	15	Wembley Arena, London
	(*British and Empire heavyweight titles*)			

*Not recognised as title by British Boxing Board of Control.

Nov. 9   John Henry Lewis   l.pts.   15   Wembley Arena, London
            (*World's light-heavyweight title*)

1937
Sep. 15   Manuel Abrew   w.rsf.   14   Glasgow

1938
Apr. 7   Jock McAvoy   w.pts.   15   Harringay Arena, London
            (*British light-heavyweight title and Lonsdale Belt*)
Dec. 1   Eddie Phillips   w.dis.   4   Harringay Arena, London
            (*Vacant British heavyweight title and Lonsdale Belt*)

1939
Mar. 16   Larry Gains   w.ret.   13   Harringay Arena, London
            (*Vacant British Empire heavyweight title*)
Jul. 10   Jock McAvoy   w.pts.   15   White City, London
            (*World's, British and Empire light-heavyweight titles and Lonsdale Belt*)

1942
Jun. 20   Freddie Mills   l.ko.   2   Tottenham, London
            *(*World's, British and Empire light-heavyweight titles and Lonsdale Belt*)

w—won   l—lost   pts.–points   ko.–knock-out   rsf.–referee stopped fight
ret.–retired   dis.–disqualified.

All contests at Plymouth took place at the Cosmopolitan Gymnasium (the 'Old Cosmo') unless otherwise stated.

'The Ring' was situated in the Blackfriars Road, Bermondsey, London, and was destroyed in a German air raid in 1940.

The National Sporting Club, was situated in the one-time King's Theatre in Covent Garden, London.

*Recognised as for vacant world light-heavyweight championship by British Boxing Board of Control only.

Index